Time
&
Idea

TIME & IDEA

The Theory of History in Giambattista Vico

A. Robert Caponigri

With a new introduction by Lisa Caponigri

Transaction Publishers
New Brunswick (U.S.A.) and London (U.K.)

Learning Resources
Centre

12590401

New material this edition copyright © 2004 by Transaction Publishers, New Brunswick, New Jersey. Originally published in 1953 by Henry Regnery Company, Chicago.

This book is printed on acid-free paper that meets the American National Standard for Permanence of Paper for Printed Library Materials.

Library of Congress Catalog Number: 2003066319
ISBN: 0-7658-0553-7
Printed in the United States of America

Library of Congress Cataloging-in-Publication Data

Caponigri, A. Robert (Aloysius Robert), 1915-
 Time and idea : the theory of history in Giambattista Vico / A. Robert Caponigri ; with a new introduction by Lisa Caponigri.
  p. cm.
 Originally published: Chicago : H. Regnery Co., 1953. With new introd.
 Includes bibliographical references and index.
 ISBN 0-7658-0553-7
  1. Vico, Giambattista, 1668-1744. I. Title.

B3583.C28 2004
195—dc22   2003066319

To the
VERY REV. MARTIN C. D'ARCY, S.J.
who in building
Campion Hall, Oxford
has realized the dream of Newman

CONTENTS

INTRODUCTION TO THE TRANSACTION EDITION

This year, 2003, marks the twentieth anniversary of the death of my father, A. Robert Caponigri, author of the present work. It seems impossible that twenty years have passed since he stepped on this campus, his beloved University of Notre Dame; twenty years without hearing his perceptive and essential interpretations of Giambattista Vico and Benedetto Croce's works; twenty years without his mind and his spirit in our midst. Although A. Robert Caponigri, the man, is gone, A. Robert Caponigri the scholar lives on through his work. When asked to write the introduction to this republication of *Time and Idea: The Theory of History in Giambattista Vico*, I was filled with both duty and humility. Duty to honor a man whose work, twenty years later, is still highly regarded as a major influence in the introduction of Vichian Studies in the Anglo-Saxon world. Duty to honor a man who spent his entire academic career bringing the shadowy figure in the history of philosophy, Giambattista Vico, to renown as a major and original thinker. Duty to honor a man who in his role as father, taught me countless values that continue to influence my life on a daily basis. Humility, at the honor to allow my words to appear alongside his.

History played such an important role in my father's life. His life was strangely and ironically parallel to that of Giambattista Vico. In chapter 1, "An Obscure Life," my father describes Vico's early years: the intervention of the Jesuits in his life; the poverty and chaotic life in which he lived; the precociousness of the young Giambattista. Antonio Vico, Giambattista's father, was a young "*contadino*" who moved to Naples in search of a better life. So, too, did my grandfather, Nicola Caponigri, move from the "*campagna*" outside of Naples in search of a better life. But my grandfather's journey was much longer—and led him to America, specifically

Chicago, with his twenty-one year-old "*contadina*" bride, also "*assai melanconica*"as Giambattista's mother has been described. Antonio Vico raised his eight children in poverty with the hope of education as their salvation and the grace of the intervention of the Jesuits. So, too, did Nicola Caponigri hope that education would save his son, and turned my father, his thirteenth child, over to the care of the Jesuits when my father, A. Robert Caponigri, was only twelve years old. My father writes of Giambattista Vico, the precocious young man who "longed for nothing so much as for a period of withdrawal in which, freed from the uncertainties of his domestic and economic situation...he might find the path right for him" (p. 13). So, too, did my father long for this withdrawal and found solace and a great peace in a life with the Jesuits until he was well into his twenties. My father states in his opening remarks regarding Vico's life that the life which Giambattista Vico, "...not without misgivings, ventured to communicate to the world was an obscure life, its riches wholly inward and of the spirit..." (p. 12). The life of A. Robert Caponigri could be described in the same way—the essence of his being, the manner in which he lived his life was one in which he sought, through his scholarship, riches wholly inward and of the spirit. He sought a catholicity of both mind and spirit. He sought Art and Philosophy, Science and Theology not as separate areas of inquiries, but each as a segment of the whole. Each a manifestation of a common creative force. My father looked always to history as his guide and was described, at his death, as one who possessed a cosmic instinct, whose vision was historical and aesthetic, rather than metaphysical or analytical. He proceeded from the primacy of "*sacra historia*" and "*sacra doctrina*." And thanks in no small part to his early Jesuit training, possessed a knowledge of the history of theology, history of philosophy and ecclesiology which few could match.

Genius, it has been said, emerges from that rare mind which admits consideration of all theses digesting each in the light of a comprehensive spirit and intelligence. This is granted to precious few, and I am grateful and humbled that one so granted was my father.

"Well done, good and faithful servant.
You were faithful in matters small and great.
Come, share your master's joy."
Matthew 25:21

With eternal gratitude to my father.
Historia magistra vitae.

LISA CAPONIGRI, J.D.
Notre Dame, Indiana
September 2003

REFERENCES

References to the works of Vico are to the following editions and under the following symbols:

Auto.: *L'Autobiografia, Il Carteggio e Le Poesie Varie* a cura di Benedetto Croce. Bari, Gius. Laterza e Figli, 1911.

OI: *Le Orazioni Inaugurali, Il De Italorum Sapientia e Le Polemiche*
DIS   a cura di Giovanni Gentile e Fausto Nicolini. Bari, Gius. Laterza e Figli, 1914.

DU: *Il Diritto Universale* a cura di Fausto Nicolini. Bari, Gius. Laterza e Figli, 1936, 3v.

SNP: *La Scienza Nuova Prima* a cura di Fausto Nicolini. Bari, Gius. Laterza e Figli, 1931.

SNS: *La Scienza Nuova Seconda* a cura di Fausto Nicolini. Terza Edizione Riveduta. Bari, Gius. Laterza e Figli, 1942, 2v.
  The New Science of Giambattista Vico translated from the third edition (1744) by Thomas Goddard Bergin and Max Harold Fisch. Cornell University Press, Ithaca, New York, 1948.

References to other editions are noted as they occur. Citations from the *Autobiografia*, the *Orazioni Inaugurali*, the *De Italorum Sapientia* and the *Scienza Nuova Prima* are by pages; of the *Diritto Universale* by volume and page; of the *Scienza Nuova Seconda* by marginal numbers which correspond in the Italian edition and the English translation.

ACKNOWLEDGMENT

ONLY in retrospect is it possible to realize how much is owed to so many for the completion of even so modest a work as the present. In appreciation of generous aid and courtesy acknowledgment is made to the agencies of the Fulbright Act both in the United States and in Italy; to the Italian Institute for Historical Studies in Naples and especially to its founder and president Senator Benedetto Croce, for access to the unique collection of Vichiana housed there; to the eminent Vichian scholar, Fausto Nicolini; to the Very Rev. Martin C. D'Arcy, S.J., of Mount St., London, for encouragement in the most difficult stage of the work; to the Committee on Publications of the University of Notre Dame for a partial subvention toward publication and finally to the many friends both in the United States and in Italy who by generous acts have in many ways made the work lighter, among whom it is impossible to pass unnamed the Very Rev. Christopher O'Toole, C.S.C., of New York City, Professor Raffaello Franchini of the college of the Nunziatella in Naples, Dr. Eduardo Sturchio of Villa Sturchio, S. Giorgio a Cremano, the Rev. Leo R. Ward, C.S.C., and Professor Paul E. McLane of the University of Notre Dame.

A. ROBERT CAPONIGRI

Capri
October 1952

INTRODUCTION

THE course of European thought, the eminent historian Paul Hazard has written,[1] must surely have been different had Giambattista Vico, in his own day, achieved a truly European audience. This is indeed tremendous homage to a thinker who for two centuries has remained, for the most part, a shadowy and uncertain figure in the annals of philosophy, and of itself might well afford ample justification for the re-examination of his opinions. Nor does Hazard stand alone in his appraisal of Vico. The Italians, among whom there exists an unbroken tradition of Vichian scholarship, have in the latest transformations of this tradition advanced a view of the history of modern philosophy in which the conventional perspectives are altered radically to bring Vico into proper focus; they discover in him both the fulfilment of the Renaissance and the anticipation of the Kantian revolution. This may appear to observers of different cultural background somewhat exuberant, if not chauvinistic. There is, however, nothing exuberant in the steadily widening circle of interest in Vico attested by an ever-increasing reference to his thought and by such major ventures as the translation of the *Scienza Nuova Seconda* into English.[2] This interest, moreover, reflects at every turn a sense of that alternality which Hazard suggests. The present essay, consequently, might with justice find its *raison d'être* in this accentuated sense of the historical stature of Vico.

To a certain extent it does. Part of its purpose is to contribute, so far as it may, to the just conception of his place in history. This is not, however, the basic nor the final reason of its being. This lies rather in a persuasion of the immediate relevance of Vico's thought to the urgent problems of contemporary philosophy. Such relevance, in-

[1] Paul Hazard, *La Crise de la Conscience Européenne*, Paris, Bonvin e Cie, 1935, I, 432.

[2] *The New Science of Giambattista Vico*, translated from the third edition (1744) by Thomas Goddard Bergin and Max Harold Fisch, Cornell University Press, Ithaca, 1948.

I

deed, alone could justify the appraisal of Hazard. Only the problems which the actual course of the development of European thought has engendered can make it meaningful to suggest that Vico's speculations bore the seeds of a genuine alternative. Hazard's sentiment is, consequently, so far as it can be justified and in its profounder meaning, an attribution of just such contemporary significance to Vico.

The point of contact between Vico and contemporary thought is the problem of man. The key to the modern problem of man, the problem of man at the mid-point of the twentieth century, lies in the naturalism of contemporary speculation; modern man has consented to think of himself as continuous with and as immanent to the process of nature. This would not seem, at first glance, peculiar to modern man. Classical man, too, viewed himself in this same context and manner. The difference lies in the conception of nature of itself. The concept of nature upon which the classical notion of man was predicated possessed one characteristic which sets it off sharply from the concept of nature in modern thought. The nature of classical thought was able to sustain, within certain limits, the notions of spirit and of subjectivity. It did not demand of man, consequently, a total alienation from himself as the price of his continuity with nature. On the contrary, it envisaged man as the immanent *logos* or rationality of nature and as the proximate end, or *telos*, of its processes and thus sustained and vindicated his intimate intuitions of his spirituality and subjectivity. The modern concept of nature, by contrast, demands of man precisely the surrender of these insights. This transformation in the concept of nature itself has been effected by the course of the development of the sciences of nature in modern times. This development seems at first glance to suggest and to demand a trenchant assertion of these qualities or attributes in man; this was the intended force of the Kantian critique. In fact, however, this intention was frustrated because it moved against the profounder implications of modern science. It was presently made clear that the innermost speculative demands of the modern natural sciences involved the elimination of all subjectivity from the structure of nature. Transcendent subjectivity is eliminated by the very openness of the universe of modern science; the subjectivity of man is logically cancelled by the inclusion of the processes of human consciousness in the subjectless process of nature and matter. The universe, the nature, which modern science envisages is essentially independent of the presence of any subject; the 'anonymous subject' of which some philosophers

2

of science have spoken logically suffers the same fate as the 'thing-in-itself' of Kantian criticism. The modern problem of man, consequently, is the recovery of the subjectivity of which the modern concept of nature has divested him and to recover it, not as mere persuasion, but as science and truth.

One course to this end has appeared to lie in a reversion to classical naturalism and not a few have attempted this catabasis. Such, however, was not Vico's way. The modern temper was too thoroughly his own. Instead, Vico offers to modern man an alternative principle for the vindication of his own spirituality and subjectivity. That alternative is history.

The dichotomy which Vico establishes between nature and history is very nearly absolute and rests upon a single principle. While the modern concept of nature may demand by its inner logic the dissolution of the human subject, history is wholly man's presence to himself as subject and as spirit. If man would discover himself, therefore, he must look not to nature but to history. History is the work of man's hands, or rather, of his whole spirit; it is, moreover, a work in which man creates, not an order extrinsic and alien to himself, but his own being in its ideal plenitude and its existential concreteness. Finally, Vico offers this alternative to man not at a late moment in the development of the modern predicament, but at a relatively early stage, indeed almost at its inception. The prophetic overcast is never absent from his thought. Vico's own enterprise, upon which he entered, by his own account, as early as the composition of the *Orazioni Inaugurali*, and which finds its fullest expression in the *Scienza Nuova*, is precisely the recovery of the spirituality and the subjectivity of man in history.

The *Scienza Nuova*, by the very vastness and complexity of its structure and by its exuberant detail has won for Vico a reputation for obscurity akin to the reputation of the scholastic doctors for casuistry and subtlety. Much of this obscurity may be dispelled, however, by the observation that, by the very conception of the work, Vico's thought is compelled, almost simultaneously, to move in two at least superficially, opposed directions. The work is orientated, in the first place, toward the concreteness and particularity which is the reality of history; it is concerned with the positive, concrete structures of human society as these have appeared in the temporal, existential movement of history. At the same time, the movement of the work lies in the opposite direction, toward the elaboration of the theoretical and methodological principles which must sustain

3

concrete historical research and construction; in a word, toward the elaboration of the theory of history in both its ontological and its methodological dimensions. This diversity of movement generates the basic tension of the work. Both these concerns are essential and integral to the *Scienza Nuova* as Vico conceived and executed it; both are not, however, of equal relevance to modern thought. It is in the theory of history elaborated in the course of the *Scienza Nuova* that the relevance of Vico for contemporary thought resides. For this reason, the present essay conceives as its primary purpose the disengagement of this theory from the vast material in which it is incorporated.

In this undertaking the essay has from the first encountered both encouragement and obstruction. The strongest encouragement derives from Vico himself; indeed, it may be said quite truly that the essay would continue an effort initiated by Vico. The 'second' and definitive form of the *Scienza Nuova* is characterized by the disengagement of its speculative and methodological principles from the concrete 'philological' investigations which constitute its positive programme and the restatement of these principles as the axioms, principles and method of the book of 'Elements'. The disengagement is only partial; it constitutes *prima facie* evidence, nevertheless, of Vico's conviction that the distinction could and should be made.

The obstructing circumstances appear in the powerful schools of interpretation which have grown up about Vico's thought, especially in Italy, where, as it has been noted, the tradition of Vichian scholarship is long and unbroken. The schools now regnant may be designated the idealistic and the realistic, more, it must be noted, by way of convenience than by way of accurate identification. The first centres about the Vichian scholarship of Benedetto Croce; the second, or realistic, is somewhat a reaction against the first and is inextricably associated with the vindication of Vico's Catholicism which Crocian scholarship seems to many to have impugned. The debt of all Vichian study to the work of Croce, it must be said at once, is immeasurable; singlehandedly, he has founded modern Vichian scholarship, and no step can be taken in Vichian studies without immediate recourse to his work. The realistic school of interpretation in its turn rests upon authority and scholarship almost equally awe-inspiring. Together, consequently, these schools or tendencies may be said to define the masterlines of Vichian study.[1] At the same time, however, they run

[1] Croce's basic contributions are the volume *La Filosofia di G. B. Vico*, Bari, G. Laterza, 1911 (4th ed. 1947), and the comprehensive bibliography continued by

a grave danger of imposing obstructing and inhibiting limitations of the horizon of inquiry and of becoming a veritable Scylla and Charybdis for one who would attain the thought of Vico himself. The strong influence which emanates from the one and from the other tends to deflect inquiry from its proper object, Vico, and to cause it to founder on the shoals of partisanship in a new war of the schools. The present essay has undertaken to run this Scylla and Charybdis. It seeks to be neither crocian nor amerian, neither idealistic nor realistic, but simply Vichian, so far as this purism is at all meaningful and attainable.

The form of the essay has been dictated by the historical and philological circumstances surrounding its objective. Because Vico's life is practically unknown save in a very limited sphere and because his thought grew, not only with a certain necessity, but even with a certain passion from the preoccupations of his own life, a brief biographical account is first essayed. Vico, as he is approached not only through the pages of the *Autobiography* but also through the detailed information which the devoted research of Nicolini has brought together, grows in human stature. The mere facts of the biographical narrative take on colour and warmth and it becomes highly relevant, even to the most abstract consideration of his thought, that this philosopher whose thought was always of mankind was so passionately attached to his native place that nostalgia could overwhelm him the moment that Capri passed from his line of vision. The story of Vico pawning his solitary possession of value to pay the costs of the printing of the first *Scienza Nuova* is so humanly moving as to cast a human warmth over the very pages of his laborious treatise.

From this concern with the man the essay passes abruptly to its proper concern, the theory of history which Vico elaborates as the archetectonic principle of his 'New Science'. The abruptness of this passage is, perhaps, regrettable. It might have been better, as it would certainly have been more grateful to the writer's personal taste, to view the theory as growing out of the life of the thinker. To do so, however, would have involved the composition of a work of quite a different quality and tone. Above all, this alternate procedure would have repressed the aspect of Vico's thought which the present essay

---

Fausto Nicolini: *Bibliografia Vichiana*, Napoli Ricciardi, 1947-8. The definitive edition of Vico's work by Fausto Nicolini is also Crocean in principle. All subsequent discussion has been influenced by Croce's treatment of Vico. The monumental document of the 'realist' school is the work of Franco Amerio: *Introduzione allo Studio di G. B. Vico*, Torino Soc. Ed. Internazionale n.d. (1947).

has sought to throw into clearest relief, its relevance for contemporary speculation. The emphasis would necessarily have been upon the relevance to Vico's own experience and growth. A more grateful task, consequently, was surrendered to one which appeared more urgent.

In the exposition of the Vichian theory of history which constitutes the body of the essay, one purpose has dominated all other interests and considerations. This is the purpose of exhibiting Vico's theory of history as a genuine philosophical undertaking and not as the construction of a 'philosophy of history' nor as a mere treatise on the methodology of historiography. The disrepute into which the 'philosophy of history' as a philosophic discipline has fallen is deserved; injustice is involved only in the inclusion of the *Scienza Nuova* among works of this description. The clarification of the distinction between the 'philosophy of history' and the philosophical theory of history is perhaps the greatest debt which Vichian study owes to Croce. The great merit of Vico is to have stated and, within his own terms, to have resolved the philosophical problem of history as the basic problem of the philosophical study of man. It is this problem, in the authentic form in which it appears in Vico, that the present essay addresses.

The Vichian theory of history, it was noted above, is elaborated as the archetectonic principle of the 'New Science'. As such, it possesses both a speculative and a methodological dimension. This articulation is inherent in the theory itself. It is very nearly mandatory, consequently, that it be preserved and respected in the exposition of the theory. Accordingly, the speculative dimension of the theory preoccupies the first five chapters of the expository portion of the essay. The chapter entitled 'The Natural Law' endeavours to fix the context and the first form in which the speculative problem of history suggests itself to Vico; this context proves to be the speculative problems of jurisprudence, with especial reference to the problem of the natural law, and in this context the basic terms of the problem and of the theory of history, time and idea, appear, inchoately, but incisively. What is projected inchoately in the context of the natural law is clarified and elaborated to its definitive form in the context of the 'Science of Humanity'; time and idea are seen to be the radical terms in which all historical process of culture is comprehensible. The chapter bearing the title 'The Science of Humanity' follows the process of elaboration. The introduction of the human subject as the principle of the synthesis of time and idea and the exploration of its dynamic structure is the intent and purpose of the Vichian doctrine of the 'Modifications of the Human Mind'; in this doctrine, which is the subject of the fourth chapter of the essay, Vico identifies history unambiguously as the presence of the human subject to itself and describes its pure phenomenology. The historicity of the human subject involves that subject, in Vico's view, in radical contradiction; this view leads to his elaboration of the concept of 'providence', which is, in essence, the rectifying principle of human history. Finally, in the chapters entitled respectively 'Ideal and Eternal History and the Course of the Nations in Time' and 'Ricorsi', Vico's treatment of the time structure of history, both the universal history of mankind and the particular histories of the nations, in themselves and in their relation to universal history, is examined. With this chapter the exposition of the speculative dimension of the theory of history is naturally concluded.

The consideration of the methodological dimension of the theory is compressed into the chapters entitled 'Philosophy and Philology' and 'Poetry, Myth, and Language'. The unity of philosophy and philology in the processes of the 'Science' supplies the primary methodological concept of Vico's theory of history. This unity rests upon certain characteristics of the human subject of history, especially upon the duality, existential and symbolic or expressive, of every historical act of spirit. Every existential form of human culture and group life, that is to say, every institution and law and above all language is by its very character as an act of the human spirit the expression and the symbol of that spirit. Philology, taken simply in itself, is the science of these existential forms and of their interpretation and historical comprehension. But philology, conceived thus autonomously, is powerless to effect its own purpose without the aid and action of philosophy; for it is philosophy that by its reflective action defines and clarifies the inward ideal principles of the spirit whose living movement is realized in the processes of culture. If philology is powerless without philosophy, so too is philosophy impotent once it essays its own task of ideal penetration of spirit outside the structure of the concrete, existential and symbolic forms which philology identifies for it. The definition of the forms of the spirit independently of this existential frame of reference would constitute an empty gesture of the spirit itself; philosophy can be, in its authentic character, no formal *a priori* construction or imposition, but the inward discernment by spirit of its own ideality within the existential processes of history. Philosophy and philology are thus united in the theory of history as the irreducible members of a dialectic of distincts whose movement must prove the only effective method of history as historiography.

Poetry is the term by which Vico designates the synthetic and active character of the first historical form of the human spirit which he has distinguished in the doctrine of the 'modifications of the human mind'. It is for him the veritable 'key' to the entire project of the 'New Science' because the documents from which that science, in its positive programme, must take its point of departure are all poetic in this sense. The essential poetic activity is the generation of myth; the first forms of human history are, therefore, pervasively and substantively mythical. But the myth is for Vico no idle evocation of the dreaming spirit of man; it is the spontaneous, imaginative form under which man symbolizes to himself the historical processes of his culture in their universally relevant features. Every existential form of the spontaneous human consciousness is, consequently, myth; and the interpretation of myth is the primary methodological principle of the 'New Science' in the execution of the first phases of its positive programme. Language, in its turn, is for Vico the system of signs generated for the communication and preservation of myth. As poetry is the key to the mind of primitive man, that is to the human spirit in its first expressive and existential time-form, and myth is the key to poetry, so is language the key to myth.

It is clear that the Vichian theory of poetry, myth and language within the framework of the total theory of history needs to be completed by the theory of the expressive and symbolic processes of the reflective form of spirit, the second which he had distinguished in the doctrine of the modifications of the human mind. Although there are many adumbrations of such a theory in Vico and though he shows himself at every point completely aware of the necessity of this development for the integrity of his 'New Science', the work was never actually carried out. It is for this reason that the 'New Science' remains essentially a fragment, and it is precisely from the point of view of the theory of history as the archetectonic principle of the 'Science' that one is especially sensitive of its fragmentary character.

Among the 'discoveries' of the 'New Science' in which Vico took especial complacency was the 'discovery of the True Homer'. The significance of this discovery for the general theory of history is explored in the chapter of the present essay entitled 'Homer'. The immediate frame of reference within which Vico conducted the positive programme of the 'New Science' was classical culture. This, as the essay strives to make clear, imposes no essential relativism on his theory. Homer is the primary document, in his view, of the early history of classical man, from which he may make the transition, essential to his whole project, to universal history. The Homeric poems open to him the culture and the soul of classical man in his heroic age and prove to be 'two histories' of civility in the heroic age of Greece. In the establishment of this character of the Homeric poems lies the essential Vichian claim to the discovery of the 'True Homer'. In Homer, conceived in this manner, he sees vindicated all of the speculative and methodological principles of the theory of history which he has developed; at the same time, the poems prove the most effective instrument of the positive research of the 'New Science'.

The fragmentary character of the 'New Science' has been noted; so too has Vico's sensitivity to this character and the tentatives and adumbrations of the integral science with which the actual 'Science' teems. The final chapter of the present essay, in order to illustrate the total operation of the theory of history, selects for exposition one area of human history within which Vico achieves at least a relatively complete effectuation of the programme of the 'New Science'. This is the area of the theory of the state, or political philosophy. Upon this material Vico deploys the resources of the theory of history contained in the 'New Science'. The result most nearly approaches the achievement which he envisaged for the 'New Science'; it embraces the construction at once of a history, a pure phenomenology, and a philosophical definition of human polity, according to the speculative and the methodological principles of the 'Science'. Such a 'vue d'ensemble', in which the full impact of the theory of history might be felt, appeared to be the most fitting conclusion to its exposition.

The purpose of the essay will be achieved, from the writer's point of view, if it contributes in some small way to the growing conviction that the inclusion of Vico in the perennial dialogue which is philosophy must add to it a fresh and vital dimension.

I

AN OBSCURE LIFE

ACASUAL suggestion of Leibnitz, whose influence pervaded the intellectual life of his time must, in all probability, be accounted the remote cause of the composition of Vico's *Autobiography*. In a letter to the Italianist, Louis Bourguet, praising the scientific work of the Padovan, Antonio Conti, Leibnitz expresses the wish that writers 'nous donnassent l'histoire de leurs decouvertes et les progrès par lesquels ils y sont arrivés'. This letter was, without doubt, shown by Bourguet to the subject of its eulogies and it was from the latter that the enterprising Conte Gianartico de Porcía, again in all probability, received the first suggestion that such a proposal might be realized among the scientists and scholars of Italy. Thus far conjecture. It is fact, however, that in 1724 Porcía began, through various channels, to solicit such 'histories' from his countrymen. Among those solicited were eight Neapolitans, of whom five are unnamed in the records, while two, Paolo Maria Doria and Nicola Cirillo, already enjoyed a certain reputation beyond the immediate pale of Neapolitan culture. The eighth was Giambattista Vico.[1]

Vico, it would seem, at first received the invitation with some misgiving, nor is his reluctance difficult to understand. The harrowing experience of the university competition of 1723 was fresh in his memory. More recently still, the trials accompanying the publication of the first *Scienza Nuova* had subjected him to injustice and indignity. He knew the little esteem in which he was held by his colleagues and his own university. Reassurance came only from the inclusion of his friend, Doria, in the list of those solicited; Doria's reputation was such as to insure the seriousness and dignity of any project with which his name might be associated. Early in 1725 Vico indicated his compliance. He set about the composition immediately and, with his usual dispatch in writing, had brought it to comple-

[1] The letter of Leibnitz (22 March 1714) is cited by Fausto Nicolini, *Bibliografia Vichiana*, vol. I, 61, after Croce, 'La Critica', XVI (1918), 216.

tion by the June of that same year. The life which he thus, not without misgivings, ventured to communicate to the world was an obscure life, its riches wholly inward and of the spirit.

I

Santa Chiara, beloved of Neapolitans, lifts its ruined but still graceful tower above the serried rooftops of the city. About it, the unmoving mountains and the gently troubled bay draw a magic circle of serene and smiling nature beneath the intense and throbbing light of the Mediterranean sky. At the feet of Santa Chiara's tower, however, nothing is untroubled, nothing serene. Here the restless life of the poorest quarter of Naples seethes and bubbles and sometimes roars along the narrow and tortuous streets. Before the gates of decayed palaces street vendors hawk their wares; plodding donkeys, laden almost to the breaking point, dispute the way with men who stumble under burdens hardly less onerous. A pastry-cook, balancing a tray of smoking *pizza* on his head, is followed by the hungry, and sometimes plotting, glances of clamouring boys and idle men, while in the tower's shadow a legless, sightless creature lifts imploring arms and voice to God and passers-by. Along the narrow street which leads past the palace of the Filomarino toward the square of San Domenico the tenders of the tiny, shabby shops lounge in dim doorways while here and there on the pavement, before the airless *bassi*, a mother stoops above a minute fire, preparing the family meal. It is the life of the Neapolitan poor, lived out in all its contradictions, without reticence or apology; a life basically unchanged through centuries, the first life Vico knew and the life from which, in outward circumstances, he was never wholly delivered.[1]

For part of its length between Santa Chiara and San Domenico Maggiore this street is called by a new name, Mariano Semmola; but beyond, where it opens on the Largo San Domenico, it retains the name as well as the character it bore when, in the middle decades of the seventeenth century, a young *contadino* from the region of Maddaloni, one Antonio Vico, first stumbled on its unaccustomed cobbles. San Biagio dei Librai, it is still called, and the tiny bookstalls from which the name derives are still, as they were then, prominent among its dim and cluttered shops. Here Antonio Vico found occupation at a succession of humble tasks; but he was, in the manner

[1] The circumstances and environment of Vico's youth are described by Fausto Nicolini, *La Giovinezza di G. B. Vico*, Bari, G. Laterza, 1932, 1–23.

of his kind, both shrewd and ambitious. Although himself almost illiterate, he painfully accumulated a small capital and in his turn set up as a vendor of books in one of the section's dark *stamberghe*. To the single dark room above his shop he led first one, and on her death, a second wife from the families of the district. And here, the second, a woman, on her son's testimony, of temperament 'assai melinconica' bore him eight children, of whom the sixth, born 23 June 1668, was baptized Giambattista, and lived to become the subject of the *Autobiography*.

This Giambattista pictures himself as precocious, and so, indeed, he must have appeared among the laggard and buffoonish boys who carved the benches and played at dice during the teachers' lectures in the dusty halls of the Jesuit college. In fact, however, his genius was laborious and late-flowering, his early training fragmentary and chaotic. A three years' incapacitation, it is true, was remedied somewhat by completion of the entire elementary course in a year. Impatient of dawdling methods and pedantic masters he struggled alone, in the night solitude of his father's shop, with such heterogeneous matter as his Alvarez, his Peter of Spain and Paul the Venetian, with the Spanish subtleties of Suarez. Committed by his father, still ambitious, but now for his children, to the law in the studio of one Verde, a master of the procedures of the law courts, he tore himself impatiently away to return to his solitary meditations now over the tomes of Voltaeius and Canisius on the *due ragioni*, the civil and the canon law. It is even recorded that, a beardless Solomon, he went into the courts on his father's account and confounded the doctors.

All this is literally true; it is also true, therefore, that in a literal sense Vico was precocious. Yet in the final analysis, all this added up to nothing. The matters which jostled each other in his capacious memory were heterogeneous and unrelated; from his long hours of application no genuine discipline had ensued; no trace of the emergence of a distinctive *forma mentis* was in evidence. And no one, happily, appreciated this situation more fully than Vico himself. He longed for nothing so much as for a period of withdrawal in which, freed from the uncertainties of his domestic and economic situation, and above all from the unilateral pressures of his own education, he might find the path right for him. It can occasion no surprise, consequently, that he should consider providential the offer made to him at this juncture to go as tutor to the family estate of the Rocca, at Vatolla in the remote Cilento, where he would be assured both a salubrious air for his own delicate constitution and ample leisure for the programme of self-education which he envisaged. Not, indeed, that from an absolute point of view this should be considered an ideal arrangement; no one, as Nicolini has observed, was in reality less suited to be his own preceptor than Vico. The historical fact, however, is that without these years at Vatolla the *Scienza Nuova* is inconceivable; both in its strength and power, and in its abundant defects and lapses, it is the faithful expression of the *forma mentis* shaped during this germinal period. The significance of Vatolla, in the last analysis, must depend on one's evaluation of the *Scienza Nuova* itself.

It is with respect to this sojourn at Vatolla that the critics, and especially the relentless Nicolini, have discerned in the *Autobiography*, that 'distortion of perspective' which renders it a document, if not suspect, then at least difficult to interpret.[1] Vico depicts these years as a period of unbroken withdrawal from his native city, during which its culture, and especially the movement of intellectual resurgence at that precise moment reaching its apogee, had become alien to him. On neither point can his account be sustained. The habits of the Rocca family made residence in Naples a portion of each year obligatory, while the whole form of his personal culture, as well as the patterns of his associations, demonstrate, not only his familiarity, but his profound sympathy with, and acquiescence in this movement, the elements of which become, in considerable measure, the elements of his own thought. Setting aside for the present the problem of the possible source of this distortion in Vico's mind, it will be of profit to retrace the shape of these years.

The cultural 'risorgimento' (the term is that of Ferdinando Galiani) in Naples which reached its zenith in the last decades of the seventeenth century had its first stirrings in the work of Camillo Colonna and received a major impetus from the return from Rome, in 1649, of Tommaso Cornelio. In its negative aspect, it constituted a revolt against the medievalism which in Naples, more, perhaps, than anywhere else in Europe, still maintained itself. In its positive and dynamic aspect it was an attempt to bring Neapolitan culture as swiftly as possible abreast of the general cultural life of Europe, and especially of France, England, Holland and Tuscany. In substance it was a vast eclecticism, in tone and style imitative and puristic. This voracious eclecticism embraced extensively every area of cultural life. Neapolitan scholars threw themselves with equal en-

---

[1] Nicolini's statement is to be found in *La Giovinezza*, p. 95.

thusiasm into the cultivation of the natural and experimental sciences, of mathematics, of the new medicine; into speculation in the fields of morals and jurisprudence, and into the practical reform of juridical and forensic procedure; into controversies over literary style and, finally, into the encyclopedic assimilation of foreign cultures through the assembling of libraries of foreign works, through correspondence with foreign scholars and academies and by journeys of self-instruction beyond the Alps and even to the Orient.

Within the special area of philosophical speculation the eclectic character of the movement is very clear: the diverse currents of the Italian Renaissance, neoplatonism, brunianism, the philosophy of Telesio and Campanella, the atomism of Gassendi, with its democratian and epicurean elements and its deterministic and free-thinking tendencies, experimentalism of the type both of Galileo and of Bacon, and finally, the rationalism of Descartes and its various derivatives found ardent and even sectarian disciples. In literature this period witnessed the strong revival of the Virgilian, Horatian and Ciceronian cults, a return to the golden latinity as reflected in the high Italian Renaissance, while in the vernacular, it brought to birth the poetic neo-petrachianism of Porcella and the puristic prose movement of capuanism, called after Leonardo di Capua, both of which were directed against the cult of the baroque but which they did not succeed entirely in dislodging. These interests and enthusiasms found social expression in the formation of numerous academies and *salotti* and, on a less formal basis, the spontaneous appearance of numerous gathering places, in bookstores, pharmacies, etc., each with its special attendance, where the questions of the hour were discussed.

Of all this activity and ferment the young Vico was not the remote, passive and even slightly disdainful spectator of the *Autobiography*, but an alert and responsive participant. The eclecticism of the movement became, in fact, the *forma mentis* of his youth and early maturity, an attitude which persisted until the second renewal of his legal studies, and was faithfully reflected in his studious pursuits. There was no area of learned discussion and dispute into which he did not enter and, indeed, sometimes intrude himself: mathematics, physics, the new medicine, all claimed his attention. Conceiving himself, according to the admission of the *Autobiography*, as above all a poet, he entered most ardently into the disputes about style, becoming in verse a porcellian, in prose a capuist and purist, in whom, indeed, the mannerisms of the purist were to become second nature, and, above all, a passionate cultivator of the golden latinity. Even at this time, however, the radically philosophical temper of his genius manifested itself in his special sensitivity to the philosophical currents which swirled about him. He absorbed, with a primitive hunger of the mind, every viewpoint presented to him. The neoplatonism of the Italian Renaissance became at this time, as Nicolini has so strongly expressed it, 'blood of his blood';[1] Lucretius could move him to the desperate lines of the *Affetti* and, more importantly, so deeply impress his imagination as to dominate certain material details of his thought even to the formulations of the second *Scienza Nuova*; Descartes and his method, as late as the revised form of the *Orazioni*, could stir him to eulogy, while he could boast in 1725 of Leclerc's commendation of the mathematical form of the proofs of the *Diritto Universale* and in the second *Scienza Nuova* speak with pride, if also with a considerable amount of delusion, of its geometrical form. Nor was he absent from the informal discussions, the *salotti*, the academies, which constituted the social expression of the new culture; his acquaintance and friendship among its exponents and leading figures was both wide and warm and he retained even to the time of the *Autobiography* a sincere devotion to their memory and merits. Nor was he, to credit some accounts and conjecture, wholly absent from the councils and associations of those 'jeunes fous' (the term is Arnauld's), who by their professions of atheism brought about their heads and upon their lives the fury and the blight of the inquisition; indeed, certain lamentations of his later life would seem to testify to such association, testimony, in a man of Vico's temper, stronger than any account or conjecture.

Nevertheless, at this same time, and mainly in the semi-solitude of Vatolla, Vico was pursuing other philosophical studies which were later to enter into dialectical conflict with the elements of the new culture and was laying the foundations of the vast, though less than flawless, erudition which was to provide the 'philological' dimension of the 'New Science'. This period, under the compulsion of his tutorial duties, saw the first renewal of his legal studies, the area of learning most fruitful, perhaps, in the total perspective of his thought. In the *Autobiography*, it is true, Vico dismisses this direction of his interests in a few lines and without details; but it is most credible that here, in addition to his 'penetration of the laws and the canons', he began that study both of feudal and of Roman law and

[1] Nicolini, *La Giovinezza*, p. 103, and on Lucretius, p. 120. Vico, on his reading of Lucretius, *Auto.*, p. 19.

history which provides the field for the most imposing developments of his method. In connection with the dogmatic questions underlying canon law he developed his interest in theology and became acquainted, though at second hand it would seem, with the intellect with which, in the summation of his old age, he was to express the most genuine and profound sympathy, that of St. Augustine. He applied himself 'seriously' to the study of moral philosophy in the ancient Greeks, 'beginning with Aristotle' and continuing, with the necessary recurrence to Plato and the Platonic Socrates, through the Stoics and Epicureans.[1] At this time, no doubt, he first read the philologists of profession, the Scaligers, Casaubon and others, as well as the *Elegantiae* of Valla which were to exercise a permanent effect on his latinity. And here surely must have begun those studies which were to give him an excellent command of Greek language and history, a rudimentary but usable knowledge of Hebrew and that mastery of Latin style which, he asserts, not less than a decade of unremitting application could promise anyone. Within the framework of his eclecticism, in a word, there began to take form, in the years at Vatolla, that hard core of humanism which in the end, and in so original a manner, defines his true *forma mentis*.

These years at Vatolla had, however, to end; when his charges had arrived at early manhood, Vico's work was over, and in 1695 he returned to his father's house in Naples. Here he immediately became active in cultural circles, forming friendships, frequenting academies and *salotti*, often among the extreme elements of the new culture and of the anticurialist circles whose power, because of the harsh conduct of the inquisition and the condemnations of 1693, had gained considerable force in the city. As evidence of the fact that his attachment to these circles was purely cultural and erudite, free from political overtones, is the fact that at the same time he was cultivating those elements of the older culture in which humanistic echoes and vestiges were strongest. These activities and the exciting associations which they brought him could not, however, disguise the problem which confronted him nor long defer its solution; he had to choose a career, or, to phrase it more prosaically, to secure a livelihood. Return to the practice of law, begun so precociously and so auspiciously a decade before, was urged upon him, but the initial repugnance which he had felt had with the years only grown stronger. He turned as the readiest, but not as the definitive solution, to the task he knew best, instruction, in the meanwhile remaining

[1] *Auto.*, p. 11.

17

alert for some position in which his accomplishments might bring a just recompense. Such seemed to offer when the post of secretary-general of the city fell vacant; in the tradition of the Renaissance, the chief requisite for this position was a mastery of Latin style, and so it would seem only justice that it should fall to him as the reward of those years of strenuous cultivation of the golden latinity. He saw it pass, however, through political manipulations, to one whose competence was obviously inferior—an experience he was to know more than once. In 1697 a second opportunity offered itself, and this time Vico did not fail. Announcement was made of a competition to select the successor to the recently vacated chair of rhetoric in the University of Naples, and Vico, encouraged by his friend, the influential Caravita, determined to present himself. On the twenty-fourth of October, 1698, he successfully demonstrated his competence in an hour-long disquisition on a passage from Quintilian and on the third of January 1699, was officially notified of his appointment to the post. His success, though certain, was not to be thought brilliant; of twenty-two possible votes, Vico received twelve, a narrow margin. But with this appointment a new phase of life, both in the intellectual and the material spheres, opened before him. The stipend, though small, gave him some measure of competence and independence; the chair itself, though a minor one, provided both the stimulus and the direction of fresh intellectual labours. With this success, consequently, there opens the second phase of his life which finds its natural term in the publication, in 1725, of the *Scienza Nuova Prima.*

II

Vico introduces his account of this new era in his life and career with the intriguing problem of his 'authors', those writers to whom he attributes a supreme influence over the formation of his thought. To this time he had had acquaintance with only two of them, Plato and Tacitus; the one had attracted by his rugged humanistic realism which penetrated without illusion and yet without despair to the motives which moved men in history, the other by that supreme idealism which, above the welter and conflict of human motives, could contemplate man in his eternal idea. Their power over Vico's mind derived, however, not from these respective attributes taken in abstraction from and in contrast to each other, but rather from the image they evoked of a science of man which would unite these antithetical principles in a cohesive whole which would reveal, within that welter, the immanent activity of that eternal idea. Now Vico associates to their company a third, Francis Bacon, for the compelling reason that in him he discerns, though in an inchoate and unsymmetrical form, precisely that union of the normative and the realistic, as well as a profound criticism, both analytic and programatic, of the system of the sciences. To this trinity there will presently be associated Hugo Grotius. This association of 'authors' is important, obviously, more for the insight it provides into the history of Vico's own thought than for any individual or comparative evaluation of these writers. It indicates, in an oblique manner, the emergence of the speculative problem which will dominate his mature thought, that is, the quest of a speculative concept of history, a process which is reflected clearly in the abundant writings of this period, and the record of which forms, in a way, what has been called the 'external' history of Vico's mind.

According to a custom which Naples shared with almost all the universities of Europe, the scholastic year was opened with a solemn discourse delivered by one of the ordinary professors before the assembled students and faculty—a convocation from which only the permanent professors were free to absent themselves. The pronouncement of this discourse fell to Vico's lot six times during the period 1699–1710, and provided the occasions for the so-called *Orazioni Inaugurali*, documents rich in interest, as the interpretations of Gentile, Corsano, Donati and others have shown, for the history of Vico's thought.[1] These discourses, with the exception of certain earlier, fragmentary passages, are preserved in a revised form dating from shortly before 1710. Vico conceived their purpose as the discussion of universal, metaphysical arguments of civil import; according to this purpose he selected their central theme, learned pursuits, and treated in turn their method and their ends in the light of their relation to human nature, to society and to the Christian conception of man's existence and destiny. Essentially occasional pieces, it is unlikely that in their original form these discourses possessed the organic unity which Vico attributes to them. This character was taken on rather in the process of revision. This process itself, however, is highly revelatory of Vico's development and it is, conse-

[1] Giovanni Gentile, *Studi Vichiani*, Firenze, Le Monnier, 1927; Antonio Corsano, *Umanesimo e Religione in G. B. Vico*, Bari, G. Laterza, 1935; Benvenuto Donati, *Nuovi Studi sulla Filosofia Civile di G. B. Vico*, Firenze, Le Monnier, 1936.

quently, in this revised form that the orations possess their interest for the history of his thought.

With the inaugural dissertations there is sometimes associated, perhaps because of the similarity of occasion which inspired, the *De Nostri Temporis Studiorum Ratione* of 1708. Its occasion was the solemn extraordinary convocation of that year; in form consequently, it offers similarities to the *Orazioni*. In Vico's opinion, however, it clearly possesses a distinct and superior importance. This superiority derives from the character of its theme. In the *Orazioni*, Vico asserts, it is 'clearly apparent' that some great and new argument was exercising his mind, though the specific themes of these discourses were themselves remote from it. In the discourse of 1708, on the contrary, he proposes to treat this theme specifically.[1] This argument of the *De Studiorum Ratione* is associated with his study of Bacon, whom he had recently raised to the rank of his 'authors', at the same time that it reflects that quarrel of the ancients and the moderns which, raging beyond the Alps for some time, was now finding its echoes even in Naples and in Vico's own meditations. It proposed nothing less than the discovery of a common principle about which might be unified 'the whole of divine and profane wisdom', and to secure this end by a comparative analysis of the classical and the modern *rationes* (as distinct, Vico insists, from *methods*) of study, to weigh the advantages and the disadvantages of the modern, to discover in what way its disadvantages might be remedied by recourse to the ancient, and all so as finally to insure a university of studies in which each might sustain and complement the others and the whole by a single spirit.

In this discourse, retrospectively and not programatically, Vico discerns the first outlines of the argument of the far more complex work, known to us now as the *Diritto Universale*;[2] the relation between them turns directly about the insertion into the *De Studiorum Ratione*, for reasons which Vico confesses with great frankness, of an essay on a system of jurisprudence based on the principles of Roman government. This essay, which evoked a protesting reply from one Monsignor Vincenzo Vidania, the prefect of all royal establishments of study, enunciated a thesis, which Vico was never to abandon but later to elaborate and which constitutes one of the chief principles of that dimension of the 'New Science' which he was to call 'Poetic Politics', to the effect that the jurisconsults of Roman antiquity had all been patricians. To Vidania, Vico made a

[1] *Auto.*, p. 31.   [2] *Auto.*, p. 32.

private reply, the public counterpart of which he considered to be the *Diritto Universale* itself. The *De Studiorum Ratione*, though the ends of the inserted essay were never gained, brought Vico considerable satisfaction: first, in the form of the praise of the Dutch scholar Brenckmann; but even more, in the form of the praise and the friendship of his university colleague and former opponent in Capuist dispute, Domenico Aulisio, the man who, according to Nicolini, above all others in the Neapolitan scene might, as a teacher, have corrected the basic faults of Vico's mind and temperament.[1]

Though he characterizes the *De Sapientia Veterum* of Bacon as 'più' ingegnoso e dotto che vero', he found in it as well as in *Cratylus* of Plato the point of departure of those investigations which led to the composition of the lost treatise *De Aequilibrio Corporis Animantis*, dedicated to Aulisio, and, more importantly, of the *De Antiquissima Italorum Sapientia*. He proposed, through investigations into the origins of Latin terms, to gain a clearer understanding of the 'Italic wisdom' which in the school of Pythagoras had anticipated and perhaps surpassed in profundity the later wisdom of Greece. The audience to which he first communicated the results of these investigations was the circle of scholars at whose centre stood the figure of Paolo Doria. Under the encouragement of this group, and especially in response to the enthusiasm shown by Doria himself, whose chief competence lay in mathematics and the natural sciences, Vico determined to apply these principles to the clarification of a system of theoretical medicine, at the same time incorporating into the system the Cartesian physics of the hot and the cold, that the one is movement from without inward, and the other, the reverse. This theoretical system of medicine which Vico calls 'la medicina egiziana del lasco e dello stretto' formed the theme of the *De Aequilibrio Corporis Animantis*. The second work stemming from this inspiration, the *De Antiquissima Italorum Sapientia*, was more ambitious in plan. It was intended to comprise three books, dedicated respectively to metaphysics, with an appendix on logic, physics, or philosophy of nature, and, finally, ethics or morals. The third book apparently remained in the realm of mere intention; the contents of the second unpublished book, now lost, would seem to correspond closely to the speculations recounted in this connection in the *Autobiography*. Only the book on metaphysics appeared, under the comprehensive title, in 1710; dedicated to Doria, it has the form of an open letter to him, but omits

[1] *Auto.*, pp. 33, 37; Nicolini, *La Giovinezza*, passim.

the proposed appendix on logic. This work, within the framework of the delineation of an hypothetical prehistoric italic culture, whose metaphysical concept it proposes to determine, advances a theory of 'metaphysical points' which Vico calls Zenonic, as well as the first form of the gnoseological thesis of the 'convertibility of the truth and the act' which the idealist interpretation makes so fundamental to his philosophy. The adverse reviews of this work which appeared in the *Giornale de' Letterati d'Italia* of Venice in turn provoked the two 'Risposte' of Vico, in which the original theses are elaborated and defended; the one of 1711, the other of 1712, are both now considered integral to the work.

What Vico intended to convey by the designation of certain writers as his 'authors' is not entirely clear; one point, however, is beyond doubt, that he intended by this term to signify a relation, not of direct dependence, but of dialectical opposition. Thus it is to the inadequacies of Bacon's treatment of the nature of myth in the *De Sapientia Veterum* that he traces the inspiration of his own theories of poetry and mythology, while Bacon remains to the end secure in his place among the authors. The same is true of the writer whose influence is even more profound and whom Vico now associates as the fourth and last of these ideal mentors of this thought, Hugo Grotius.

Every evidence supports the belief that Vico was acquainted with the work of Grotius as early as 1713–14; in the *Autobiography*, however, Vico himself places this acquaintanceship somewhat later, allying it with the work undertaken in conjunction with the composition of the Life of *Antonio Carafa*, a relocation which ideal considerations no doubt justify. The life of Carafa was a commissioned work, undertaken at the request of Don Adriano Carafa, the nephew of the subject and a former pupil of Vico, and for its composition access to the family archives was given him. It appeared in 1716, in magnificent format, as Vico says 'in the Dutch style', and won for its author the praise of Pope Clement XI as well as the friendship of the Italian scholar Gianvincenzo Gravina.

Vico, in all his historical writings, was never the archivist; the philosophical and the psychological aspects of his subject always achieved an easy and immediate ascendency in his interest. As a consequence, the preparation of this biography led him to the study, which was no doubt a second or third reading, of Grotius' *De Jure Belli et Pacis* and to his consequent election to the ranks of Vico's authors. In Grotius he discovers, in an eminent degree, precisely that fusion of the philological and the philosophical which is to become the ideal of his own 'New Science' and which he had found lacking in Plato and Tacitus and only inadequately realized in Bacon: for Plato merely 'adorned his philosophical wisdom with the vulgar wisdom of Homer'; while Tacitus 'strews his metaphysical, moral and political (speculations) among the facts as they were handed down to him'; and Bacon did not rise to the consideration of the 'universe of civilization, in all times and among all nations'. Grotius, by contrast, 'unites in the system of one universal law the whole of philosophy and of theology in both of its branches, that is, the fabulous or certain history of events and the history of the three languages, Greek, Latin, and Hebrew, which are the three learned languages which the Christian religion has handed down'. This interest in Grotius extended even to the undertaking of an annotated edition of his work (in which he should be defended against the charges of Gronovius), a project abandoned by Vico 'on the reflection that it was unbecoming a Catholic to adorn with notes the work of an heretical author'.[1] In his turn, however, like Plato, Tacitus and Bacon, Grotius and his thought assume a dialectical function in the formation of Vico's views; it is about Grotius that Vico's anti-intellectualism, in the immediate matter of the theory of history, namely, jurisprudence, is to crystallize.

The extended field of his learned interests and the meditation of his four authors precipitated in Vico's mind the first form of the argument which was to become the core of his mature work, namely, in his own words, 'the conviction that there was not yet in the world of letters a system in which the highest form of philosophy, that is the Platonic subordinated to the Christian religion, was set in accord with a philology which might carry the force of science in both its parts, the two histories, the one of languages, the other of events'. To him, retrospectively, it seemed that it was toward just such a synthesis of philosophy and philology that his own thought from the crude beginnings of the *De Studiorum Ratione* through the metaphysics of the *De Antiquissima* had been tending. With fresh vision he determined upon a more definitive formulation of the principle of such a synthesis and thus set his hand to the composition, to extend over four years, of that complex of treatises which is designated, in Vico's own term, as the *Diritto Universale* and which is so central in the formation of his thought.

Although complex in structure and heterogeneous in its parts,

---

[1] *Auto.*, p. 39.

the *Diritto Universale* presented itself to Vico's mind from the very beginning as a unified and organic work. Evidence of this is furnished by the general introduction to the work which, under the title of *Sinopsi*, he published in the middle of 1721 when the first major section, the *De Uno*, was as yet in manuscript and the others existed only in intention. The purpose of the *Sinopsi* was, in Vico's words, 'to set out beforehand an idea of the work which might demonstrate that such a system (as he contemplated) could actually be effected'. It had a provisional character, looking backward, on the one hand, to the lost university prolusion of 1719, and forward, on the other, to the *De Uno* and to the other portions of the complex work which was to come. In Vico's account this lost university prolusion of 1719 is the key to the entire structure of the *Diritto Universale*, for in the theme of that prolusion there is announced both the central idea and the divisions of that idea which the *Diritto Universale* as a whole and each of its parts respectively were to develop. This theme, as stated in the *Autobiography*, asserts the basic thesis that 'the elements of all human and divine wisdom are three: to know, to will, to be able; of these there is a single principle, the mind, whose eye is reason, to which God directs the light of eternal truth'. This thesis is in turn divided into three more specific propositions asserting, respectively, that the principles of all sciences are from God, that the eternal truth emanating from God permeates all the elements of science and leads them ultimately back to Him; finally, that these propositions, together, constitute a norm or rule for the acceptance or rejection of all that has hitherto been accounted science.

Certain criticisms raised against this prolusion sharpened his determination to effect his project; and it was as a first answer to these objections that he published the *Sinopsi*. The effectuation of the projection was to be the *Diritto Universale* in its entirety. The same year in which the *Sinopsi* appeared saw the publication of the first major portion of the work, *De Uno Universi Juris Principio et Fine Uno*. Its purpose in Vico's plan was the demonstration of the first and the second portions of the theme of the dissertation of 1719. This work in its turn provoked a host of objections, touching for the most part, in Vico's opinion, not the principle of the system, but particular points and again, for the most part, simply repeating the opinions and attitudes against which his new synthesis was directed. For this reason, he made no special attempt to meet these objections, but deferred their substantial refutation to the portions of the work to follow. These appeared in the following year, under the collective title *De Constantia Jurisprudentis*; it was the function of this work to conduct to a successful conclusion the demonstration of the third part of the thesis of the prolusion. For the purposes of this demonstration, this portion of the thesis was further broken down into two questions, which gave their titles to the respective divisions of the work *De Constantia Philosophiae* and *De Constantia Philologiae*. A chapter of this second part of the work, entitled 'Nova Scientia Tenatur', Vico records, drew the special fire of his critics. In it he advanced the first form of his reduction of philology to a science.

The criticisms (sometimes carping and trivial in Vico's view) directed against this work were all compensated by the praise of one man, Jean Leclerc, whose letter of appreciation Vico reproduces in full.[1] The praise of this great man so elated Vico that he at once turned to a fresh work which would further prove the fecundity of his principles. In the light of these principles he undertook the re-examination of the Homeric poems and demonstrated that they constituted 'two groups of Greek histories of obscure and heroic times, according to Varro's division'.[2] These Homeric readings together with the canons and principles according to which they were conducted were published in the following year, 1722; known now as the 'Notae', they bring to completion, in a surprising but logical manner, the complex structure of the *Diritto Universale*.

As early as the *De Studiorum Ratione*, Vico, by the device of the introduction of the 'essay' on jurisprudence, had signalized the attraction which the study of jurisprudence held for him and the aspirations he entertained of securing a wider field for his talents in the university through the study of the law. His subsequent studies and learned activities, down to and, indeed, culminating in the composition of the *Diritto Universale* had served only to fortify and magnify this interest and aspiration. The golden opportunity for the realization of these hopes seemed to present itself at the beginning of 1723 when, upon the death of the incumbent, the 'morning chair of civil law' in the University of Naples, inferior to the 'evening chair', fell vacant. There is some reason to believe, according to Nicolini, that Vico entertained some hope, on the basis of his seniority and merits in the university, of securing the chair by simple transfer; but of any such hope he was immediately disabused. The position was made the object of a regular competition announced on the nineteenth of January 1723; and Vico was first to inscribe

[1] *Auto.*, p. 42, and Croce's note *in locum*.   [2] *Auto.*, p. 43.

himself among the competitors. The conditions of the competition were the usual ones: the presentation of a lecture, to last a full hour, on a theme announced twenty-four hours in advance. On the twenty-fifth of the month Vico met this condition in a conference delivered before the judges in the Dominican convent situated in Via San Tommaso d'Aquino.

In principle, the issue should have been decided on the basis of what transpired there; in fact, the decision lay elsewhere, and with considerations quite different from the quality of a learned discourse on a text from the *Older Digest*. Into the normal pattern of such affairs political strategy entered. Two of the candidates, for reasons other than academic, stood out clearly above all the others, and about them opposing parties were formed. Victory would lie, it was clear, with him who had the greatest and the highest patronage. In this respect, one Gentile's star was definitely in the ascendent; he had managed through grace of his person and the easy persuasiveness of his manner to secure a chain of patronage which extended from the powerful Nicola Capasso, long an enemy of Vico, upward through the viceregal favourite to the Austrian viceroy himself, Cardinal Michele Federico d'Althann.

Vico in all such practical and political matters was notoriously inept; in this case, however, he seemed to be aware of the real basis on which the issue would be decided, and in his turn sought decisive patronage. The object of his choice was none less than the Prince Eugene of Savoy, then resident at the imperial court at Vienna. The basis of this appeal was slim; Vico had some time before sent to the prince, a famous bibliophile, a magnificently bound copy of the *Diritto Universale* and had, with some insistence, secured from him a letter of thanks which ended with a general and remote offer of good will. The strong and rather presumptuous letter which Vico, on these unsure grounds, addressed to the prince seeking his intervention in the matter of the competition was, consequently, from the first doomed to the fate which it actually met; it went unanswered or at least without effective results.

After this, events could not but follow their preordained course. Vico was even counselled by his friend Caravita to withdraw from the competition; if such withdrawal was made, it was merely oral and hence without effect. The votes were divided almost evenly between the competitors favoured by the major factions. The issue was decided in favour of Gentile only by an intervention of the viceroy which has been called an act of violence. Vico was passed over in silence, a humiliation which his long service in the university, upon which he had at the first raised his hopes, now rendered all the greater.

III

An event such as the discomfiture in the university competition of 1723, which so many factors conspired to render crucial both to his professional and his private life, might well have turned another man from learned pursuits in bitterness, or, as Vico expresses it, 'made him repent of ever having cultivated them'.[1] In Vico's case, however, its effect was quite the opposite; it opened to him the path of his supreme scientific effort and achievement. Freed now from all university ambition and delivered from the illusion that there remained for him any means of deliverance from the poverty and the humble social position which accompanied it, he returned to the subject of his meditations with a heightened scientific disinterestedness and the resolution to work out his guiding insights with no other concern than the achievements of the revolutionary results with which he felt them to be pregnant. In this spirit, which was to flag only as his life expired, the *Scienza Nuova* was conceived and realized through its complex metamorphosis until it achieved, under his dying hand, the form it presents in the posthumous edition of 1744.

To Vico's mind the composition of the *Scienza Nuova* was itself a work of that providentiality in the affairs of men in which he came to believe ever more strongly and which he establishes as the supreme principle of that science; in the light of this belief, he saw the meditations of his whole life conspiring toward this one achievement. As a consequence, to pick up the thread of the development of this 'New Science', he does not hesitate to reach back into the first pronouncements he ever made in scientific matters. He saw this unity of his life work as consisting in the quest and the discovery of a single unitary speculative principle which, employed in the method dictated by its own intrinsic speculative character, might reveal the actual process by which the forms of human culture emerge in time with eternal and ideal necessity. The quest for such a principle, it seemed to Vico, had inspired, and alone could serve to interpret, the first of his

---

[1] *Auto.*, p. 48: 'After this blow of adverse fortune which would have made another renounce all learning if not repent of ever having cultivated it, he did not desist for one moment from addressing himself to other works.'

27

scientific utterances, the *Orazioni*, and had continued, with ever-increasing clarity and force, to inspire all his succeeding efforts. In all of these earlier efforts, however, the central and animating scientific motives had been obscured and impeded by alien factors, deriving either from the negative elements in his own intellectual formation or from non-scientific preoccupations. Now, however, he might address the scientific motive directly and without distraction.

The first fruit of this fresh scientific dedication and, consequently, rightly considered, the first form of the *Scienza Nuova* is the composition which Vico notes in his *Autobiography* immediately after his philosophic reflection on the misadventure of 1723. Indeed, he speaks of this work as already devised and meditated during the very days in which he was tortured alternately by the sense of his own merits in that contest and the malignancy of the forces arrayed against him. Never published, and lost to us even in its unpublished form, this work was conceived first as *Dubbi e disideri intorno alla teologia dei gentili*, but in the catalogue of Vico's works has come to be designated as the *Scienza Nuova in Forma Negativa*, a juster description of its true character and a designation made valid by Vico's own understanding of its relation to the later, positive, forms of his thought. This work, in Vico's account, consisted of two books, 'which might well have filled two volumes of full quarto size'; in the first of these books he undertook to determine the principles of a 'diritto naturale delle genti' within the 'principles of the humanity of the nations', by means of an analysis and exposition of the inverisimilitudes, the inconsistencies and the impossibilities of all the theories and accounts which had been formulated, or more accurately 'fancied' on this material; this is the 'via negativa' from which the work takes its name.[1] The second, abandoning the negative method of the first, but assuming its results, sought to 'explain the formation of human customs by a definite chronology based on the analysis of the obscure and legendary times of Greek prehistory'. From the point of view of this second book, consequently, the work can no longer be conceived as entirely negative; its negative character was, however, dominant in Vico's mind when, after the difficulties encountered in seeking its publication, and upon reflection that the negative form of demonstration is 'uncongenial' to the understanding 'in proportion as it agitates the phantasy, since by it nothing is explained to the human mind', he concentrated on the discovery of a positive method of demonstrating the same material, a method which

[1] *Auto.*, p. 48, *Bibliografia Vichiana*, I, 34.

would be stricter and more efficacious. The composition of this work, *Scienza Nuova in Forma Negativa*, and the affairs attendant upon its attempted publication occupied Vico's attention, according to Nicolini's chronology,[1] for approximately two years, 1723-5. With far more resolution and energy, however, was this new proposal of a positive demonstration executed. The composition of the work was accomplished within the period of a month. The *Scienza Nuova Prima*, a work, as Nicolini suggests, of entirely new conception and stature, was in the hands of the printer by the beginning of September of 1725. By late October of the same year dedicatory copies of the work, which bore the portentous title, *Principj di Una Scienza Nuova d'intorno alla Natura delle Nazioni per la Quale si Ritrovano i Principj di altro Sistema del Diritto Naturale delle Genti*, were on their way to scholars throughout Italy and beyond the alps.

It is evident that to Vico's own mind the *Scienza Nuova Prima*, whatever his later attitude toward it, represented a definite turning point in the history of his thought and, indeed, a point of arrival which was to become the fixed basis of all further movement. It brings to a close the long period of questing beginning, however obscurely, with the *Orazioni* themselves, during which he had sought that unitary principle about which to construct his new synthesis. Of the *Scienza Nuova Prima* he asserts unequivocally, that 'in this work there is to be found completely explicated that principle which confusedly and without adequate distinction had underlain his previous works'.[2] For this reason, he interrupts the narrative of the *Autobiography* to present an analysis of the structure and achievement of this work.

The normative principle of the 'New Science' is sacred history; that is so, because the direct and supernatural operation of providence in the case of the chosen people preserved them from the deviations into which the gentile nations fell. All that transpired in sacred history, therefore, becomes the type of what would have transpired among the gentile nations save for certain disrupting factors. Sacred history thus provides a positive guide in determining what the deviations of gentile history actually were and what course a providential reconstruction must follow. The formal and methodological principle of the 'New Science' is a new 'art of criticism', in virtue of which it

[1] *Bibliografia Vichiana*, loc. cit.
[2] *Auto.*, p. 48: 'In this work he discovered at last in its fully developed form that principle which in his previous works he had understood confusedly and not in all its distinctness.'

becomes possible to address and interpret the 'vulgar' traditions of the peoples and to determine here the true process of their formation prior to the criticism of the written sources upon which such reconstruction had hitherto been based. This art of criticism, in its turn, changes the conception of the origin and character of all the sciences contributory to a science of universal jurisprudence concerning natural law, from which the ideas and the language of such a jurisprudence must derive. Dividing the inquiry into that of ideas and that of language, Vico believes that he has determined, at the level of ideas, fresh historical principles of geography and chronology which provides the true principles, heretofore lacking, to universal history; further, he has discovered historical principles of philosophy, and above all a 'metaphysics' or 'natural theology' of the whole human race which supplies the formal principle of the first human society, and that the basic principle of that theology was poetic. On the basis of this metaphysics he was able to determine a morality and a politics common to all the nations which in turn furnish the principles of a jurisprudence of the nations which varies through time. At the level of language, the primary discovery traceable to this new criticism is that of the naturalness and necessity of poetry as the first form of human consciousness and expression, and therefore, as the constitutive principle of all primitive institutions and documents. Upon this basis, he is able to reconstruct the language of a universal jurisprudence. These ideal and linguistic principles, in conjunction, constitute the basis for the construction of an ideal and eternal history ordered by providence, upon which the course of the nations in time is formed. The time structure of history is reconstructed about the ancient formula of the three ages, or gods, of heroes and of men. To each of these ages he assigns a typical mode of expression: to the first mute language, through hieroglyphics; to the second symbolic, or metaphoric, language, the heroic tongue, expressed through the heroic 'imprese'; and finally, to the last, the epistolary tongue. Again to each of these ages he assigns a characteristic social organization, the familial, the civil, and the popular, respectively. And upon these bases, he believes, he has established the fundamental principles of a genuine universal jurisprudence and at the same time refuted the intellectualism of the classical masters of modern 'jusnaturalism', Grotius, Selden and Pufendorf, who, because they had lacked this art of criticism, confused the natural law of the nations, which finds expression in their customs and their vulgar wisdom, with the natural law of the philosophers. And he closes this account of the *Scienza Nuova Prima* with an expression of the pride occasioned by the fact that 'in this age and in the bosom of the true church the principles of all gentile human and divine wisdom were discovered'.

The history of the 'New Science' during the subsequent twenty years is a history of transformations and revisions during the process of which the position of the *Scienza Nuova Prima* becomes increasingly ambiguous. On the one hand, there is Vico's own formal repudiation of all save 'three principal passages' for the sake of which alone he was willing to see the whole work reprinted.[1] On the other hand, as even the most casual comparison of the two works, the first and the second, together with the intermediary forms, establishes, there is no abandonment either of the fundamental character or the fundamental structure of the first *Scienza Nuova*; on the contrary the archetectonic correspondence is well nigh perfect. As a consequence, there is no difference 'toto caelo', as some would assert, between them; such an assumption raises insuperable difficulties in the interpretation of Vico's thought. On the contrary, it becomes very clear that just as it closes one period of his thought, that in which he was seeking this principle, so the *Scienza Nuova Prima* opens another, of which the *Scienza Nuova* of 1725 is in its turn the term. This second period is characterized by a continuously more astute and profound analysis of this principle and of its expression, method and consequences; a process of self-clarification in which, inevitably, each early step must be abandoned and held as nothing, while, at the same time, without them, the movement of the whole is inconceivable.

The first of these transformations, which culminated in the edition of 1730 (the third *Scienza Nuova*, if Nicolini's suggestion is entertained), had its external occasion in the invitation, offered by a group of Venetian scholars, among whom the *Scienza Nuova* of 1725 had found a ready reception, to prepare certain clarifying comments to accompany a new edition of the work to appear in Venice. This invitation precipitated the doubts and corrections which had been stirring Vico's mind about his work almost from the day it had come from the press. Consequently, he readily acquiesced in the proposal and immediately set about the task. The suggestion was made by his Venetian correspondents that the adjunctions and corrections which they most desired might best be inserted as occasion demanded in the text of 1725 edition itself so as to constitute, in fact, a revision of that work. To Vico, however, it seemed better to leave

[1] *Auto.*, p. 71.

31

the text of 1725 intact and to supplement it with a series of clarifying, amplifying and emending annotations. To this proposal the Venetian parties acquiesced; and during two years Vico was engaged in this effort which grew, under his relentless self-criticism, to unconscionable size—so great, in fact, as to constitute, in prospect, together with the intact text of the *Scienza Nuova* of 1725, a volume of close to, if not exceeding, a thousand pages. The Venetian editors, from the first somewhat dubious of this procedure, now, at the immensity of the task, grew frankly critical; Vico, offended in turn, withdrew from the whole proposal, demanding the return of all manuscript already forwarded. He found himself, consequently, in a position analogous to that in which he had found himself five years earlier with respect to the *Scienza Nuova in Forma Negativa*, that is, constrained to undertake publication at his own expense and therefore, in view of his slender means, to shorten the work. Confronted with this problem, he decided on a procedure which was identical with that suggested originally by his Venetian correspondents, namely, that the revision be made 'ab intra'. Vico achieved this revision in one extended effort, as he tells us, between Christmas day of 1729 and Easter Sunday of 1730. In this form the work saw the light in December of 1730 under the title *Cinque Libri de Giambattista Vico de' Principj d'una Scienza Nuova d'intorno alla Comune Natura delle Nazioni.*

Vico discusses the relation between this edition and that of 1725 (and it is in this conjunction that he introduces the designations *Scienza Nuova Prima* and *Seconda*) in the *Autobiography*.[1] From the point of vantage of the revision of 1730 the errors of the edition of 1725 appear to him to be dominantly errors in order. In the early edition, as he had already indicated in a passage of the *Autobiography*, the ideal principles of the 'New Science' had been treated independently of the liguistic principles. These, he now understands, were, by their nature, united and unitary. Again, he had there raised the methodological question independently of that of the ideal and linguistic structure of the 'New Science'; by a juster method, he now saw, the manner of treating the material of this science must be determined by the ideal and linguistic principles taken in strict conjunction. It was, consequently these errors of order which he sought to correct in the new edition, seeking above all a coherence of method which would enable him to relate the linguistic and ideal dimensions of the science as closely as they demanded and to treat

[1] *Auto.*, p. 72.

the individual problems raised by the material in the light of this fresh coherence of principles.

The annotating demon which possessed Vico was not laid even by this herculean labour; indeed it was at work even while the edition of 1730 was in the press, and showed itself in the 'Annotationes Primae' with which Vico felt compelled to burden the text. To these, a second series was promptly added occasioned by the remarks and suggestions of one Don Francesco Spinelli, Prince of Scalea, to whom Vico had sent a copy of the work. These remarks called to Vico's attention three errors or defects of treatment, whose effects, Don Francesco felt, could be discerned throughout the work. To these indications Vico replies carefully and at length, and expresses in the *Autobiography* the hope that these, together with others which were occurring to him continuously as he discussed the work and its arguments with friends, might be incorporated in a third printing of the *Scienza Nuova*. The fourth and final recasting of the work was already under way, with the ink scarcely dry on the third.

It is clear that as this final recasting took form in Vico's mind, it would follow closely the pattern of the formation of the edition of 1730. With the completion of the first and second sets of annotations he set himself to elaborate marginal correction, emendation, and improvement of the 1730 text, filling in this way the margins and fly-leaves of several copies. By the spring of 1731, however, this disordered manner of proceeding became onerous and he resolved to collect all of these emendations and corrections into one manuscript; this manuscript, together with the text of 1730, left intact, as at first proposed with the text of 1725, would then ideally constitute the complete expression of his thought. The project of this grand appendix was completed by the summer of 1731 and constitute the 'Correzioni, migliormenti e aggiunte terze, poste insieme con le prime e seconde, e tutte per incorporarsi nell'opera nella ristampa della Scienza Nuova seconda'. These corrections, in fact, are so extensive as to constitute, more nearly than an appendix, a genuine revision of the edition of 1730; of this latter they leave no page unaltered, increasing its scope by fifteen chapters and appending an extensive essay containing two 'Ragionamenti', the one on the purported introduction of the Laws of the Twelve Tables into Rome from Greece; the other on the law of Tribonianus, points in the history of Roman jurisprudence on which Vico was especially satisfied with the discoveries which his 'New Science' enabled him to make. In these annotations, moreover, he clarifies even further the relation of the present form of his thought to its earlier formulations, expressing with those earlier formulations a discontent which, while not constituting a formal repudiation, nevertheless emphasizes the great distance he had traversed.

From the 'Nunc dimittis' with which Vico closes the manuscript of these corrections, it might be supposed that he was finally content with the expression of his thought here achieved. This is not the case, however, for in the following year, or at the latest in 1733, he undertook a fresh revision of the work conducted in the same manner as the preceding, that is, by indicating a series of corrections, improvements and adjunctions to the text which was still to be left intact. These annotations would naturally have constituted the fourth series, but Vico, apparently with the understanding and intention that they should annul and supersede the previous, designated these also as 'third', and destined them also for incorporation in a reprinting of the edition of 1730. As time passed and this reprinting did not materialize, Vico's continued scrutiny of his thought reached a point of dissatisfaction and intensity analogous to that which preceded the recasting of the 1730 edition; and again, as he had done on that occasion, he now decided to have done with all such half measures as corrections and adjunctions, and to recast the work from top to bottom. This revision, undertaken about 1735, forms the basis of the edition of 1744. While in fact posthumous, this edition enjoyed the advantage of the author's proof revision of at least half its pages; autograph annotations are clearly discernible. Under the title, *Principj di Scienza Nuova di Giambattista Vico d'intorno alla Comune Natura delle Nazioni*, it appeared in July, 1744. The testament to Vico's genius was complete.

From an external point of view Vico's life may be said to have reached its apogee in the concourse of 1723; in the success of that competition there lay for him practically the only hope of an improvement in his material and economic conditions commensurate with the status of his genius and with the responsibilities which he bore. With its failure, these hopes were entirely eclipsed and his life became that bitter and unending round of drudgery on the brink of absolute poverty which he records in a number of places and which recalls inevitably the image of the exiled Dante 'climbing alien stairs and eating alien salt'. In Vico's case, moreover, these material burdens were exasperated by emotional and family difficulties by which even his iron virtue, so universally attested, was sorely tried.

After 1737 his health had so far declined that the burden of his university lectures was assumed almost completely by his son Gennaro. At about the same time, a petition to the sovereign, through Nicola de Rosa, the royal prefect of studies, resulted in the confirmation of Gennaro in his father's chair. A further measure of relief, not however unattended by limiting duties, came in the form of his appointment as royal historiographer.

The last days of the philosopher were especially agonizing. Deprived by general debility of the use of his senses and his memory, he lingered in a state of near coma, to revive only briefly before his final agony, which transpired on the night of 22–3 January 1744. Of the edifying character of his death and of the miserable circumstances attending his burial Villarosa makes mention,[1] and Nicolini elaborates. The obscurity of his life made men careless and contemptuous of him even in death, an obloquy which was to hang about his name in the intellectual theatre of Europe for two centuries.

[1] Villarosa's addition to the *Auto.*, p. 77 et seq.

II

THE NATURAL LAW

THE speculative problem of history arises initially for Vico in the context of theoretical jurisprudence and with especial reference to its central problem, that of the natural law. Speculations upon the nature of juridical process and especially on the ultimate logical and ideal ground of law preoccupied Vico at two decisive periods of his career. The distaste engendered by his first contact with forensic law in the studio of Verde turned him, as he recounts, to the consideration of the theoretical problems of jurisprudence in such authors as·Voltaeus and Canisius; again, but a few years later, during the sojourn in the Cilento, his duties as tutor directed his attention afresh to the 'due ragioni'. To this theme he returns, after long preoccupation with subjects as diverse as the speculations of the *De Antiquissima Italorum Sapientia* and the lost *De Aequilibrio Corporis Animantis*, in the group of heterogeneous treatises which comprise the *Diritto Universale*. It is in this latter work that the crisis in theoretical jurisprudence matures. Committed without qualification to the classical enterprise of the natural law, Vico attempts, in the initial treatise of this group, the *De Uno*, to construct such a theory on the most rigid intellectualistic lines. Presently, however, this project appears unfeasible to him, through lack of a speculative and methodological principle adequate to its authentic conditions. The determination of this principle gives direct rise to the speculative problem of history.

The chief problem of theoretical jurisprudence, that of the natural law, arises, in Vico's view, from the intimate exigencies of practical jurisprudence. The task which confronts practical jurisprudence is the interpretation of a law which is offered to it as authoritative, as 'certum', in Vico's term,[1] as embodying immediately the concrete actuality of the law. The intention of the law, however, is universal; this intention embraces a class of instances which fall under actual

[1] The term appears DU, I, 82, in the basic distinction 'certum'—'verum'; cf. SNS, 138.

adjudication, even though these instances, in all their particularity, irreducible novelty and uniqueness, could not have been foreseen or specifically intended in the law. This universal intention of the law imposes itself upon practical jurisprudence with a force equal to its authority; it must execute this universality and thus establish the relationship between the law and the instance. Failing this, it fails even in its obligation to the authority of the law.

The establishment of this relationship, however, demands that a dimension of the law other than its certitude and authority be revealed. The authority of the law is not its own interpretative norm; it is not the brute fact of the law, its mere authority, certitude or actuality which the juridical process seeks to translate, but its universal attention. This universal intention of the law itself cannot be sustained wholly by the law's certitude and authority; on the contrary, it implies, within the intimate structure of the law, the presence of a further element which is, in fact, in opposition to its certitude and authority and which is the immediate vehicle of its intentional universality. Thus there emerges the concept of the 'verum' of the law, its truth, or logical ground and ideal principle. This ideal dimension of the law enters directly into the purview of practical jurisprudence, for it is the genuine mediatorial principle between the law and the instance.

Nevertheless, the mediation of the law and the instance through the truth, the 'verum' of the law, is dependent upon a prior mediation, within the law. For the 'certum' and the 'verum', as dimensions of the law, stand in dialectical relationship to each other, indeed, almost as contradictions. For the authority and the certitude of the law, looking wholly to its immediacy, its particularity and concreteness, opposes, at the same time that, in the structure of law, it implies that universality of intention which is the assumption of adjudication in the same manner that universality of intention, the vehicle of the ideality and the truth of the law, to the degree that it transmutes and transcends the mere authority and certitude of the law, would seem to oppose and negate it. Thus there are present within the law the seeds of diremption and absence from itself, unless this opposition between the certitude or authority and the truth or ideality of the law be mediated or closed.

This latent opposition, this threatened diremption within the law, provides, in the Vichian view, the immediate context for the concept and the enterprise of the natural law. In its most immediate and concrete sense, the natural law is the mediation between the truth and

he certitude, the positivity and the ideality, the concreteness and the
iniversality of the law. It indicates the only path between juridical
narchism and juridical positivism, between, that is to say, the alter-
iate modes of the annihilation of the law. Juridical anarchism is the
lenial of an ideal dimension in the law and involves, consequently,
he conclusion that the law is incapable of interpretation or continu-
ty, with the corollary that the juridical process is continual revolu-
ion; juridical positivism is the failure to recognize any distinction
ietween the 'certum' and the 'verum' as immanent dimensions of the
iw. In either case, the jurisprudential process is annihilated. The
iatural law, by contrast, as the mediation of the truth and the certi-
ude of the law, appears as the sole sustaining principle of that process.

In this manner, the fundamental concept of the natural law is de-
ived from the intimate demand of practical jurisprudence, namely,
ie establishment of an authentic principle for the interpretation and
ie administration of the law; the law, appearing before the interpre-
itive process in the alternate modes of ideality and positivity, truth
nd certitude, demands mediation. This context is still, however,
io narrow to sustain the total concept or project of the natural law.
: represents, as a matter of fact, a highly abstracted view even of
ie process of practical jurisprudence. Actually, laws do not present
iemselves for interpretation in their stark particularity; neither is
ie juridical process concerned with the interpretation and adminis-
ation of laws in abstraction and isolation. The one and the other
ike are moments of process. The law appears in the context of the
rhole process of the emergence of positive structures of law, and
innot, for the purposes of interpretation and administration, be
istracted from the ramifications of that process. Jurisprudence, on
ie other hand, does not appear as the attempt to penetrate the
leality of single laws, but, rather, as itself a continuous process to-
'ard the idealization of the law in its universality. The 'certum' and
ie 'verum', which natural law seeks to mediate, are dimensions, not
f single laws, but of the total process of law, and represent the alter-
ite dynamisms of that process, the one toward the immediacy, the
increteness, the multiplicity of the law in its historical structures,
ie other toward its unity in idea. As a consequence, the context of
ie natural law must be redefined.

This context, in its wider terms, and as it may support the concept
id the enterprise of the natural law in their fullness, comprises, on
ie one hand, the actual historical process of the formation of positive
iridical structures and, on the other, the informing idea of all law

conceived in its unity. Further, it comprises these terms, as in intimate relationship to each other, as interpenetrating, the one informing, the other concretizing, and together as giving structure to the reality of law. Within this context, the function of the natural law is to lay bare the laws and principles which govern that dialectical process, to lay bare, that is, the ideal grounds of that concrete process of the historical formation of positive structures of law, as well as the principles of the historical concretion of the idea of law in its multiple, positive forms. These principles, controlling the process in its unity, would constitute the natural law in its content; its formal principle, in turn, must consist in that concept which defines the essential unity of concrete and ideal process, which would be the speculative principle of the natural law. In its amplitude, the natural law is the radical synthetic principle of the total juridical actuality.

Such is the character of natural law as suggested to Vico by the exigencies of the jurisprudential process both in its more restricted and in its ampler aspects: a unitary principle which would mediate the truth and the certitude or authority of the law, the historical process of the formation of juridical structures and the ideal principle of law; and such is the idea of the natural law which permeates his thought. Such is not, however, Vico discovers, the conception which had inspired classical natural law theory, from its very inception in Plato to its 'great masters' in modern thought, Grotius, Selden, and the others whom he enumerates. For this tradition, on the contrary, the natural law was not a principle of unity but of duality, not of synthesis but of dissociation between the positive, historical and the ideal dimensions of the law, between its truth and its certitude. It was, consequently, not the instrument, but the impediment to the programme of jurisprudence.[1]

The fundamental characteristic of classical natural law theory from Plato to Grotius, in Vico's account, is that it dissociates the two dynamisms of the total process of law, that toward the concretion and multiplicity of the historical forms of law from that toward the unity and total presence of the idea of the law. Instead of conceiving the natural law as the mediatorial and unitary principle between these dynamisms, it identified it wholly with the movement toward the idea. It conceived jurisprudence in its essence as the attempt to determine this idea, the ideal ground of law, apodictically; that is, independently of the actual process of the formation of the historical structures of law. The natural law, as thus apodictic and

[1] SNS, 310–13; SNP, p. 14.

transcendent, was a purely formal principle, to which the historical flux of juridical structures must be extraneous and alien.

The consequence of this classical conception of the natural law and of the natural law enterprise seemed readily discernible to Vico. In the first place, it rendered the jurisprudential process in principle non-viable. For the essence of this process lay in the mediation of the oppositions within the law, of authority, or certitude, and truth, of positivity and ideality. Only by such mediation can juridical process have any reality. The classical conception of natural law, however, rather than mediate, tended to dirempt and to alienate those opposites, not in fact only, but in principle. The authority and the truth, the positivity and the ideality of the law were set in contradiction to each other. Each was made more absolute in itself and at the same time more exclusive of the other. Thus the natural law, in its transcendental character, becomes a principle disruptive of the authority of the law; the authority of the law, on the other hand, appears not as the manifestation, but as the negation, of its ideality: 'Dura lex sed scripta; certa lex sed prorsus non vera.' [1] But the natural law, because of its purely formal and its transcendental character, is not susceptible of jurisprudential rendering, while the positive law, being dirempted from all ideal dimension, can be sustained only on grounds other than ideal, and can be referred only to principles—to force, to interest— from which ideality is seemingly absent. In a word, the administration of law, and even legislation in its genuine sense, is impossible, for these are contingent upon the mediation of the oppositions of the law which classical natural law theory dirempts.

The non-viability of the jurisprudential process which is the principal effect of the diremption of the positivity and the ideality of the law is accompanied by consequences equally as portentous. The dissociation and alienation of the historical and the ideal dimensions of law introduces confusion into both. The definition of the ideality of the law independently of its positive historical content and structure is rendered nugatory and self-defeating. The only evidence for the success of such a venture could be the power to deduce, apodictically, from such a formal structure the content of the positive law; but such deduction is manifestly unfeasible. On the other hand, bereft of all ideal illumination, the historical course of the formation of positive structures of law is surrendered to chaos. Ignorance of its own antiquities, Vico points out ruefully,[2] is characteristic of the most intel-

[1] DU, I, 83; SNS, 322.
[2] SNP, p. 24: 'They were brutally ignorant of their own antiquities.'

lectual culture the west has ever seen; to the Greek, history was closed, and the most moderate of their philosophers, Aristotle, could seriously declare history to be gnoseologically inferior to poetry 'because less universal'.

One conclusion follows from the convergence of these factors— the character of the natural law as indicated, in idea, by the exigencies of the jurisprudential process and the diremption of the elements of this process in classical natural law theory—concerning the task of theoretical jurisprudence. This task must be the healing of this diremption and the actualization of that unity which is demanded by the nature of the process of jurisprudence. The problem of the natural law must be broached in its authentic terms, as determining the principle of unity or synthesis between the process of the historical formation of the structures of positive law, of the 'certum' in its widest extent, and the correlative process toward the formation of the idea of the law, its 'verum'. In a word, the project of the *De Uno* is thus defined and related to the central and imperative exigency of theoretical jurisprudence; the *De Uno* is, in principle and idea, the first attempt by Vico to meet this demand. In fact, however, and on the basis of Vico's self-criticism it falls short of this objective; moreover, its failure is crucial. While it achieves a certain material synthesis of the 'certum' and the 'verum' of the law, it fails to achieve such a synthesis formally, because it fails to determine adequately its speculative principle.

The principle on which the synthesis of the 'certum' and the 'verum' of the law is attempted in the *De Uno* is the classical Platonic and neo-Platonic principle of participation. The 'certum' of the law, its authority, its positive historical structure and multiplicity is related to the 'verum', the unity and the ideality of the law, as part to the whole. This relationship is formulated by Vico in a system of correlations between the terms 'certum' and 'verum' and their adjuncts.[1] The 'verum', he asserts, is the proper and perpetual adjunct of necessary law and derives from the 'ratio' of the law, that is, from its conformity to the eternal order of things. 'Certum', by contrast, is the proper and perpetual character of positive or voluntary law and derives from authority, or human decision. This certitude, however, belongs to the positive law only as a certain part of its truth, the 'verum', for the certitude of the law is but a part of its truth and 'ratio' which the legislator presents to be held by authority because it falls beyond the scope or power of the natural virtue of the subject

[1] DU, I, 81 et seq.

41

of law, namely, sensitivity to conscience, or 'pudore', shame. In like manner, he proceeds to affirm, authority is a part or dimension of reason, or 'ratio', of the law; for as the 'certum' of the law, deriving from authority, is but a part of the 'verum', deriving from the 'ratio' reason and authority cannot be opposed to each other but must on the contrary, in their turn, sustain this same relation of part and whole; 'ipsa auctoritas est pars quaedam rationis'. Finally, and inexorably, the positive law, as the sum of the historical formations of law, can be but a part of the natural law, conceived as the ideal totality and unity of law. The positive law participates, or simply, is a part of the natural law; the principle of the synthesis of positive and ideal in the law is the principle of the relationship of part to whole, of participation.

The inadequacy of this mode of synthesis, and of the principle which inspires it, becomes apparent to Vico in the very process of developing its implications. Participation fails of genuine mediation because the positivity and the ideality of the law remain extrinsic, so to say, to each other. To state it otherwise, the positive dimension of law is confirmed in its mere certitude, for no genuine ideal principle for the multiplicity of the positive law is revealed, while the ideality is confirmed in its transcendence, since it is not revealed to be, or established as the unity and ideality of the positive many, but as a transcendent unity which must be opposed to it. The 'certum' and the 'verum' of the law remain confirmed in their initial opposition.

The positive dimension of the law is confirmed in its mere certitude and authority, on the principle of participation, because the relation of part to whole is an extrinsic relationship which does not overcome the otherness implicit in these terms. If the assertion that the 'certum' is a part of the 'verum', the authority a part of the 'ratio' of the law, is genuinely to mediate these terms, it must clarify a complex situation. In the first place, it must illuminate the principle of their particularity; that is to say, the principle of their distinction from the whole. It must reveal the reason, in the whole, for its deployment through its parts. In the second place, it must reveal the principle by which that particularity is overcome, and returned to the unity of the whole. Finally, it must make clear the rationale of this total process by which the whole is resolved into its parts, and the parts in turn synthesized into the unity of the whole. Only in this way will the positive character of the law, its mere opposition to the idea of law, be overcome. Concretely, this relationship of part to whole should fulfil the exigency of jurisprudence by making possible the translation, the interpretation and administration of the positive law. In fact, it does none of these things. It does not explain the particularity of the law, because the principle of that particularity is to be found adequately in the positive law itself. Every such law, in its particularity, may be adequately accounted for in terms of the forces or influences under which it was formulated. In its particularity, it is the reflection of those forces, and thus is itself the whole, with respect to them, and not a part. This particularity needs no reference to a transcendent unity or totality. Thus, to refer to an example which Vico himself adduces more than once,[1] an adequate conception of the Publilian law may be formed on the basis of Roman history and government, so long as this law is viewed thus in its positive, historical, particular character; reference to the context of a wider unity must always appear extraneous and fortuitous and it can add nothing to the understanding of this law to assert that it is a part of the general structure of Roman law. Neither does this assertion that the 'certum' is a part of the 'verum' make clear how that particularity is overcome. For it is clear that in the actual process of the formation of law, the particularity of the law is overcome by a further particularity, and not by reference to a transcendent unity or totality. One positive law displaces another; this is the concrete process of the history of the law. If any ideal transaction transpires it must do so within the particularity of these terms. The movement of the 'part' is not toward the indistinction of the whole, but toward the articulation of another 'part'. From the point of view, consequently, of the positive law the whole movement from part to whole appears alien and adventitious. At every point the particular, the positive law resists any such subsumption, and is by that very resistance confirmed in its own certitude.

In like manner, the 'verum' of the law is, by this same principle of participation, confirmed in its transcendence and unity, in its alienness to the process of the historical formation of the law. For if the 'verum' be conceived as the whole, as the unity of the idea of the law, this totality and unity must consist precisely in the indistinction of its 'parts', in their unity and not in their multiplicity. It must further, to the extent to which it is itself positive, transcend the sum of its parts, as a term toward which their mere multiplication cannot advance. The 'verum' of the law, as its unity, its totality, its ideality, must always be simply other to the particularity, the multiplicity of its

[1] SNS, 26, 104-5.

'certum'. Rather than illuminate, the reference to unity and totality must dissolve and dissipate the positivity of the law, or reassimilate it to its own indifferentiation. And as the simple other of the multiplicity and particularity of positive law, of the 'certum', the 'verum' can yield, in its turn, no intrinsic principle for its own resolution into that multiplicity. It is, in fact, in its turn, established in a hyperpositivity, for this opaque unity and totality of the 'verum' is as much a 'given', an unmediated and unmediating positivity as the hard enactments of authority.

In a word, it must be said that Vico rediscovers, here on the plane of the theoretical problem of jurisprudence, all of the difficulties which essential Platonism has occasioned during its long career. Participation exacerbates, rather than heals, the radical trauma between the world of historical process and the transcendent ideality in terms of which Platonism would unite that world. As a consequence, in the very midst of the project of the *De Uno*, Vico finds himself tending toward that immedicable dualism in which he had observed classical natural law theory to be suspended. Indeed, he even found himself closer to an understanding of the force which had swept natural law theory into that impasse, namely, adherence to that essential Platonism as the speculative principle of the natural law. From this circumstance there arises the most striking characteristic of this treatise, the *Diritto Universale*, and the principle of the heterogeneity of its component essays; in full career, as it were, Vico alters course. He veers from the reefs of participation, now all too apparent and manifest, to seek a fresh speculative principle of the natural law, a principle which might effectively realize that mediation of the 'certum' and the 'verum' of the law in which the presence of the natural law must reside.

Nevertheless, Vico's detachment from essential Platonism, like that of everyone who has once fallen under its spell, is partial, not complete. Under an altered form, it re-enters his final synthesis, to become, in fact, its constitutive principle. It re-enters that synthesis, the concept of history, as the principle of the ideal movement of history toward the fullness of an idea; specifically, as the principle that the total process of the formation of positive law moves toward the fulfilment of the idea of law, which Vico identifies as 'aequum bonum'. As one writer has remarked, what was, for Platonism, transcendental and initial, becomes, for Vico, terminal. And it is this movement of concrete process toward the idea, this radical but altered Platonism, which is the cohesive principle of Vico's resolution of the duality of the 'certum' and the 'verum' of the law, and, finally, of his theory of history. The ideality of the law, its 'verum', is identified with this plenitude of the idea, toward which its historical process tends.

The retention of this element of Platonism, the plenitude of the idea as the term of the process of the formation of positive law, involves also, for Vico, the retention in part of the notion of participation. For the elements of that process, to the degree to which they may be distinguished, remain as partial realizations of the plenitude of the idea, approximations, as it were, which stand in a relation at once of unity and opposition. Each element of the positive law is law by virtue of that approximation and participation in the plenitude of the idea of law, while, at the same time, by its partial and approximative character, it is set in eternal opposition to it. Thus the Platonic elements, as another commentator remarks, enter into the composition of Vico's thought, as 'blood of his blood'.

The retention and alteration of the Platonic notions of the plenitude of the idea of and of participation as the relation of the positive process of law to its idea establishes the widest architectonic of the notion of history, and establishes the first bridgehead between the elements of the law, the 'certum' and the 'verum', which classical natural law theory tended to alienate and render opaque to each other. These are seen now to penetrate as do process and the immanent term toward which it moves, where before they stood apart, confronting and excluding each other. Nevertheless, this mediation of the 'certum' and the 'verum' of the law as process and term remains incomplete for two reasons. It yields no principle, in the first place, which can guarantee the continuity of that movement toward the ideal within the process of the concrete formation of positive law, nor in the second, a principle which would define the order of that movement. For these principles, which he incorporates into his basically Platonic scheme, Vico turns to quite another source, namely, the tradition of Roman jurisprudence. In its fundamental insights, he finds the sustaining principles of his own resolution of the problem of natural law.

The fundamental insights of Roman jurisprudence, by which it was enabled, pragmatically at least, to resolve the trauma between the 'certum' and the 'verum' of the law, were two, in Vico's account,[1] Providence and the 'sette dei tempi', the notion of time. These furnish for Vico the sustaining principles of his basically Platonic scheme,

[1] SNS 310, 342; SNP, p. 13.

45

establishing respectively the principle of the ideality of the movement of positive law and the order of that movement.

The 'sette dei tempi', or 'divisions of the times', was the principle of the viability of the juridical process among the Roman jurisconsults. The contrasting necessities between which this process was suspended threatened, as has been seen, that viability. On the one hand, the necessity of preserving the authority of the law defined one limit of the process; the interpretation of the law could not traduce that authority, which must constitute its constant concrete point of reference. On the other, the obvious universality of the intention of law described an ulterior horizon toward which the process of jurisprudence tended. The 'aequum bonum' is the supposition of all law, and it is this which in effect is administered in all juridical process. The process had, consequently, to move between these limits and effectively to mediate their opposition, so that the character of the ideal supposition of all law, the 'aequum bonum', might be vindicated in every law, at the same time that the concreteness and the authority of that law was conserved. This mediation was effected, in part at least, by recourse to the 'sette dei tempi'.

The 'sette dei tempi' establishes a complex network of relations and correlations which closed the ground between the positive law and its universal and ideal alternate. Principal among these relations was that of the time-order of positive law, which defined the order of the positive law to the ideal and universal principle of law. Thus the continuity and the perpetuity of the law in its concrete process of formation was insured. The concrete historical process of positive law constituted, under this aspect, a temporal continuum ordered toward the 'aequum bonum'. Every moment of this continuum advanced that order, after its own fashion; as a consequence, none could be transcended in the movement toward that term. The concrete process of positive law was indeed the 'catena aurea' which linked society to its own idea through the temporal process of its history, and it is in this temporal continuity, which is also perpetuity, that the identity of the society is to be found. Thus the temporal process of the formation of positive law is made the primary link between the certitude and the ideality of the law.

At the same time, the concept of the 'sette dei tempi' sets up a dual correlation of the positive law toward the objective and total content of ideal law, on the one hand, and on the other, toward the legislating agent, the legislating mind and will. In the former correlation, the content of every positive law is conceived to stand in a relation of part to whole to the ideal content of law. There is no positive law, which has the character of law, which does not reflect within its limits the idea of law, the 'aequum bonum' in its plenitude. This reflection is, indeed, the measure of its character as law. There arises thus a second mediation between the 'certum' of the law, its positive character, and the 'verum', with specific reference to the material dimension or content. The 'verum' conceived as the ideal content or material plenitude of the law, embraces the 'certum' as its deployed elements. No genuine opposition, therefore, can appear between the 'certum' and the 'verum' of the law, under this aspect, for all such opposition is resolved when the relation of part to whole is introduced into the juridical process. But this order of part to whole within the material dimension, or the content, of the law, the 'aequum bonum' in its plenitude and the content of positive law in its particularity, is in its turn mediated by the more basic relation of the time-process of positive law to the 'aequum bonum' as the ideal term of law. Thus, within the temporal continuity, there is introduced a second continuity of material inclusion, by which the unity of law is insured.

In the latter correlation, the positive law is conceived to stand as the expression of a limited perception of necessity or utility on the part of the legislating agent.[1] The limitation of this perception, and hence of the intention and expression, defines the positivity of the law. As such, consequently, it too would seem to define or establish the positive law in its opposition to the 'verum' of the law. This is not the case, however, because in the direction of the agent there recurs a structure of universality and ideality strictly analogous to the inclusive and material extension toward the content of ideal law. For it is the supposition of the legislating mind that it wills the 'aequum bonum' in every positive law, and not the positive law in opposition to the 'aequum bonum', that is, in its strict particularity. From this formal and intentional point of view, consequently, just as from the material and the contentual, the 'certum' is seen to be the implication of the 'verum' of the law, the 'verum' in its turn, the supposition of the 'certum'. Every positive law, under this formal aspect, reflects the limits under which the legislating agent acts, but at the same time, evokes the context of the total and ideal intention of the legislating will. This total and ideal intention is the formal correlative of that material or objective totality of the 'aequum bonum', which mediated the 'certum' and the 'verum' in their material dimensions. As a

[1] DU, I, 82.

47

consequence, the mediation is effected under this aspect too, and by a reciprocal mediation. The positive law can be read only as a fragment of the ideal intention of the law, which is the supposition of all positive legislation. This formal or intentional mediation of the 'certum' and the 'verum' is in its turn mediated by the time-ordering of the process of positive law to its ideal term.

By thus establishing this complex network of relations between the 'certum' and the 'verum' of the law, the 'sette dei tempi' contributes directly and principally to the formation of that conception of the natural law which Vico conceives to be the chief glory of Roman jurisprudence and which is basic to the structure of his own thought not in this respect only, but, as will be seen, in its entirety. This conception of the natural law is characterized in the first place by a massive continuity in its material, its formal or intentional, and its historical dimensions; in other words, in every dimension of the 'certum' and the 'verum' of the law. In its temporal dimension, the natural law is characterized by the continuity between the successive transformations of positive law and positive law structures in the direction or order to the idea of law. In its material, contentual or objective dimension, that is, in what it commands or forbids, this continuity is reflected in the approximative character of all positive law to the material dimension of ideal law. Finally, this continuity characterizes the positive law as the expression of the legislating mind and will; for this legislating agent, whatever the limits under which it effectively operates, formally enunciates the universal intention of law, the 'aequum bonum'. The natural law is thus established on the principle of the 'sette dei tempi' and of the relations the continual and extensive mediation of the 'certum' and the 'verum' of the law, and provides the proper medium within which the juridical process, which must pass for ever between these terms, becomes viable. In time, in intention, in content, the law moves freely in a solid three-dimensional world between the terms which define the conditions of the actual juridical process.

This whole concept and structure of natural law, as the mediation of the 'certum' and the 'verum' through the 'setti dei tempi', is an inverted pyramid. It rests upon a single point of assurance, namely, the assertion that the time-order of the formation of the structures of positive law is indeed orientated toward an ideal term, that this order is, consequently, itself pervasively ideal; or, in other words, on the assertion of the unity of temporal and ideal process. The sustaining principle of this assertion Vico also discovers in the wisdom of the jurisconsults of Rome. It is the principle of providence; a principle, he asserts, which Christian philosophers, despite the guidance of Christian wisdom, ignore or abandon, while, to their honour, it is the unvarying lodestar of the Roman jurisconsults.

Three alternatives, indeed, solicited the assent of ancient thinkers concerning the principles which control the course of man's history; fate, chance and providence. And in this respect again, the philosophers have proven less wise than the jurisconsults. And again, it is the abstractive paths of pure philosophy, bent only upon the naked summits of truth, which have deflected the philosophers from the truth. Whether, with the Stoics, history be surrendered to fate or, with the Epicureans, to chance, the fault is identical: too great an abstraction from the actual workings of human culture, the actual processes whereby the ligatures of community are effected. But this abstraction is a temptation from which the jurisconsult is immune. Immersed in the very process with which he is concerned, himself, as it were, weaving the living web of law which is the strongest bond of community, he cannot fail to perceive in its temporal movement the sure and pervasive flow of the idea; to feel, in the erratic patterns of human conduct, in the vacillations of human will, in the obscurities of human understanding and the uncertainties of man's decision, the sustaining power which through all these deviations, hesitations and vagaries, propels the processes of history toward its ideal term. The evidence he needs is not the abstract ratiocinations of the philosopher, but the living evidence, as it were, of his very senses: the actual growth and refinement of the structures of law and of the societies which those structures sustain.

Providence is, consequently, for the tradition of Roman jurisprudence, essentially not a metaphysical doctrine, but the urgent assertion of this urgently perceived movement of ideality in history itself. It is sustained by no subtle logical arguments, but is compounded of the innumerable cumulative perceptions of the growth and the destiny of nations toward an ever ampler appreciation of the 'aequum bonum' and its ever more complete expression in the forms of legislation and of social life itself. If there is a deficit of argument, or any metaphysical obscurity, with respect to Providence, there is, on the other hand, no obscurity concerning its function. The function of Providence is precisely the assurance of this ideal direction of the temporal processes of law and social life, the movement, through the complexities of partial insights, partial utilities, partial necessities, toward the summation of the idea.

In its more specific character and function, Providence is the principle which purges the area of the 'certum' of that opaqueness which inheres in it and which appears to dirempt it so fatally from the 'verum' of the law. This opaqueness, this brute givenness of the 'certum', derives from the fact that it is the work of human will; and the human will, by the character of its ultimate freedom, or autonomy, would seem to exclude from its very heart the illumination and the counsel of the idea. What depends upon man's will must always be marked by this ultimate obscurity, and its movement toward an ideal goal be subject to the thousand alternalities which can sway that will. Under this aspect providence appears as the supreme rectifying principle of man's will, and hence as the guarantee of the ultimate ideality of the order of the 'certum'. It is that power which counteracts, in the total movement of history, all the distracting forces of interest, of passion, of failure of vision, to hold that movement, in its total advance, on an ideal course. It is, in the largest sense, the assertion of the pervasive presence of a supreme wisdom in man's affairs, a wisdom which in its total effects transcends his own, and in which the complex alternalities of history are finally mediated. Such a wisdom alone could sustain that ideal movement which is reflected in the natural law; and it is of such a wisdom actually, that the natural law itself is the supreme evidence.

The mediation of the 'certum' and the 'verum' of the law by the 'sette dei tempi' and the notion of providence drawn from the jurisprudential tradition of Rome resolves for Vico the knottiest problem of theoretical jurisprudence, that of the natural law. Even more, it transforms for him the concept of the natural law and of jurisprudence as a science. And this transformation is effected by the force of the philosophical concept of history immanent in those principles of time and providence.

By this mediation, the theoretical problem of the natural law is resolved, because this mediation establishes the ground for the complete convertibility of the 'certum' and the 'verum' of the law. The 'certum' and the 'verum', as it has been observed, present themselves as the irreducible elements of the juridical process. At the same time, they appear in opposition to each other, for the properties of the 'verum' appear to be established in opposition to those of the 'certum' of the law. The viability of the juridical process, on the other hand, demands their conversion, indeed consists precisely in that conversion. The natural law, as the most intimate problem of theoretical jurisprudence, is precisely the problem of establishing that convertibility in principle. It is this conversion which is effected, for Vico, by the appeal to these principles of the 'sette dei tempi' and of providence.

These principles effect the conversion of the 'certum' and the 'verum' by disclosing them to be, not the abstract elements of an analytical situation, but dialectical moments of one continuous and dynamic process. Their opposition is not abstract, but immanent to the concreteness of this process. Classical natural law theory had set these elements in opposition, an opposition which proved to be irreducible and to involve their complete diremption, because it viewed them thus abstractly and analytically and not in the matrix of the total process of the formation of structures of law in history. The essential structure of this process is established by its inner tension between the pure ideality and unity of the law and the exigencies of the concrete and historical moment, of human decision, in which law is enacted, between the unity of the law in idea, that is, and its particularity and multiplicity in fact. Viewed abstractly, the terms of this tension appear in absolute opposition; viewed in the concreteness and continuity of the historical process, however, they are seen to be reciprocal conditions of each other. The unity and continuity of this process is established by the principle of providence, its particularity, by the principle of the 'sette dei tempi' or the time-structure of the process. The elements of the process are convertible, because, within the context of the total process, every positive law, the 'certum' in its multiplicity, particularity and authority, is seen to be pregnant with the intent of the whole; the unity of the idea, on the other hand, to be pregnant with the ideality of the infinite variety and diversity of the concrete moments of history. The convertibility of the 'certum' and the 'verum' of the law signifies, not their reduction, but their inclusion and reciprocity within the unity of this process.

This conception of the conversion of the 'certum' and the 'verum' of the law alters profoundly the classical conception of the natural law itself. Classically, Vico recognizes, the concept of natural law is a static and normative concept merely. This is due to the fact that, ultimately, for classical natural law theory, the natural law is identified with the 'verum' of the law. As a consequence, the natural law was viewed as the 'unwritten law', or the law written in heaven, in the pure expression of Antigone; more precisely as the summation of those positive enactments which are implied normatively in the ontological nature of man. Viewed thus, it is clear the natural law is but an unenacted positive law, or a positive law by implication and deduction. For this reason, the natural law in this sense appears in irreducible opposition to the positive law in history, because it confronts that positive law simply as another positive principle and not as a principle of ideality. For this reason also, the natural law in the classical sense represents a perversion of the 'verum' of the law; for it construes this 'verum' as an alternate, though purely normative and unacted, positivity, to the positive law in history, rather than an immanent ideality of the historical process of the formation of positive law.

By contrast, Vico views the natural law as the concrete mediation of the positivity and the ideality of the law. It is identifiable neither with the pure positivity of the formations of history nor with the pure idea of the law, but with the actual process whereby the one, the continuity of the historical formations, is inwardly and progressively transformed, qualitatively, by the operation of the other and at the same time whereby the idea itself is clarified and established by the historical processes of positive law. To demonstrate that there is a natural law, for Vico, is consequently, not, in the classical sense, to demonstrate that there is a 'cosmos' of positive law implied in the ontological structure of human nature, but rather that such a process of historical transformations actually transpires.

This transformation of the conception of the natural law is pregnant with the conception of a transformed jurisprudence. For Vico jurisprudence is neither the deductive science of the natural law, in the classical sense, nor the mere technique of the administration of the positive law, which may be synthesized in the procedural rules of a digest. It is, rather, the historico–philosophical science of the natural law. Classical jurisprudence was much preoccupied with the derivation, from its basis in the abstract concept or definition of man, of the implied body of normative legislation; this was conceived to be the proper preoccupation of theoretical jurisprudence. Ideal structures of law, and ideal republics, which represented just such derivative and deductive structures, exercised over classical jurisprudence the fascination of Medusa, and rendering it as sterile as the stone. Meanwhile, pragmaticism with respect to the administration of the positive law was the rule.

Jurisprudence as the historico–philosophical science of the natural law, by contrast, addresses itself to quite a different and more difficult task. It seeks to establish, in one concrete synthesis, that actual process of historical, qualitative transformation whereby the structures of positive law move toward the ever greater and closer approximation to the idea of law, which for Vico remains always the 'aequum bonum' of Roman law. The science of jurisprudence, in this sense, would have its feet planted firmly on the matter of the history of law, that is, would have its foundations in the actualities of the historical process of the formation of positive law. At its other extreme it would embrace that ideality which had hitherto been conceived to be the proper object of a philosophy whose method transcended the processes of history. Its real concern, however, would be the area between, in which these extremes meet and are synthesized, and into which it would absorb alike mere historical fact and mere idea, and from which it might move both in the direction of the reconstruction of historical fact on its ideal ground, that is toward the generation of history in its true sense, and toward the expression of the idea as the immanent informing principle of concrete historical process. Or again, in its extremes, such a science would be, before all else, a science of the origins of law, for its most intimate principle is time, and, with equal emphasis, a science of the ends of law.

An example of this science in action, as it were, is afforded early by Vico in the 'essay of jurisprudence', which he tells us[1] he inserted in the *De Studiorum Ratione*, for reasons not wholly scientific. The ostensible subject of this 'essay' is a fine point of Roman political history, the mode and circumstances under which political power was conceded by the patricians to the plebeians. In fact, however, it is a demonstration of a science which might in one synthesis unite history and philosophy and write the history of law for the first time.

The very conception of such a science of jurisprudence is clearly predicated on the rudimentary theory of history worked out with reference to the natural law and contained in the synthesis of the principles of the 'sette dei tempi' and of providence. The essence of this theory of history, inchoate though it be, is the synthesis of time and idea. The movement of the formation of law, natural law itself in its most intimate character, is seen to be an ideal process in time. To be sure, such an insight is not so much a theory of history as an insight into the philosophical problem of history. It may rather and better be said to be the first formulation of the problem of history in the terms dictated by the exigencies of theoretical jurisprudence. For if the Vichian insight is here that history is a time-ideal process,

[1] OI, p. 100.

this is but to raise the still profounder problem of the basis and the possibility of such a movement. This he does not do, specifically and extensively in this context; but it was the question which must inevitably draw him on.

III

THE SCIENCE OF HUMANITY

THE speculative problem of history which, in this way, reveals itself, for Vico, to lie at the heart of the natural law concept recurs with greater urgency and clarity of structure and implication in a second context, that of the science of humanity. This project of a science of humanity constitutes the widest frame of reference of Vico's thought; it is the definitive commitment of his intellectual effort and it is only with reference to this project that the unity, the continuity, and the actual direction of his thought can be established. In its essential character, as conceived by Vico, the project of the science of humanity is but the extension, materially and formally, to its logical and programmatic limits, of the concept and the enterprise of the natural law. Law, as the type of the bonds of human community, is extended to include the whole process of civilization, of the formations of society, and hence of the 'humanization' of man. The 'certum' of the law is extended to embrace the whole content of culture and of social process in its positive aspect. The 'verum' of the law, in turn, is broadened to include, not the idea of law, the 'aequum bonum', alone, but the idea of society, of man himself. Finally, as the culminating mark of this extension and continuity, the speculative problem of the science of humanity reveals itself to be identical with that which lay at the heart of the natural law concept, namely, the speculative problem of history.

The idea of a science of humanity, which is the final informing principle of Vico's thought, has its historical and its ideal roots in the tradition of classical political humanism. From this source it draws, at least initially, its conception of humanity as well as its conception of science, the science it aspires to be. For Vico, as for the classical tradition of humanism, man's humanity is quintessentially his sociality, his power, that is, to generate, to sustain and to fructify the relations of community. In these relations, man finds the fulfilment and realization of his nature, in a word, himself, his own reality; outside of these relations, he is, at best, an hypothesis, at worst, simple alienness and absence from himself. The proper study of mankind is, indeed, therefore, man; not, however, man in that abstract individualism which so fascinated the centuries between which Vico's life was divided, but man in society, because here alone, in the social structure, is the reality and fullness of man to be discovered.

Again, it is from the tradition of classical political humanism that Vico draws the conception of science which pervades and informs his project of a science of humanity. For Vico, as for classical humanism, science is wisdom, that is, presence as idea and as power. The formal structure of wisdom is presence as idea, that is, as totality, in any order of being or nature, and finally in being itself. Presence as idea, however, cannot be taken in abstraction from presence as power, from will and control. The idea is not a mere object of contemplation; it solicits to action, and the first token of its presence is the power with which it endows the active principle which it solicits. In science as wisdom, the idealistic and the practicalistic or activistic elements are completely synthesized. And finally, wisdom, which defines science, is itself defined by Vico, anthropologically, as the unity of thought and action, of intellect and will.[1] Science finds its wholeness in life, in action.

The science of humanity of which he speaks is, consequently, a wisdom, the supreme human wisdom, in which man's being is fully realized, fully present, in idea and in power. And since man's humanity is defined for Vico by his sociality,[2] man is present to himself as idea only in the idea of society. This idea, therefore, is the formal principle of the science of humanity. But conformably to the structure of wisdom, such a science would be incomplete, would be but half itself, in Vico's words,[3] did it not deliver to man power as well as presence. It must, therefore, find completion in the control with which it can endow him over the processes of sociality. The science of humanity must be in substance intelligent control of social process, through the total presence of its idea and the command of its forces. In this wisdom, man possesses the actuality of his own being; and it is thus that Vico describes the science of humanity as it is the informing principle of his mature thought, 'to meditate upon certain principles of the humanity of the nations . . . that by such principles might be established . . . a certain state of perfection of which the extremes and the gradations may be measured . . . whence with scientific certitude there might be understood the means by which

---

[1] SNS, 364–6; SNP, p. 39; DU, I, 201.   [2] DU, pp. 53–4; SNS, 134–6.
[3] I.e. intellect as well as will; SNS, 364.

the humanity of a nation, after its inception might arrive at such perfection and, having fallen from it, might lead itself back again'.[1]

The dominant Platonic tonality of this conception of science as wisdom, as the wisdom of the city, is evident, and fully justifies both Nicolini's remark that Platonism was to Vico 'blood of his blood' and Vico's apotheosis of Plato as the first of his four 'authors'. The controlling formal principle of that wisdom is the notion of perfection, of the plenitude of being and existence in an order of nature. This notion of perfection, of plenitude as formal presence is the Platonic idea; and it is such an idea of humanity and society which would control the science of humanity as Vico conceives it. Toward such an idea the science, by its method, would be directed; in such an idea its formal character and actuality would consist, and from such an idea, finally, its character as power would flow. In a word, the notion of science has its metaphysical basis in that conception of total presence which is the ultimate principle of the Platonic idea. To this notion Vico's conception of his science of humanity is initially, finally, and consistently faithful.

At the same time, and again quite consistently with the spirit of classical political humanism, and the humanistic attitude in general, Vico's science of humanity has another centre, another nucleus, as it were, which counterbalances the attraction of this pure Platonic idea and forces the science into an elliptical path. This element is an immediate, complete and even joyful sensitivity and receptivity (in Vico unlimited by that inherent aristocratic restriction which, in antiquity and in the Renaissance, gave rise to the classic disdain for the vulgar) to the multiplicity, the variety, the partial, even the conflicting and mutually contradictory forms of society and culture, and for the limited, the unideal, even the selfish, utilitarian, and brutal motivations which inspire men's action and thus enter into the composition of the social structure of humanity in its concrete historical reality. It is the element which Vico himself, and in contrast to the Platonic, characterizes as the Tacitean theme of his science and which, in certain of its aspects might even more truly be called Odyssean. For what it holds before the eye is at once the μάλα πολλὰ of the far wandering hero of Homer, the ready acceptance of all the diversity of man's world, in custom, law, language, belief, and the character of Odysseus himself, compounded of guile, of power, of will and phantasy and in every act pregnant and instinct with the fullest humanity. Nourished in the same spirit which has its eye fixed stead-

[1] SNP, p. 11.

57

fastly on the pure unity and homogeneity of the Platonic idea, this sensitivity and receptivity might appear to some the seed of romanticism fostered in the bosom of classicism; in Vico, however, it is more truly the source of that transcendence alike of the romantic and the classic which his theory of history achieves.

It is this dualism between what again may be described as positivity and ideality which reflects in the science of humanity the structure of the speculative problem of the natural law. For these two elements of sociality: on the one hand, the idea of human society, as distilling the plenitude of humanity, and on the other, the multitude, the diversity of the forms of sociality historically existent and historically possible, that power of wisdom, wholly controlled by that idea, and the lush, unideal force which is actually the motive power of historical social structures reflect almost perfectly the diverse elements of the situation of law, the 'certum' and the 'verum'. So perfect, indeed, is this correspondence to Vico's mind that it is treated as simple identity; that fluid, positive, unideal dimension of sociality becomes the 'certum' of the science of humanity or of society, that idea of perfection in society its 'verum'. Under these, respectively, the 'certum' and the 'verum' of the law fall inclusively as ulterior specifications. Thus there is actually effected in Vico's thought a material transformation of the terms of the problem of theoretical jurisprudence into the primary terms of the speculative problem of the sciences of humanity.

Even more importantly, this translation of the basic terms of theoretical jurisprudence into the science of humanity opens the way for, and is itself completed in, the more characteristic duality of that science, namely, the duality of philology and philosophy. Philology, in its most extensive sense, and the sense basic to it in Vico's employment, is simply the science of the 'certum'. It is that science whose concern is to fix or to establish the order of the 'certum' in its certitude and positivity; it is the science of authority, in the sense that the world of the 'certum' to which it addresses itself is the world whose actuality is derived from the 'arbitrium' of men, from their free decisions.[1] Of this world man may call himself the 'author', the originator, because to this act of his decision its positive character and its reality, as a fact, is to be wholly traced, so that no other 'authority' need be sought. The material object, consequently, of philology is precisely that various world of positive forms which man generates as the immediate expression of the basic property of his nature,

[1] SNS, 350, 137.

'd'essere socievole'. Moreover, philology, in the first instance at least, addresses this world precisely in its positivity, variety and multiplicity; nor can it, despite whatever transformations it may undergo as a science, abandon this primary orientation. To adopt a phrase coined much later, but whose legitimacy, in this restricted area, Vico would readily have acknowledged, the aim of philology is simply 'that which transpired'; as a science, philology may yield, as its proper fruit, not the idea, but a ground sufficient to remove all reasonable doubt, and thus to duplicate, at the level of science, that positivity which is its object in the order of facts, of historical transactions.

In like manner, the 'verum' of the situation of law is transformed and completed in the idea of philosophy which pervades and sustains the Vichian science of humanity. In itself, and in its abstract self-identity, philosophy is the science of the 'verum' now understood not merely in the limited and restricted form, in which it appears in the area of law, but in its widest and most inclusive sense as ideality in itself. Its object is that notion of perfection, of totality, pursued through all the reaches and orders of being and rendered present in its most intimate character. In this area of the science of humanity, its more limited object is that idea of man which glimmers through and beyond all the positivities of history; but this it pursues under the same seal as it does all being, the seal of its total presence and self-identity. The orientation of philosophy is fixed toward the 'verum' as that of philology is toward the 'certum', nor can it depart from this bias save under the penalty of surrendering its own character.

The duality of philosophy and philology thus represents the projection on to the plane of the science of humanity of the alternality of the 'certum' and the 'verum', in the first instance, materially. Such projection could not be effected materially, however, without entailing a formal projection as well, a projection, that is, of the 'rapport' which had been established between them at the level of the natural law. The concept of the natural law demanded, as its fundamental condition, the synthesis of these dimensions of law, the 'certum' and the 'verum', the positivity and the ideality; the classical natural law theory had tended to sustain them in a radical opposition. As a result, the actual problem of the natural law became for Vico the discovery or determination of a principle of mediation between these dimensions of the law. It is this pattern, extended and clarified to meet the extension of the material, which recurs at the level of the science of society.

The salient characteristic of classical political humanism, and of Vico's thought, as well, as it renews and exercises that tradition afresh, is its openness at once to the unity and the self-identity of the idea and to the multiplicity and the variety, indeed, the very contradictions of the concrete order of existence and becoming. From this characteristic was born its profoundly moral or ethical character, its devotion to the concept of wisdom; for ethics, and wisdom, as its fullest expression, is essentially the pursuit of the idea in and through that multiplicity, variety and contradictions of human presence, within which it seeks to induce these properties of the idea, its unity and self-identity. Wisdom is thus the primary informing principle of that humanism. Wisdom, in turn, however, must possess as its own formal principle a theoretical synthesis of that duality of idea and concretion. Its informing principle must in its turn be a science in which that synthesis should be achieved in theoretical terms. And since the idea toward which that humanism in its fullness is turned is the idea of man in society and the concretion on which it rests is the concrete process of the formation of the structures of social life as expressing and realizing man's humanity, the science of humanity, in these synthetic terms, would seem to correspond to the most profound exigency of classical political humanism.

In fact, however, here again, as in the instance of the more restricted, though typical, area of the natural law, the historical practice of classical humanism has been in diametrical opposition to its theoretical exigencies. These exigencies are wholly for unity and synthesis; its practice wholly in the direction of opposition and diremption. Specifically, Vico indicates, it has sought to define the unity and the self-identity of the idea of man, of society, transcendently to the process in which the concrete forms of society have arisen. It has sought to define this idea and to entertain it as the logical presupposition of that process rather than its intimate direction and result. It has fallen consistently into the type of abstract naturalism which defines the nature as a system of abstract relations and identifies this system with the idea. Inevitably, by contrast to this idea, the concrete process of the formation of social structures must appear as pure otherness. Rather than the vehicle of an ideal process, it must be conceived as without formal or ideal direction or immanent movement. Any correspondence with the idea which it might display must be fortuitous and as rationally inexplicable as any other dimension of that process. At very best, the relationship between the idea, the nature, and the concrete process must be extraneous and accidental; at worst, the one or other must be conceived as exclusively the 'real' while the corresponding member must be consigned to the realm of illusion.

This trauma at the heart of classical western political humanism, in which its most intimate exigencies are frustrated and its actualization inhibited, is illustrated by Vico from the plight into which those elements of the ideal science of humanity, philosophy and philology, respectively, had fallen. These, as he has distinguished and identified them, should constitute the warp and the woof of the fabric of a true science of humanity, the one, philosophy, supplying the basic ideal structure, the other, philology, orientated toward the realm of the 'certum', of authority and concreteness, the density, the colour and the texture of one fabric whole and without seam. As a matter of fact, however, as a consequence of this alienation, confusion is the character of both, and deviation from their natural term.

Philosophy, turned wholly to the consideration of what ought to be, and describing the abstract structures or systems which it calls into being as the idea and as the plenitude of presence, becomes, as he remarks, of use to but a few, those few who are content to dwell in the heavenly city of Plato. The normative character of this world of ideas toward which the gaze of philosophy is turned is itself deceptive; rather than normative, that order of ideas is vacuous and irrelevant, akin, it might be suggested, to that realm of essences to which a latter-day philosopher, under the relentless pressure of his naturalism, has reduced the ideal world of Plato.[1] For the normative character of such ideas, their very 'oughtness', must imply a realizable relation to the concrete process of the formation of social structures. That 'oughtness' must be the palpable bond of the unity of idea and process; it must express at once the intimate formality of that process and its intimate exigency and provide, in like manner, the dynamic principle of its order. As a matter of fact, however, that 'oughtness' describes nothing more than the inward self-consistency of those ideas as systems of abstract relations, abstractly constructed and synthesized. As such, they are purely tautological and redundant with respect to their own character; every such idea is but the eternal and abstract reiteration of itself, in an extensive form which is essentially redundant. To define justice as giving every man his due is to utter sublime irrelevancy and platitude; indeed, it is but the repetition of identical sounds with no increment of idea. Such an enunciation could achieve ideal status only if it might be demonstrated to be, not

[1] George Santayana; cf. *The Realm of Essence.*

61

a transcendent intuition, but the actual term of the concrete process whereby structures of justice are formed, destroyed, replaced and rebuilt; it might have meaning and sense, only if it could be demonstrated that such a definition enunciated the inward movement and reality of that process, so that it might have as its meaning the whole range of the otherness and the complexity of that process. In such circumstances, far from being redundant, it would be the immanent word or 'logos' of that process, enunciating its own reality in contradiction to, and at the same time, in realization of all the tensions and contradictions of that process. Such it is not, however, on the lips of the classical philosophers; on the contrary, it is set by them over against that concrete process as the uncontaminated idea to which that process must ever form the ludicrous contrast.

These abstractively normative concepts are not merely, however, irrelevant and redundant; they become positively mischievous when, in response to a genuine demand of the unity of man's consciousness, the effort is made to employ them, apodictically, as the principles of the ordering of the 'certum' of man's humanity, that is, of social process. This apodictic intrusion of the normative idea into concrete process is the true principle of 'myth' in that pejorative and pseudo-poetic sense in which it is repudiated by Vico and which his own doctrine of poetry and myth is designed, to a great extent, to counter-act and depose, that is, of myth as the phantastic reconstruction of concrete process on the pattern of an abstract and apodictic idea. To the order of myth, in this sense, belong, from Vico's point of view, practically all of the theories of social process which had been advanced to his day. He singles out for especial reprobation in this relation the three masters of recent political and jurisprudential theory, Grotius, Selden and Pufendorf; but this signalization is merely a matter of immediate preoccupation, for as occasion arises, he extends this essential criticism backward in time to include Hobbes, Spinoza and Bacon, the Stoic and the Epicureans of antiquity, and does not hesitate to lay the fallacy at the door of his own, often acknowledged supreme master, Plato. The common crime of all of these is pseudo-mythologizing. Whether, with Hobbes, we reconstruct the process of the socialization, which is at the same time, on the premises from which none of these authors depart, the intimate process of the humanization of man, on the hypothesis 'homo homini lupus' or, at the other extreme of possible supposition, with Plato on that of the 'sapienza riposta' of the ancients, the semi-magical ascription of an explicit, philosophical wisdom to the founders of nations, the root fallacy which vitiates the argument from its inception is the same: an abstract, normative idea is apodictically intruded into the context of social process, into the order of the 'certum' of humanity. Instead of genuine history there is generated pseudo-myth, which in its turn, like the poetry against which Plato directed his classical arguments, is at two removes from the truth. Such myths are productive of false principles of every science; of political science, for example, such as the proposition that monarchy was the first form of human polity; of the science of the human spirit itself, such as the assertion, so important of Vico's own theories, that poetry is the late flower of a culture and belongs essentially to the pleasurable dimension of human awareness; or finally, and most monstrous to Vico's eyes, of history in the proposition that the first man was innocent of the idea of God. Such mythical constructions are the pure contradiction of genuine science and represent the complete degradation of the idea. Nevertheless, it is a degradation which the abstract idea cannot escape, since its only possible area of validation lies in the concrete process, and here only can it turn to escape from the barren monotony of its own tautology. Pseudo-myth is the inevitable accompaniment of such philosophizing. Finally, in addition to the confusion which this activity of pseudo-mythologizing induces in the order of the human 'certum', it constitutes, at the same time, a complete nullification of the philosophical process itself. For if the legitimate object of philosophy as a science be the idea, it is obvious that in this process it ends, not with the idea, but with its caricature, the pseudo-myth. And if the whole reality of the idea be the presence which it realizes, the end product of such philosophy is the very opposite of idea, since the pseudo-myth is a mode of absence and not of presence.

If such be the plight of philosophy, which has frustrated the inner movement of classical political humanism toward a genuine science of man, that of philology is to Vico's mind, little better, characterized by equal confusion and productive equally of that absence of man from himself which is the negation of humanism. Philology is, according to his conception, the science of the 'certum' in its own character. Its term, consequently, might legitimately be thought to be the establishment of the order of the 'certum' in its positivity; that is, that it should be able to furnish indubitable evidence of the positive character of the structures and ligatures of society. In the order of polity, for example, what might be expected of philology, among whose exponents Vico numbers the poets, the historians, the orators, the grammarians, in general the 'erudite'[1], would surely be an indubitable account of the founding of the cities and the nations of the past, the determination of the order and succession of the forms of polity, in their positive character. In the order of morals, it would be equally legitimate to expect an indubitable determination of the customs of the various times and peoples, with some account of their convergences and divergencies: in the order of the arts and sciences and the disciplines of culture, an equally certain account of their positive process. And of the wider and more elastic ligatures of community, language, poetry, the movements of expansion and contraction of the nations, on all these accounts it would be only legitimate to expect philology to speak out with certainty and to generate that dimension of man's presence to himself which must consist in the certain knowledge of his origins, of his history and of his concrete relations in the structures of community.

As a matter of fact, however, on all these counts philology is dumb, or rather, speaks with that uncertainty and hesitation, that contradiction and confusion which is the substantive denial of its reality. There is, for example, no subject on which doubts are so multiple and multiply so rapidly as on the problem of the origin of language; yet no single bond of community is of equal ontological importance or historical necessity. Of the origin and propagation of the nations, the doubt is equally enveloping and dense. No principle of the continuity of gentile and sacred history can be established, while chronology, which would seem to be the fundamental philological construct, displays the profoundest confusion. The people most advanced in intellectual culture in the classic world, the Greeks, are the people most brutally ignorant, and careless, of their own antiquities, on the testimony of their first historian 'veritiero e grave', Thucydides. The history of Rome, in its origins and its antiquities, with respect to its own constitution, the formation of its institutions, its language, its propagation and chronology, is by the testimony of its own authority, the historian Livy, a mass of conflicting and contradictory assertions. In vain, in a word, may one seek in the area of philology that indubitable knowledge of the order of the human 'certum' which should be its characteristic mark.[2]

The source of this obscurity and uncertainty in the very heart of the science of the 'certum' is to be traced to that conceit of philosophy by which it had substituted the transcendent and apodictic idea for

---

[1] E.g. SNS, 138–40.   [2] SNP, p. 24 et seq.

the ideal movement of concrete process. The fact is that the concept of a science of the 'certum' independent in its principles of all philosophical illumination is self-contradictory; as self-contradictory as the concept of a pure jurisprudence of the 'certum'. Such a science is non-viable not merely in the sense that it can of itself yield no ideal conclusions (for these in fact should never be demanded of it any more than of the 'certum' of the law should there be demanded a 'ratio naturalis' of the law), but in the more important sense that it cannot, without such illumination, yield the certitude proper to it. The concept of a science of the 'certum' in its own character arises by reaction against the pseudo-mythology of transcendental philosophy. It evinces a need, rather than an authentic possibility; the need, that is, of a science which will establish the 'certum' in its certitude as against the fantastic structures of that mythology. But such a science is impossible save in the closest conjunction and identity with philosophy itself. Directly and indirectly, that is, by way of the extravaganza of pseudomyth which it has produced in place of history and by reason of the extremity to which it has reduced philology, the extremity of conceiving itself as an inquiry independent of the inquiry of philosophy, transcendental philosophy stands convicted, before Vico, of a complete frustration of the intimate exigencies of classical political humanism and as generative of that absence of man to himself, both in fact and in idea, in history and philosophy, and, consequently, in wisdom, which is characteristic of the western mind.

It is on the ruins of this critique of the tradition of classical political humanism that Vico erects the image of the science of humanity as it would correspond to the speculative and methodological requirements of such a humanism. It is, above all, a science in which the duality between positivity and ideality in the social process and between philosophy and philology would be definitively closed. It is a science which should be both history and philosophy, in the sense that it would render man's presence to himself total and positive in idea, as informing the process of the formation of the positive structure of sociality, and in fact, in the concrete, in that process as reducing to its existential state the fullness of that idea. Concretely, on the basis of the exigencies revealed in this critique it is possible to evoke, as it were, an image of that science in its most fundamental lineaments.

The movement of this science would be oscillatory. The terms of its movement would be, on the one hand, the idea; specifically, the idea of that humanity which is realized in the relations of community; on the other, the concrete forms of sociality. These latter must include not merely those structures which are most patent, such as the structures of polity, of economy, of law; but as well, those other, more tenuous, but no less vital ligatures of community such as the arts, the sciences, the customs, the languages, the ideologies, which weave the connecting tissue, as it were, between the grosser social forms. Thus, to illustrate, Vico lists as the most fundamental and originative of all social forms, three of the most tenuous: a belief, that is, the existence and power of God, a custom, itself resting on the generation or substance of a belief, the burial of the dead, inseparably associated with the immortality of the soul, and a primitive rite, marriage, whose chief function he believes to be to insure the sense of origin and perpetuity, in which presence and idea must reside. These concrete forms, which collectively constitute the material dimension or substance of philology, are present to the science of humanity, or constitute its term, in two ways: first, in their individual character, for this is the irreducible form of their positivity; secondly, and more importantly, as process, that is, in that dynamic relationship in which they sustain a continuity, even in their positive character, and thus induce a totality. Between these terms, the science of humanity would trace its oscillatory path.

Nevertheless, its movement between them is not indifferent, the mere path of forces perfectly equalized and hence rendered neutral. The primary orientation of the science of humanity must lie toward the idea; this it is which it would evoke in its plenitude, as the total presence of man to himself. For this reason, the idea may be called the positive pole of that science. Yet as a positive pole is such only in the presence of the negative, the idea can be generated only in the field established by the presence of concrete process. Even more precisely, the idea which the science of humanity seeks to evoke is but the immanent ideality, the 'logos', of that process. It is, therefore, nothing distinct from that process, but the process itself seen in its totality. The humanity which man achieves in the process of society and civilization is not a humanity transcendent to that process, but the very reality of that process seen and existing in its continuity, perpetuity and totality. From this, too, it may be seen that the science of humanity itself, in which, according to its notion, that humanity would be rendered totally present to itself, is not itself an act transcendent to the process it synthesizes, but as it were the 'culmo', the immanent culminating point of that process of civilization itself. The path of the science leads back from the idea to the concreteness of social process not as the something extraneous to that idea but as to another dimension of it. For the first time, in such a science, a genuine philology would be achieved; that is to say, the order of the 'certum' of humanity would be established in its true certitude, the certitude which can accrue to it only from its illumination by the immanent presence of the idea. Man's past, the whole concrete process of the formation of society and culture might in such a science be rendered present, in its factual character, in its chronology, in its inner dynamic. That absence of man from himself in that concrete process, or, more simply, that gross ignorance of the past, which, as Vico had indicated, characterized the highest intellectual culture of antiquity, would be overcome; for the most tangible and substantive fruit of such a science would be precisely that knowledge of the past as ordered to, as constituting and sustaining the present, which is history. For the first time, also, within the structure of such a science, would authentic philosophy be realized, a philosophy in which the antique transcendences by which the idea had been rendered a principle of alienation, rather than a principle of presence, of duality and otherness, rather than of unity and identity, might be themselves transcended and the unity of the real be recognized. In such philosophy, the idea might be recognized in its true character as the inner movement of process seen in the perspective of its totality. The final fruit of that science must be an authentic wisdom, that is, a union of idea and power, which would overcome once and for all that disdain for action which had characterized classical humanism and which discovers in action illuminated by the inner light of the idea the fullness of liberty and the vindication of authority.

But if the image of that science, and of its possible fruits, is clear, what is not clear, Vico recognizes, is the conditions under which it may be realized. It is, as he asserts, a 'New Science'; a science which, while alone corresponding to the exigencies of political humanism, has nowhere in western thought found the establishment of its principles. It is a science, consequently, which must be founded 'ab ovo', a 'New Science', as he calls it, not, as has been asserted, as an echo either of the proud epithet of Bacon's *Novum Organon* nor of the equally complacent designation of the *Two New Sciences* of Galileo, but simply in conformity to its intrinsic character, to the actualities of western thought, and above all to the labours involved in its establishment.

These labours, which Vico, with Dantean directness, tells us were the object of a quarter century of rude and unrelenting mediation, were principally two. Its possibility must be established in principle with reference, in his own words,[1] to its two parts, idea and language. By these terms, Vico intends, on the one hand, the ontological and the gnoseological bases of such a science, on the other, its methodological conditions. There must, in other words, lie at the basis of such a science both metaphysical and methodological conditions, a theory of the processes of being and of knowing involved in the historical processes of sociality and a theory of the instrumentalities and procedures involved in the final transmutation of that process into the mode of presence of science. But that these are not in reality two, but one, and in their unity constitute the speculative problem of the 'New Science' is equally clear. For the science of humanity, as it has been suggested, does not stand outside or beyond the process of which it is the science, the process of the incivilment or civilization of man through the development of the forms of social life; it is itself a moment of that process, the moment of its total presence. As a consequence, it must be, in its structure, continuous and extensive with that process and its conditions must be identical in principle with the conditions of that process itself. It is in the speculative problem of this science of humanity that the unity of the real finds preliminary expression. Its methodological and metaphysical dimensions are, consequently, only abstractly distinct.

Seen thus in its unity, this speculative problem of the 'New Science', or the science of humanity, is the speculative problem of history; and it is at this level that the transmutation of the theoretical problem of jurisprudence into that of the science of humanity is completed.

The crucial theme of this transmutation is again the relation of time and idea. The resolution of the theoretical problem of the natural law, revolved, as pointed out above, about the concept of the 'sette dei tempi'. Derived originally from the tradition of Roman jurisprudence, this concept was extended and enlarged by Vico to sustain the whole weight of the concept of natural law. The natural law he understood to be, not that transcendent and unenacted normative law, allegedly implied in the concept of 'human nature', but the movement of the process of the historical formation of the structures of positive law toward an immanent ideality. The natural law is a law which emerges in and through the formation of the customs

[1] SNP, p. 9.

68

of the nation. It may be looked at indifferently as the movement of that process toward the idea or as the immanent operation of the idea as presence within that process working its qualitative transformation. In either case, the concept of the natural law depended directly upon the validity of this initial insight into the speculative concept of history, that is, into the concept of time-ideal process.

Translated to the plane of the 'New Science' or the science of humanity, this speculative concept of history is given a wider arena of activity and a correspondingly higher office. From its validity depends now, not merely the concept of the natural law, but the whole concept of political humanism itself as well as the possibility of that science of humanity in which that humanism must find its formal and theoretical realization. For that process of the formation of the positive forms of human sociality, in all their diversity and multiplicity, is the vehicle of the positive presence of man to himself in which, formally, his humanity is realized. Humanity, like the natural law, is not a transcendent idea. Like the natural law, it arises in and through that positive process of the formations of the structures of community and constitutes the inner movement of that process toward its ideality, which is the total presence of man to himself in society. This process, again like the process of the natural law, is essentially an ideal process through time.

The cardinal question of the science of humanity is, therefore, evident. It is the problem of determining in the first instance the validity of this concept of an ideal process through time; and in the second place, of the character and conditions of a science of that process. The radical speculative problems of the science nakedly confronted, these are seen to be each an abstraction, the abstract negation each of the other, whereas in the actuality of that science they should be each the assertion of the other.

The science itself, consequently, can be fixed at neither pole of the process. It can consist, in its proper character, neither in the establishment of the idea in its pure ideality, nor of that process in its positivity, but must fix, before all else, the law of their inner reciprocity, unity or mediation. It consists, to Vico's mind, in principles, in eternal ideal principles, which establish the law of the immanence of the idea of humanity in the concreteness of the social process, or the rule of the appearance of the idea under definite concrete forms. Such, to illustrate, is to his mind that 'eternal principle of fiefs' which he considered a chief glory of his 'New Science' and which is the type of the principles in which that science is embodied. These principles are the 'eternal maxims', in which the science of humanity must consist and which are the authentic form of the total presence of man to himself, in idea and fact; from these principles, also, flows that power which transmutes that abstract presence or science into wisdom, presence as idea and as power, in which the fullness of that science must consist and which may make man potent over the very processes of his humanity.

Such is the image of the science which Vico evokes as corresponding to the profound exigencies of political humanism and in which, formally, that humanism alone can consist and be actualized. The achievement of that science would be three—of humanity, or the speculative problem of history seen in its fundamental dimensions, the antology of historical process and the gnoseology of historiography. For it is the ontology of history alone which can provide the ontological basis of the science of humanity, while this science, since it is the science of an historical process, is historical or historiographic in its formal structure.

Together the ontology of history as ideal process in time and the gnoseology of the science of such process constitute the positive dimensions of the Vichian theory of history. Together, they provide the positive basis of that science of humanity which the 'New Science' aspires to be. This science, in turn, finds its actualization in those ideal and eternal principles which in systematic relation delineate the 'eternal and ideal history upon which is patterned the movement of the nations through time'[1] and which defines the 'New Science' in its idea.

[1] SNP, p. 66; SNS, 349.

IV

THE MODIFICATIONS OF THE
HUMAN MIND

THE philosophical problem of history as it arises in the dual context of the natural law and of the project of a science of humanity is thus fixed for Vico. It is the problem of the synthesis of time and idea. In this formulation, time is the general formal principle of the positive structures of society and culture; that is, time defines the most general order which pervades the realm of these structures. They appear in temporal succession, manifesting in this medium that variety and diversity, those transformations and dynamisms which are the characteristics of their positivity. Idea, by contrast, in this formulation, defines that plenitude or perfection which would seem to be the implication of that positive movement and over against which the process of the formations of the concrete structures of sociality and of humanity are to be measured. The error of classical political humanism has appeared to Vico as the attempt to fix this ideality apodictically, that is, independently of that temporal order in which concrete forms of society appear. This attempt has led, and must lead, in the first place to the diremption and the alienation of process and idea and, even more disastrously, to a distortion of the idea of society and of the character of its concrete forms. Neither the one nor the other can be determined or established independently. The idea established apodictically is pseudo-myth; the concrete form established 'empirically' is mere nature, the object of awareness but never of science. Science must fix the relationship of the process and the idea; that is, the ideal principle for the appearance of the concrete forms in their temporal order. Such appearance alone is truly 'nature', and the object of true science, while the product, or more precisely, the very substance of science is the total presence thus evoked. The idea is no timeless essence; it is the eternal law of the appearance of concrete forms in time. But the speculative problem which inheres is this notion of an eternal law of temporal appearance, stated in its most abstract form, is the relationship of time and idea. The Vichian theory of history, consequently, as a positive theoretical construction, is the determination of the principle, or principles, of the synthesis of time and idea, or, as it may also be stated, of time and form.

The first effective principle of the synthesis of time and form, and, consequently, the first positive element of the Vichian theory of history, is the doctrine of the modifications of the human mind. One thing alone is certain and indisputable concerning that positive process of the emergence of the concrete forms of sociality and culture in time: that world of the 'gentile nations' is surely the work of men.[1] It is the work of man's thought and represents in all the diversity of its positive character the insights into the idea which have guided his life in society. It is the work of his will, of his decision and determination, of his freedom, for these alone establish and sustain those forms in existence. This is but to reiterate the authenticity of the order of the 'certum' in its human character. This order is fixed by no transcendent principle, whether nature or another; as a consequence, the principle of this world of social forms is to be sought, in the first instance at least, within the structure of the human mind and the force of the human will. It is here, again in the first instance at least, that the synthesis of time and idea transpires; though whether this principle may ultimately suffice to establish this synthesis unambiguously remains to be determined.

The readiest interpretation of this dictum that the principles of the synthesis of time and idea are to be sought within the modifications of the human mind or consciousness, would seem to offer two possibilities. The determination of the modifications of the human mind may constitute a psychology of group consciousness. If this be the case, it is essentially an attempt to distinguish and to classify the acts of the mind by their content and on this basis to erect classifications of the contents of culture. The group psyche is assumed to be the agent in the formation of social structures, and the laws for the appearances of these forms would be identical with the laws which govern the psyche as a natural principle. The structure of the psyche and of the world of culture will faithfully reflect each other. That such is the nature or character of the Vichian doctrine is to a great extent indeed the case; at least, it is true in the sense that, from the material content of the 'New Science', such a psychology of the group consciousness can be derived, and, consequently, that the

[1] SNS, 331.

whole of the doctrine of the science can be reconstructed on these terms. That such is in fact the intention of Vico is, however, more difficult to establish; on the contrary, the erection of a psychology of group consciousness would seem to be in opposition to his wider purposes. For such a psychology would be, in the last analysis, in gross opposition to the primary concern of the Vichian theory of history, for it could not by any conceivable standard provide the principle for the synthesis of time and idea. These psychological laws, while they might establish the relationship between positive concrete forms of social organization and determinable attitudes of the human psyche, would still be, on the one hand, without reference to the time-structure of the process of culture and, on the other, equally without reference to a normative ideality of society or humanity. They would have no reference to the time-structure of that process because such laws would have as the terms between which they establish relations or correlations the abstract psyche and the generic culture structures; they would possess, consequently, that essentially atemporal character which is proper to 'laws of nature'. Again, such laws would be without essential reference to idea; for idea, in the Vichian context, which is, as we have suggested, unalterably Platonic, is normative; these laws, however, would be powerless to indicate or to determine any normative quality or direction in the movement of the agent psyche itself or in the process of cultural and social formation which it initiates. Every such modification of the human mind and every social structure corresponding to such modifications would possess, not normative, but purely descriptive value. More concretely, conceived psychologically, the modifications of the human mind would make it possible to establish neither a genuine history of humanity nor a philosophy or idea of humanity; the projected science of humanity, which the determination of those modifications is clearly intended to serve, would be defeated in both its fundamental dimensions.

Alternately, this problem of the determination of the modifications of the human mind may readily be conceived as the establishment of a 'metaphysic' of the human mind. To this understanding Vico himself lends a certain literal authority, for he speaks repeatedly of the central undertaking of the 'New Science' as a 'metaphysic' of the mind and even more specifically of the group mind.[1] This authority, in turn, has encouraged the daring constructions of the contemporary idealistic interpretation of Vico. Such a metaphysic

[1] E.g. SNP, pp. 28–9; SNS, 338 et seq.

73

of the mind, spurning the approach of psychology, would seek to determine *a priori* the ideal and eternal forms of human consciousness and the interrelations between them, dynamic and dialectical. This construction might then be offered, as Croce has offered it, as the true significance of that 'eternal and ideal history', the pattern of the histories of the nations in time, which Vico suggests must be one of the central achievements of the 'New Science' of humanity.[1] The dubious character of this undertaking, from the Vichian point of view, would, however, seem readily apparent. For such a formal and abstract dialectic of human consciousness would in its turn be pervaded by that eternism and atemporalism which it is Vico's purpose at every point to oppose. And this is recognized, moreover, by both the foremost exponents of the thought of Vico as such a metaphysics, Gentile and Croce alike.[2] By contrast, Vico's intent is indisputable; he is concerned, by this determination of the modifications of the human mind, to fix the law of the temporal appearance of the idea, or of the temporal movement toward the idea in the concrete process of the formations of human society. And his thought is especially opposed to that recrudescence of cultural positivism for which that metaphysics of the human mind effectively paves the way.

These alternatives do not, however, exhaust the possible avenues of approach to the Vichian concept of the modifications of the human mind. A third offers itself, much closer to Vico's own spirit and continuous with the whole texture of the 'New Science'. It is this: that the propositions concerning the modifications of the human mind are themselves propositions of the science of humanity, of the type, therefore, of those 'eternal' principles in which that science, according to Vico's conception, must find its complete expression. They are, consequently, historico-philosophical statements which realize the scientific expression of the synthesis of time and idea at the same time that they enunciate its cardinal principle. These 'modifications' are therefore neither empirical and descriptive classifications of human acts on the basis of the formal properties of their contents, nor are they eternal forms of consciousness or spirit which underlie at the same time that they transcend all phenomenal content of human acts. They are, rather, to be interpreted as historical statements in the Vichian sense of the term. They assert, consequently, before all else, the historical structure of the human mind itself. The human mind

[1] Benedetto Croce, *La Filosofia di G. B. Vico*, 4a ed., pp. 40–1; 136.
[2] Croce, ibid.; Giovanni Gentile, *Studi Vichiani*, p. 115.

does not produce history as something extraneous and contingent to itself; it produces itself in history, and its modifications are the concrete principles of its temporal-ideal actuality. The system of its 'modifications' expresses the laws of its own temporal process and movement toward its own ideality.

The first principle of the modifications of the human mind is to be found in the definition of man which Vico advances in the *Diritto Universale*: *posse, nosse, velle finitum quod tendit ad infinitum*, a finite principle of possibility, of knowing and of willing which tends to the infinite.[1] This definition of man is the supposition of all the ulterior modifications which Vico seeks to establish. In its own structure, the definition is complex and marked and characterized by the tensions which exist between its terms.

The most apparent of these tensions, and the one which will pervade the whole structure of spirit, appears between finite and infinite. Indeed, the notion of a finite principle whose tendency is toward the infinite must finally appear as pure contradiction and the need to resolve this contradiction presents perhaps the most profound speculative problem of Vico's thought. But little less apparent is the tension existing between the terms possibility and tendency; the passive overtones of the one, possibility, and the activistic flavour of the other, tendency, suggest an opposition only slightly less radical than the contradiction between finite and infinite. Finally, there appears the tension between *posse* and its own modes, knowing and willing; these would seem to attach themselves much more readily to the notion of tendency with its activistic associations.

The force of the *posse* of this definition is to express Vico's constant insight into that character of man's being which, in another place, he calls his 'indefinite nature'. This is the insight that the being of man cannot be enclosed within a determinate structure of possibilities, such, for example, as might be fixed by any law of cause and effect, but that it moves, rather, among indeterminable alternatives, and even further, by its own movement, generates these alternatives. It is the quality of this *posse* which makes it impossible to say what man is save by indicating what he has been and has become, while, at the same time, indicating that the centre of his being is not here either, but essentially in the possibility of transcending even his own history. It is the *posse* of man which establishes him in his essential being, which is precisely the power to transcend any assignable form or limits and to generate unlimited alternatives for his own

[1] DU, I, 44; cf. also 'Sinopsi' and 'Proemium', passim.

action. It is, in a word, the root of man's historicity, his character as the subject of history.

The possibility which thus constitutes the being of man, is not, consequently, to be associated with the classical concept of potentiality. Potentiality, which is ordered to a form, and which is but the abstraction of that form with respect to its actuality, is opposed in its very idea to actuality so that, where actuality is pure or complete, no element of potentiality may be present. The possibility which is here asserted to constitute man in his fundamental character, is, by contrast, closer to the idea of act or actuality itself. It is, so to say, the active principle of possibility, embracing within itself latently the abundant and varied forms which it possesses the power to generate and sustain. Yet in itself this radical and constitutive *posse*, or active and generative principle of forms, is not identical with the forms which it generates or creates, either in their specific and diversified character or in their presumable plenitude; it is rather the inexhaustible presupposition and spring of those forms, incommensurate with the flow of their concreteness, which arise within, and actualize, but never adequate or exhaust that fundamental act.

It is to man as *posse* in this sense that the contradictory terms of finite and infinite are to be related. The tendency of the radical constitutive activity or actuality of man is toward the infinite, because it is essentially incommensurate with the flux of actual concrete forms which it generates and in which it realizes itself, and because, as a result too of this incommensurability, it has as its own supposition a plenitude or pure actuality toward which its own creative force is orientated. This irrepressible tendency, which in its wake draws the authentic exigency of the infinite and the absolute, is the most intimate and constitutive principle of man as spirit, and opposes him to nature, from which such a tendency is, with equal force, excluded. For nature is always commensurate with itself and with the diversity of forms which may arise within it; and for this reason nature has no history, but returns ever upon itself in the endless cycle of the deployment and reabsorption of its forms and energy, with no window on the infinite.

At the same time, however, this incommensurability of the human act or spirit with the plenitude of the forms and the infinite which is its supposition is the source, the reality of its finiteness. For were this act of man pure act, commensuration in all dimensions would be its character; it would at once, and in a single burst of absolute and self-sustaining energy, as it were, actualize that plenitude, and in that plenitude, itself. And with the self thus realized it would be completely commensurate. The perfect expression of this plenitude would be its total and absolute presence to itself which must exclude all otherness, all change and all diversity which is not at the same time identity. Such, however, is not the character of the act which is the human spirit; this is rather, not realization, but tension. Its act is not, but endlessly becomes. It generates the forms latent within it and in them itself, not, as it were, in a single creative flame of energy, but distributively and through succession. As a consequence, its character is ever both presence and absence, sameness and otherness. It is always a limit to itself, and other and absent to itself, albeit that it moves, by that irrepressible tendency toward plenitude and the infinite, toward presence and identity. This inextricable and immedicable admixture of presence and absence is its essential finitude.

The human spirit, man, is consequently, according to this view, distended between these terms of its own finitude and that infinity toward which it tends, between total presence toward which it aspires and the absence which inheres fatally in it. This distention, in turn, is the very essence of time. And it is for this reason that time identifies precisely the relationship of man at once to his own actuality and to that infinite and absolute which is the supposition of his actuality. Time is the form or order of that radical and constitutive tendency of man toward the infinite from the basis of his essential finitude. It is the pattern according to which that finite principle perpetually transcends its determinate actuality in its movement toward a plenitude and absolute which it apprehends as its perfect double, a completely identical and completely other to itself. For this reason, the spirit of man is the time-spirit, suspended between the limited timelessness of nature and the unbounded and timeless self-commensuration of God.

In this way, the definition of man as *posse finitum quod tendit ad infinitum*, contains the basic principle for the radical synthesis of time and idea, and must, therefore, be considered the constitutive principle of the Vichian theory of history. This synthesis is clearly, for Vico, the very substance of man's spirit. For from this conception of man neither dimension, the infinity toward which the human spirit irrepressibly tends, nor that finitude which defines precisely his relation to that infinite may be eliminated. But that infinite, under its aspect of plenitude of form and presence, is the idea, and as such it enters constitutively into the distended being of man as the defining term of that tendency. At the same time, that movement of the human spirit, which is substantial time, without reference to that infinite is not movement, but inertia. This movement toward the idea in time is and must be the ultimate definition of the human spirit, in which all of its dimensions are present and synthesized.

The term *posse* is associated in the Vichian definition of man with two others, *nosse*, *velle*. Together, these constitute the basic modalities or forms of spirit, formalities so pervasive as to be identical with the *posse* itself. For the knowledge which is indicated by the *nosse* is essentially that presence which is as intimate and constitutive of spirit as that actuality or activity which defines its primary being. In spirit being and knowing cannot be other, but must be identical. The being which is spirit, cannot be a being which can stand to itself as object, but rather a being which must be essentially present to itself. Here the dualism between being and knowing, which is characteristic of nature and which characterizes man's knowledge of nature, has no place. Spirit is being which knows and knowing which is. *Nosse*, consequently, in the Vichian formula, may be designated as the first formality of the actuality of spirit, commensurate with spirit and constitutive of it. In like manner, is the *velle* related to spirit, to the *posse* which defines spirit. In its radical character this *velle* is identical with that energy or power by which spirit sustains itself in being; as such it is as pervasively identical with spirit, as is that *nosse*, from which its being cannot be distinguished save by a formal distinction. For the act which is spirit sustains itself and the world of forms, the time world of forms, which it generates; and this sustaining power, in its constitutive character, is the *velle* of which Vico speaks; not an empty velleity, but the active sustaining principle of spirit and its time world. Quite justly, therefore, Vico includes these terms in his definition on an equal plane with the principle term *posse*; for any distinction which would render them principles of the absence of spirit to itself would manifestly be false. And since they are the primary modes of spirit, *nosse* and *posse* are, like spirit, time principles; because they, too, like spirit, are essentially distended between finite and infinite.

This tendency of finite spirit toward the infinite conceals a paradox and contradiction. In this, the profoundest influence of his thought, the Christian, detaches Vico from his first allegiance to Plato. He might, with Plato, have conceived this tendency as a form of inner and linear determination of the movement from finite to infinite, to be impeded only by some external principle, such as the body provided for Platonism. Such a linear determination of tendency between finite and infinite would constitute a radical optimism which would link Vico both to classical Platonism and the forms of expansive infinitism associated with romanticism and with the progressivism of the enlightenment. In fact, however, his view is removed from both alike; to understand it, one must turn rather to the Christian insight, especially as developed by Augustine in his polemic both against the Manicheans and against the Pelagians. The essence of the Augustinian insight is that the tendency of the finite toward the infinite is essentially one of paradox; the finite and the infinite are both continuous and contradictory. The tendency of the finite has as its presupposition and its term the infinite and the absolute; this is precisely the sense of *tendency*, that at every instant the infinite presuppositions reveal themselves. At the same time, the infinite as such can never become the explicit term of the finite; the latter is always orientated toward another aspect of the finite, thus involving itself in the essential contradiction of finitude. It must be said that the nothingness of the finite forever cuts across the path of its initial movement toward the infinite and drives it back upon itself. It is for this reason that some, who also would not deny affiliation to Augustine, would see in this tendency of the finite toward the infinite, not its salvation, but its radical sin, not unrelated to the classic *hybris*. The profound need of the finite, consequently, is a power which might overcome this paradox and this contradiction within the movement of finite spirit. It is precisely in this guise, as will appear more clearly later, that the principle of providence enters into Vico's theory of history.

The definition of man as *posse, nosse, velle finitum quod tendit ad infinitum*, it has been suggested, constitutes the first, and the principal of those modifications of the human mind in which Vico discovers the clue to the synthesis of time and idea, and thus to the philosophical problem of history and the idea of a science of humanity which should be both history and philosophy, yielding the total presence of man to himself. Nor has he failed in this; for as it has been seen, the concept of *posse* as finite act whose tendency is toward the infinite yields directly the notion of time which embraces its movement toward the idea. Nevertheless, this definition deserves to be called not so much the first of the modifications of the human mind, as the archetectonic principle of the human spirit, within which the modifications which he intends arise. For the concept of ideal movement through time provided by this definition of man provides also the general principle for the definition of those modifications. These must be, in their essence, nothing other than those successive stages of self-transcendence whereby spirit seeks to advance existentially its radical tendency toward the infinite. That these stages must be, in the most primitive character, time-ideal movements is clear; since they are on the line between finite and infinite which essentially defines the time-ideal structure of the human spirit itself, they must in turn partake of the same character.

Again, this definition of man as *posse finitum quod tendit ad infinitum* also provides the terms in which those modifications may be identified. These transformations must be such within the primary formalities of spirit, namely, thought and action, *nosse* and *velle* and through these in that actuality or activity which is ultimate spirit itself. What therefore the determination of the modifications of the human mind constitutes is the determination of the pure phenomenology of the time-ideal movement of finite spirit toward the infinite, toward, therefore, the realization of its ultimate presuppositions and toward its total presence. A pure phenomenology, because it must be Vico's purpose to determine these time-forms of the human spirit not descriptively, with respect to their content (though this will be included in the total project of the concrete science of humanity), but in their principle and laws. This pure phenomenology, in its transcendence, must constitute that ideal and eternal history of which Vico speaks as one chief fruit of the 'New Science'.

As it has been seen, however, although *nosse* and *velle*, thought and action, must furnish the terms of these modifications, they cannot do so in isolation. In isolation, *nosse* and *velle* are abstractions; they find reality in their mutual relation through the *posse*, the basic and constitutive activity of spirit. The actual term of the modifications, consequently, must be one which expresses this mutuality and basic unity. This term has already been encountered, for it is integral to the tradition of classical political humanism from which Vico's thought takes its point of departure. It is wisdom. Wisdom is the unity of spirit, of *posse, nosse, velle*, in its idea, and consequently, in any of its time-ideal modalities or modifications. The modifications of the human mind, are, in the last analysis, the articulations of the pure phenomenology of human wisdom which support the structure of history.

The concept of wisdom has already been encountered in Vico's thought; it may here be specified more completely. Wisdom represents the degree of unity or integration which is achieved between the principles *posse, nosse, velle* at any moment in the movement of the human spirit on the line from finitude to infinity. Since, however, these terms cannot be taken as of equal value in the definition of the human spirit, the unity or integration which constitutes wisdom is something more complex than mere equilibrium. Thought and action, it has been noted, arise as primary formalities within the metaformal activity of spirit and are themselves metaformal with respect to the forms which arise within them. For this reason, wisdom may indeed constitute an equilibrium between thought and action, but never with respect to that more primitive activity, which remains incommensurate as the inexhaustible well-spring of all further formalities and of the successive modes of wisdom itself. The actual structures of the human mind, its modifications, with which Vico deals and to which he traces the actual formations of culture and society in history are those totalities of group consciousness embracing as components thought and action or will in the matrix of the constitutive activity of the human spirit. Every 'wisdom' consequently appears as a moment of synthesis which human group consciousness achieves within its pure activity and between its primary formalities on the continuum between finite and infinite which describes its life movement. Each such synthesis finds its realization and expression in a complex of expressive forms which phenomenologically constitute a society, a culture. These syntheses are interrelated further on that continuum, not in simple, progressive determination, but, as with the whole relationship between finite and infinite in Vico, as contradiction, demanding rectification.

These moments of synthesis express most clearly the *storia ideale eterna*, the ideal and eternal history, which the 'New Science' seeks to enunciate and constitute its ideal and eternal moments. Again, it is these phenomenological structures of wisdom which provide the point of departure for the entire analysis of society, culture and history in Vico, and precisely as complexes of expressive forms or signs which express the syntheses of thought and volition within the boundless constitutive activity of human spirit. In tracing the modifications of the human mind, both formally and historically, Vico is concerned, consequently, to disengage these moments of synthesis and to employ them methodically for historical analysis. For this reason, also, the quest of the modifications of the human mind presents itself in the complex form, first of the distinction between vulgar and civil or rational wisdom, and secondly in the modalities of thought and will or action, and finally the determination of the

81

dynamic time-relation between these forms of wisdom. Under this aspect, the 'New Science' presents itself concretely and programmatically as the reconstitution of the moment of vulgar wisdom and of its components, poetry and passion, myth and phantasy, will and authority, as against that civil wisdom in which reflective thought so pervades will and action as to generate the form of perfect freedom; yet this is accomplished in no primitivistic or romantic sense, but as rational and historical necessity. In a word, it is in this context that one must understand that approach to the poetic, the mythical, the authoritative, which has been called the anti-intellectualism of Vico, but which is, in reality, but the integrity of his humanism; for this humanism would achieve the total presence of the human spirit to itself, presence from which all element of absence must be excluded. Vico restores poetry, not in opposition to philosophy, but in the name of the integrity of the human spirit in its time-ideal actuality.

It has been suggested above that the propositions which enunciate the modifications of the human mind are themselves to be understood as propositions within the structure of the 'New Science', conformable in their character as propositions to its canons. This is illustrated clearly by the method which Vico follows in establishing these modifications concretely. It is the method of the synthesis of philology and philosophy, the central methodological principle of the 'New Science'.

The philosophical principle upon which he initiates this process of the determination of the modifications of the human mind is axiological, concerning, that is, the order of values as these solicit human appetition and volition. Man, Vico writes,[1] or rather mankind, seeks first the necessary, secondly the useful, and finally the commodious or pleasurable. Finally, he adds, they yield to luxury, while their substance is dissipated and dissolved. The philological point of departure of the process is an axiological criticism of the neo-classic attitude toward poetry. It is a common maxim of poetic and literary criticism, Vico notes, that the language of poetry and the language of common life are to be distinguished; again, he observes, it is commonly advanced that in the structure of a culture, poetry is a late-blossoming plant, and represents that inclination of the spirit of a nation away from the stern necessities which surround and determine its youth and vigorous period and toward that pursuit of pleasure which marks its maturity and perhaps decline. In covert manner, this is clearly a sophisticated play theory of art. These

[1] SNS, 241.

maxims Vico confronts with a further philological observation. It is uniformly to be observed, he notes,[1] that in the histories of all nations, poetry appears as the first and primary mode of expression as the vehicle of their first articulate life and expresses, not the peripheral, the pleasurable, or even the commodious dimensions of life, but the most intimate, stern, and fundamental necessities of the life of the people, that is, their laws, their wisdom, their religious rites, their sacred formulas of birth, marriage and death, of initiation, of war and peace, and their rude speculations on the cosmos.

In the confrontation of these opposed and contradictory philological propositions in the presence of the axiological principle of the necessary, the useful, the commodious and the pleasurable, the axiological principle acts as a catalyst, so to say. The resultant precipitate is the fundamental principle of the concrete determination of the character and the order of the modifications of the human mind, and indeed, as Vico says, of the whole science of humanity. It is the principle of the logical and the temporal priority of the poetic moment and principle in the life of the human spirit. For if, axiologically, the necessary is primary, and if, philologically, the poetic is the primitive mode of expression, the conclusion is inescapable, that the poetic principle is the co-principle with the necessary of the temporal-ideal movement of spirit. The reconstruction of the modifications of the human consequently finds here its key: the primacy of the poetic moment in the structure of the human spirit.[2]

The consequences of this principle are little less than revolutionary. Its first effect is the re-examination of the total structure of the human spirit as it had been conceived by western thought since Plato and the restoration of the prelogical moments of spirit to an integral function in its life. The second, is to put an effective end to that æstheticism which also had characterized western thought and which had assigned to art either a peripheral or a transcendental value in the life of spirit. Finally, it effects the temporalization of the processes of finite spirit, while establishing their ideal dimension and orientation. For this reason, Croce is most correct in characterizing Vico as the founder of the science of aesthetics;[3] it might justly be added the founder also of the modern philosophy of spirit.

The Vichian revolution in the domain of the philosophy of spirit consists in the transcendence of classical intellectualism and the reestablishment of the prelogical or æsthetic moment of spirit. The

[1] DU, II, 379; SNS, 173 et seq.　　　　　　　　　[2] SNS, 34.
[3] Benedetto Croce, *Estetica*, Bari, G. Laterza (1945, 8a ed.), p. 242.

dominion of the intellect over the life of spirit had been established for western thought effectively by Plato; with utmost truth it might be said that no later thinker had seriously departed from the conception of the structure of spirit which Plato had developed. This is true despite the fact that the panlogism, which is the inescapable conclusion of the Platonic theory of spirit, has not been accepted readily, nor with it, that radical ethico-psychological dualism, which follows from it with equal force. This dominion of the intellect as Plato had established it had a dual basis, ontic and logical. The ontic principle was the unity of being; being is asserted to be one, multiplicity, consequently, the absence, and not the presence of being. The logical principle was the corresponding unity of the idea, which alone reflects the unity of being. This principle in turn established the transcendence of the intellect as the spiritual faculty of the idea, while the senses, as related to multiplicity, were correspondingly characterized as the agents of illusion. The ethical dimension of this dualism in its turn is established at the level of the passions, which, as dominated by the image, are equally with it allied to non-being in the order of appetition and the good.

This Platonic dualism is replaced in Vico's thought by a vision of the organic bond of the spirit which, while surrendering nothing of the chaste unity and identity, would enrich its sterile self-containment with the inexhaustible diversity of the multiple. There is re-encountered at this level, it may be said, that same insight which characterized Vico's treatment of the problem of the natural law: namely, that the idea, the 'verum' in abstraction from the wealth of the concreteness of the 'certum' is absence and not presence, non-being, therefore, and not being. This organic unity is made possible radically by the notion of the human spirit as finite *posse*, act and tendency. In this dynamic matrix it is possible to conceive the human spirit as moving toward the unity of the idea through the diversity and multiplicity of the senses, toward the unity of the good, through the diverse motions of the passions. And it is further possible to specify the bond of this movement toward unity, namely, time. In this manner, the vast resources of the senses and the phantasy, of the passions and the impulses, are brought within the pale of the life of spirit, and spirit grasped in its purest idea, as the temporal process of the generation of the idea, or, more simply, as history. The abstract dualism of which classical Platonism has been the agent is resolved, with no sacrifice of the irreplacable values of the Platonic insight into spirit as ultimately presence and being, whole and without seam.

The seeds of spirit as presence and idea must be sought, in Vico's view, in the depths of the obscurity of the senses, the phantasy and the passions; and the life of spirit, in its essence, is its movement toward that idea through the processes of time, or history.

Similarly, this primacy of the poetic brings to an end the strain of aestheticism which has also marked the tradition of western thought. This is the proposition that art as the expression, and indeed, the expressive actuality, of the pre-logical or pre-intellectual life of spirit, lies outside the scope or province of truth or science. This notion is in turn associated with the antinomies between unity and multiplicity, the illusory character of the senses and the phantasy, and, in Plato himself at least, between passion and the good. Art is thus radically and effectively dissociated from the highest aspirations and movements of the spirit, the attainment of the true and the good. From this dissociation of art from the vital interests of spirit there spring two forms of æstheticism, both of which have found eloquent advocacy in western thought. There is, in the first instance, that aestheticism which would carry this dissociation of art from life to the extreme of a cult, making of art a refuge from life, a realm into which the human spirit may retreat from the task of the discernment of values, of the real from the unreal. There is also that æstheticism (in reality a variant of the first) in which the relationship of art to life is conceived extrinsically; art is made an external appanage of life, with the function of pleasure, of instruction or edification, or finally perhaps simply of relaxation or amusement. By contrast to both, the Vichian theory of spirit would integrate art and life, recognizing in art the first movements of the spirit toward the idea and toward the fullness of its own being in total presence.

Finally, there is overcome in this theory of the human spirit the radical trauma between spirit and its own phenomenology. This trauma, it has been suggested above, has its roots in another, the diremption between time and idea, which in turn is radicated in that intellectualism against which the principle of the primacy of poetry is a direct protest. The eternism which flows from the Platonic insight and which has indeed become, in the course of western thought, the hallmark of true spirituality, is transcended. The time form of the human spirit is clearly established, but with no prejudice to its eternal and absolute orientation. Time as the distention of the human spirit between finite and infinite is recognized as the very form of human life, the modality of its inexhaustible richness in those particular forms which themselves define the idea and constitute its existential dimension; even more, the modality of the self-generation of the human spirit in history.

This conception of the integral and organic structure of the spirit opens two positive questions for Vico, that of the internal structure and the qualitative character of the modalities of the *nosse* and the *velle* and that of the character of the movement toward the idea, toward total presence in which, precisely, that integrity and organicity consist. The fundamental image is that of human consciousness as a continuum, of which Vico speaks.[1] The terms of this continuum are, hypothetically, the pure sensual life of the animal, which is the absence of humanity and of spirit, and the pure possession of itself by spirit, as idea and as power, which is total presence. Between these terms, the movement of human life is continuous because the terms imply each other. The minimal moment of humanity, that which Vico depicts in his 'uomini bestioni', is radically distinguished from the animal life of sense which is its nearest term, and made completely discontinuous with that life, by the implication which pervades it of the possession of the idea; this implication Vico calls at one time 'vis veri', at another the 'semi' of eternal truth.[2] At the other extreme, the possession of the idea, total presence, equally implies that minimal moment of consciousness; for the human idea, or the human possession of the idea, has always about it the marks of its origin or point of departure in the initial moment of quasi-animal awareness, and for its fullness of expression must return to that point of departure in the transfigured image of poetry or art. Between these terms, consequently, human life moves. And the law of this movement is stated by Vico in the supreme rubric of the modifications of human mind: men first sense without advertence, secondly advert with perturbed and commoved spirit, and finally reflect with a pure mind.[3]

The qualitative characterization of the modalities of spirit, of the modifications of the human mind, according to this law follows a double pattern; that of the division into the moments of spontaneity and reflection, and that of the distinction of sense, phantasy and reason. The correlation between these divisions is present, though most difficult to fix exactly. Spontaneity and reflection are, clearly, the wider terms; yet they are not terms which may be taken at the same level of significance. For radically, the human spirit is wholly spontaneous; this is the inescapable implication of its definition as *posse*, or act, and the ontological basis of spirituality as such. In this

[1] SNP, p. 11.   [2] DU, I, 49; SNP, p. 41.   [3] SNS, 218.

sense, consequently, spontaneity is a more radical term than reflection, and is synonymous with the self-creative process of spirit in all its forms, or more simply, with spirit itself. Reflection, by contrast, denominates a movement within the spontaneous life of spirit; precisely, it is that januan movement whereby spirit, by advertence to the rich complexity of its immediate and spontaneous life, is at the same time freed from that immediacy and multiplicity, and advanced toward the unity of the idea, toward its own unity, therefore, because it is still identical spirit. The members of the threefold division are correlated with this double movement of spirit, but the correlation is not rigid or exact. Pervasive spontaneity is again the basic notion; within this, reason is recognized as the especial faculty or organ, so to say, of the reflective movement of spirit, though it is clear that reason can be nothing more than spirit in its reflective movement. Similarly, sense and phantasy are associated more closely to spontaneity; but here ambiguity presses close. For sense, taken in itself, cannot be considered spontaneous, possessing as it clearly must a passive moment. For this reason, sense in this structure of spirit can be taken only as sense-phantasy as a complex moment, therefore, in which that passive moment of sense is wholly transcended and transfigured.[1]

This analysis is complicated further by the fact that these designations of the modifications of the human mind or spirit would seem to be in dominantly gnoseological terms; spontaneity alone is free from such overtones. This fashion of reference or designation does not accurately reflect Vico's intention. Actually, as has been suggested earlier, the reference of these terms must be to the basic definition of man as *posse, nosse, velle*; the terms of this definition, in turn, may not be taken in abstraction, but constitute an inseparable complex. Human consciousness is integral. The term expressive of this integrity in Vico's lexicon is wisdom. Consequently, the definitive modifications of the spirit are to be made in terms of wisdom. Here too the patterns of discernment are double and not amenable to ready correlation. The widest division of wisdom, corresponding to the division of spontaneity and reflection, is that into vulgar and philosophical. In this sense, continuing the correlation, vulgar wisdom is that moment of synthesis in the life of spirit of which phantasy and passion are the elements, while philosophical wisdom has as its components reason and will. Superimposed on this, and only partly correlated with it, is the division of wisdom into divine, heroic, and

[1] Franco Amerio, *Introduzione allo Studio di G. B. Vico*, p. 171.

87

civil. Finally the term, poetic wisdom, is applied by Vico equally to the first two members of the latter division and to vulgar wisdom. Nevertheless, throughout this tangle of distinctions and correlations, the significance of wisdom is assured; it signifies the moments of synthesis of the human spirit and it is these moments of synthesis in their qualitative differences which constitute the genuine modifications of the human mind.

One it is recognized that wisdom is the actual term or principle of historical analysis for Vico, a further important fact is elucidated, namely, that, for Vico, historical consciousness is group consciousness. Considerable obscurity, to this point, has adhered to this aspect of the problem of the modifications of the human mind, due in part to his fidelity to the traditional terms of gnoseological analysis and in part to his repeated comparison between the historical structure of consciousness and the consciousness of the individual and, with reference to the poetic moment, the consciousness of the child. Vico is therefore confronted with the dual problem of the structure of that group consciousness which sustains history and of its relationship to the individual consciousness.

That the wisdom of which society and culture are the expressions is a group wisdom is clear to Vico from the fact that the career of institutions pursues a different path from that of the individuals who participate in the group life. A language, for example, is always a structure which stands over against the experience and the intentional activity of the individual; it is the expression of a consciousness in which he shares only obliquely and which has a determining power over the formation of his own mind. This is the first level at which the paradoxical structure of historical reality appears. Its root, obviously, is the fact that the absolute, the infinite, the idea, is the presupposition of all individual manifestations; with reference to language, it is the idea which is the presupposition of all discourse, and not the individual impression. So with all the structures of social life and culture; they reflect this group consciousness.

Nevertheless, the group and the individual consciousness do not stand in a simple relation either of identity or of contradiction in Vico's theory. They are related, rather, in that paradoxical system of continuity and opposition which is encountered on the plane of the relationship of the historical consciousness and providence. The historical consciousness is both contradicted by and realized in the individual conscious, while the converse is equally true. It might seem possible, on the ground hitherto adduced, to proceed in the study of history without reference to the individual consciousness or will. This is not, however, the case with Vico. This relation may be illustrated most clearly from Vico's political theory, which represents perhaps the most powerful analytic effort of the 'New Science'.[1] For Vico, political institutions are wholly the product of group consciousness; when, however, he comes to determine the ideality of the political form, he departs radically from any of the forms of absolutism which might be thought to inhere in such a principle in favour of a humanistic monarchical constitutionalism in which the state finds its legitimacy and function as the safeguard of the individual and person who is the ultimate repository of all right. This political doctrine, as a matter of fact, simply reflects in this area a wider and more profound character of Vico's thought, namely, that the emergence of the individual is, for him, the logical term of the historical process and the evident mark of its rationality. The individual consciousness detaches itself from the group consciousness; that is not, however, a movement toward anarchy and unreason, but toward ideality itself. The value of the individual ultimately resides in his power to reflect in monadic fashion the whole, the idea, the absolute. In this way, the whole, the absolute, is itself immeasurably enriched. In this manner, the anti-individualism which would seem to hang like a cloud over his theory of history is revolved. Nevertheless, it is not to be supposed that this relation between group and individual and between individual and absolute is a relation of simple continuity. On the contrary, it is here, more than anywhere else, that the complex relation of continuity in contradiction stands out. The group and the individual, the individual and the absolute, even as they reflect and reveal each other, stand in contradiction to each other. Of this radical tension there is in Vico no absolute relaxation.

In the 'New Science' he addresses the analysis, on philological and philosophical principles, only of the poetic wisdom of man or of humanity. As a consequence, the work, as it stands, and indeed, the science in its positive achievement is but a fragment. Nevertheless, it is a fragment from which the structure of the whole is readily enough discernible. This whole would include the analysis of the philosophical wisdom, as well as the ordered movement of spirit through time from the one to the other. It is also readily clear why the analysis of the poetic wisdom is the necessary point of departure of the science of humanity. The reason is that such a science must be, before all else, a science of origins, or, as Vico says, of authority. This is to say, again

[1] Cf. infra, Chapter XI.

in an expression of Vico's own, that this science must begin with its material[1]; but its material, in the last analysis, is the living process of the human spirit as it moves, through temporal process, to its total presence to itself, as idea and as power. Its point of departure, therefore, must be in time, for the human spirit is essentially the time spirit, though its term be in eternity.

From this it is also clear in what manner the theory of the modifications of the human mind closes the trauma between time and idea which the classical political humanism had opened. This reconciliation of time and idea is achieved in principle in the conception of the human spirit as *posse, nosse, velle finitum quod tendit ad infinitum*; concretely, it is achieved by the discernment of the time-form of that active tendency in which the reality of spirit consists, and the articulations of this form. Finally, it is both achieved, and, as it were, transcended in the concept of the historiographic moment of spirit, that is, in the moment in which by its supreme reflective act, the fulfilment of the philosophical wisdom in its formal character, the human spirit renders present to itself, in idea and in fact, the totality of its being, its universal history, in its eternal principles and in its temporal course: *storia ideale eterna, sopra la quale corrano le storie delle nazioni in tempo.*[2]

---

[1] SNS, 314, 394. [2] SNP, p. 66; SNS, 393.

V

PROVIDENCE

THE doctrine of the modifications of the human mind constitutes the first principle of the synthesis of time and idea and, therefore, the first positive element of the Vichian theory of history. This synthesis is achieved in terms of the human subject of history. Time and idea are related as dimensions of human presence. The human subject is finite subject and hence partial presence. It is, however, the finite subject whose whole being is dynamically orientated toward the infinite, that is, toward the plenitude or totality of presence, of the idea. In this tendency, which is not passive drift, but constitutive activity, resides the most intimate reality of the human subject. Time, in turn, is but the distension of the human subject between the terms of this tendency, that is, between partial and total presence; or, more precisely perhaps, time is the measure of the absence of the human subject from that total presence which is its idea. Of time in this sense the idea is a constitutive principle. Time process is process only to the degree to which it is measured by the idea; the idea is more intimate to time than time itself, for it is that which measures time. And as it is the human subject which in history becomes, that subject becomes only in its dimension as idea, as total presence. The modifications of the human mind, consequently, are the articulations, the successive 'demarches', the modes, of the human subject of history as it moves toward that total presence. They constitute, in their ensemble, the pure phenomenology of the time-ideal process of the human subject of history.

The synthesis of time and idea which is thus achieved is, however, incomplete, or only speciously complete. Speciously because it countervenes the very terms of the definition of the human subject which have made the synthesis of time and idea possible. The definition of the human subject of history upon which this synthesis of time and idea reposes is that definition analysed above: *posse, nosse, velle finitum quod tendit ad infinitum*. For the synthesis of time and idea in terms of this definition to be complete and sufficient, it would have to be assumed or established that the tendency which is the nerve of that definition indicated a movement, linear and inwardly determined between finite and infinite. A purely humanistic progressivism would then accurately depict the inward structure and dynamic of human history. The sense of tragedy, actual, imminent, or transcendental, which envelopes that history would be dissipated. Dependent for that ideal direction of its movement on no principle other than itself, the human spirit could be impeded in its attainment of that goal by no effective power. It would possess, in its own right, resources adequate for its ideal actualization. The temptation to this progressivism, it must be confessed, is always present in Vico's thought and at times rises close to the surface. But Vico is restrained from succumbing, in the first place, by the profound sense of the ever-imminent tragedy of human history and even more, by his insight into the roots of tragedy, resident in the very definition of man which he has advanced. The whole sense of the tragedy of human history resides precisely in the frustration of that constitutive tendency toward its own ideality; but this, Vico is aware, is not a frustration which threatens it from without, but one which lurks within, which is implicit in its very terms. Finite and infinite cannot sustain a movement of linear progress because these terms are in contradiction. This contradiction the concept of 'tendency' may conceal but cannot resolve. It becomes apparent, consequently, that in order to sustain this ideal temporal movement a second principle of synthesis is needed, whose function must be to resolve this contradiction at the heart of the definition of man and to rectify the movement of the finite principle toward its infinite term. This function belongs, in the Vichian theory of history, to providence.

The Vichian concept of providence, like the speculative or philosophical problem of history itself, appears first in the context of the theoretical problems of jurisprudence. Its appearance in this context is of primary importance, for it is here that there is revealed, for the first time and unmistakably, the basic function which this concept performs in the complex structure of the theory of history, its function in the theory, we suggest, as distinct from its ontological and theological implications. Function and ontological reference are both integral to the concept of province in Vico; nevertheless, their premature association has occasioned considerable obscurity and controversy. Nothing is more effective for the clear understanding of the concept in its integrity than attention to the context in which it appears and the speculative purpose with which it is introduced. In the first introduction of the concept the ontological and theological implications of the concept are singularly in abeyance, the problem of its function wholly to the fore.

The concept of providence which is so important to Vico's reconstruction of the natural law and from which the providence of the theory of history derives, is not the providence of Christian theology, with its unambiguous theistic basis, but the providence which he discovered to be so important to the principles and procedures of Roman jurisprudence.[1] It is true that even in the context of Roman jurisprudence the problem of the ontological reference of the concept of providence lies immediately beneath the surface. Nevertheless, in this context, the concept had achieved a certain operative freedom from these metaphysical and ontological implications. It is this operative freedom of the concept which Vico emphasizes. The immediate occasion of the introduction of the concept is the contrast, which Vico establishes, between jusnaturalism and Roman jurisprudence. It is Vico's accusation against the principal exponents of jusnaturalistic theory that they had systematically and methodically excluded all traces of the concept of providence from the province of the natural law. In this, he remarks, they display a marked inferiority of insight to the jurisconsults of Rome, who, independently of all revealed aid, had determined this concept and placed it at the heart of their jurisprudential theory. This concept, he asserts, in turn placed in the hands of the Roman jurisprudence superior logical and methodological instruments for the common and central task of theoretical jurisprudence and of juridical procedure, the determination of the natural law. For this reason, the consideration of the concept of providence in the Vichian theory of history must take its point of departure in the role which Vico assigned to it in his interpretation of Roman jurisprudence.

The function which Vico, in his interpretation of Roman law and jurisprudence, assigns to the concept of providence is precisely the function of reconciling the ideal and the temporal orders; or, more concretely and in terms of the immediate material, the function of determining a natural law which arises within and with the movement of the actual formation of structures of positive law and which is, therefore, an ideal process transpiring through time. The natural law is one which has arisen and arises with the customs of the peoples. It is an eternal law, precisely in this, that having begun with the very origins of religions, it proceeds, through certain 'divisions

[1] SNP, pp. 13–17.

93

of time'—the term is that of Roman jurisprudence itself—and through the same stages, to reach a certain clarity such that, for its perfection, it needs only to be established by philosophy in maxims or principles based on the idea of an eternal justice.[1] This movement of the principal parts of the law toward ideal clarity and formulation in eternal principles, which is a movement by ordered stages through time, is ordered by providence. Here, clearly, providence appears in its logico-historical function, that of insuring the steady emergence of the idea through the time-process of the formations of the structures of culture. In fact, the sense of providence in this context is nothing else than the actuality of that process. Its entire significance is the actuality of the movement by which this transformation takes place; its entire force is to close the diremption of time and idea which was the dualizing principle within classical naturalism, but which Roman jurisprudence, by its saving closeness to the actual processes of social change had in fact, if not always in theory, escaped. The concept of providence which is operative in the Vichian theory of history is the extension of the concept of providence which he associates with Roman jurisprudence.

In this initial context of jurisprudence the concept of providence labours under one grave limitation. While the providence of Roman jurisprudence indeed governs the emergence of the idea through temporal process, it does so without explicit reference to the contradiction which characterizes that process. In order, consequently, that this concept become available for the general theory of history, it has to be projected against that contradiction which Vico has discovered to lie at the very heart of the definition of man as *finitum quod tendit ad infinitum*. To effect this translation, it is necessary for him to establish in what sense that contradiction inheres in the definition of man, and for what reason. The sense of this contradiction for Vico is clear; every movement of the finite principle, of the human spirit, in history toward the infinite and the idea is abortive and evokes a time-form of sociality which is a caricature, if not the unequivocal negation, of the idea which is its supposition. The reason why this contradiction clings to the definition of man is no less clear; the existential conditions of the subject of history are never absolute or ideal, but limited and finite.

Vico develops this insight concretely in two contexts, both exceedingly delicate in the emotional reverberations which they arouse, but both, at the same time, vital to his entire theory. The first of

[1] SNP, p. 11.

these contexts is religious, the other political. In either case the sense of this contradiction is the same; every attempt of the finite subject to form or to define, on the one hand, the concept of religion and of God, and, on the other, of political justice as the ligature of community and of human sociality, must not only fall short of the idea of the one and of the other, but appear in actual contradiction to them.

Religion is, for Vico, the unshakable basis of human society. The idea of God, and the whole pattern of attitudes which the presence of this idea, in however attentuated and even erroneous form, awakens, alone has throughout man's career served to awaken in him the movements of humanity and maintained him in those movements and alone, in principle, has sufficient force and power to do so. At the positive, or philological, level he is, consequently, concerned to refute the notices, bruited abroad in the century immediately preceding his own, of the purported discoveries of godless peoples living in social harmony and innocence.[1] The philosophical principles of a science of humanity, he maintains, confutes the possibility of such a phenomenon, while every purported establishment of its actuality is traceable to misapprehensions in the reporter. On the contrary, only the sense of an overweening power suffices to set limits to the essential egocentricity of the finite subject and to awaken in it that sense of its own limitedness, of its own finitude, and the corresponding sense of the other, which is the ultimate basis of the social consciousness.[2] This egocentricity is for Vico, the ineradicable mark of the activity of the finite subject which, at no stage of its social emancipation from the self, leaves it entirely. In his own expression, man, the finite subject and worker of history, seeks first and always his own utility; if it be the solitary man of Lucretius or Hobbes, in his solitude he seeks that utility in terms of that solitude; entering into the primary associations of family, he seeks only the utility of his own; into the wider association of his class, only the utility of his class, or into the amplest associations of the nation, of his own nation.[3] But deeper than all these partial transcendences of solitary egocentricity, Vico seeks to fasten attention on that initial impact which alone can shake that constitutive self-concentration at its very roots. This is born alone, he holds, of that initial act in which the egocentric principle is brought, by some inward or outward cataclysm, of nature, that is, or of the spirit itself, face to face with its own inner and constitutive nothingness and calls out, in a loneli-

[1] SNS, 334.　　　[2] SNS, 338.　　　[3] SNS, 341.

ness which now has become infected with terror, to that initial and primitive other 'che lo salvasse',[1] which is the primitive and constitutive sense of God. It is this awareness which is the root and well spring of that transcendence of the self and its emergence into the world of community in which the humanity of man consists. What radically compels man to look upon other men, not as upon legitimate objects of his own predatory ego, but as other in the same order of being is the sense of the presence of that supreme other, before which all men stand at a common level. In a word, the primary sociality into which man enters is community with God; it is only the continuity of that presence which can insure man's humanity, that is, the secondary community with his fellow men. In this way, religion, as the immediacy of the recognition of that supreme other, which is a presence and a power, is the root of all sociality and hence of man's essential humanity. For this reason also, in Vico's view, atheism is the destruction not of an abstract doctrine of the philosophers or of the primitive belief of a people but of the humanity of man in its root and spring.

Nevertheless, every attempt to translate this primitive religious insight into expressive image, or reflective concept, or social institution, must inevitably distort and, to a degree at least, negate it. For every such translation is a reflection or projection, not of that reality toward which that insight is directed, but of the finite presence within which it is formed. From this limitation neither brute savage nor the sophisticated philosopher is wholly delivered. With Lucretius, Vico recognizes that 'primos deos fecit timor'. The conclusion he draws is not, however, the conclusion of atheism, but rather the conclusion that the god who is thus worshipped, or perhaps hated, in fear reflects neither the reality of God nor the attitude which that reality might and must in its idea inspire, but rather the limits of the finite consciousness within which that reality is compressed. Nor is the theological concept of the most refined philosopher freed from this same limitation and distortion. For the concept of a Plato, removed *toto caelo* from that rude image of the Lucretian savage, is still but the reflection of a finite principle, unable to sustain the full weight of the reality toward which it is orientated. The limitation and the distortion of the one and of the other are thrown into relief when the translation into the social is attempted. The brutal theocracy of a primitive community, translating a rude insight into the origin of social life into a structure of tyranny and using the liberating

[1] SNS, 339.

idea of God as a bond of enslavement, and the immoral idealities of a Plato, such as the conception of the community of women, reflect these limits and distortions in the medium of humanity itself, society. If we gaze only at the multiplicity of religious images, ideas, forms, in their positive character, cynicism, scepticism are almost inescapable. But neither the rude image of the primitive phantasy nor the distorted concept of the reflective intellect reveal this essential character of the finite so clearly as the atheistic hypothesis itself. For here the retreat of the finite upon itself and its self-immurement is complete. For this reason, Vico does not hesitate to elevate above the princes of the natural law of the modern day the jurisconsults of Rome; for with no revealed religion and little enough philosophy, they yet intuited this self-limiting character of the finite and the eternal contradiction in which it stands to the infinite and the idea by which it must be measured.

This same characteristic is displayed by all the forms of political sociality which men erect; each is at once a movement away from and a denial of that idea by which alone it can be measured. The idea of justice alone can measure human policy and can legitimize the force in which polity must ultimately and effectively reside. Yet every concrete and positive political structure is a structure of injustice, as well as of justice. It is a compression, to the point of distortion and negation, of the idea of justice into the positive conditions of a limited agency of policy. And inescapably so. For political power must have a *locus* and a system of instrumentation. These instruments can be employed ideally only in the name of the idea of justice itself. It is inevitable that under necessity, every structure of power should identify that ideality with its own positivity, the infinite with its own too apparent limitations and that, consequently, in its positive character, it must stand quite simply as the negation of that idea in whose name it seeks to justify itself.

Thus, finally, there comes to light the real source of this contradiction in which the finite stands to that infinite toward which it is thought to tend. It is the inescapable mechanism of the finite to contract the infinite, the idea, to the limits of its own finitude. This mechanism has for the finite the quality of necessity; it is, in fact, but the effective reality of that finitude and as such may no more transcend itself than a man may elevate his stature by a cubit. If, consequently, that tendency of the finite toward the infinite, in which the dynamic reality of man's nature is said to consist, is to be actualized, if, that is to say, there is indeed a movement toward ideality in the very positivity of the structure of human history, this movement must be the effect of a principle whose whole operative character is to transcend these inescapable limits of the finite, and to direct the finite to that infinite and ideal term, by way of that movement of the finite back upon itself.

And such, precisely, is the operative conception of providence which sustains the Vichian theory of history. It is a force in history by which the finite subject of history is directed to the ideal term of its own nature by way of those movements back upon its own finitude by which it would seem to alienate itself from its own reality. Providence is for Vico not only that power which insures the ideal direction of the activity of the human subject of history in the formation of the positive structures of sociality; it is even more the power which converts to that direction a movement whose momentum, so to say, impels in an opposite course. Its action is a genuine resolution of the contradiction latent in the definition of man as *finitum quod tendit ad infinitum,* because it achieves the rectification of the movement of history by way of the conversion of the finite movement and not of its denial, or its resolution into illusion, or its absorption into a transcendent movement in which it is lost or negated. Of this character of providence, Vico is fertile in illustrations. It is from and by way of the erroneous images of the deity which are formed in the fervid phantasy of primitive man, that the way lies to that greater clarity and ideality of the concept of the philosopher. It is by way of the brute structures of power which were the first polities of men that the way lies toward the juster conception and the more effective realization of the sense of the sociality and humanity of man. Finally, it is in and by way of the rude images of the phantasy and the shadowy presence which these constitute that the way lies to the clarity and the total presence of the idea. The reality of providence is this essential rectificatory movement within human history. As such it is the final sustaining principle of history conceived as the time-ideal process of humanity; for by this principle the intrinsic contradiction of such a movement is effectively resolved.

In the presence of this principle, obviously, the linear movement of history from finite to infinite, from image to idea, from power to justice, is negated. It is replaced by the image of the movement of history as essentially a tension between that retrogressive movement of the finite back upon itself and that rectifying force by which that movement is converted in an ideal direction. Nevertheless, Vico depicts this action of providence as above all else suave and without violence.[1] It is a natural movement, within the movement of history itself and not interjected from without. It insinuates itself into the very movements of the human subject of history so intimately as to become indistinguishable *in actu* from the movements of his own powers. It is only in its effects, and not in the violence of its activity, that providence is in evidence. Where, on principle, there could be only conflict there is peace; where only retrogression, advance and progress; where mere positivity, the glimmer of the ideal. Its channels are the liberty of man, his passions, his will and wilfulness, even his brutality and malice; within each of these, it works its silent magic.

As such, Vico is right in asserting that no demonstration of providence is necessary; or, more accurately, in asserting that a science of humanity as he conceived it would itself be the supreme demonstration of providence.[2] For effectively, and as it could be established by the method of such a science, providence is the movement of human history toward its own ideality. Wherever image surrenders to idea, power to justice, privilege to law, ignorance to science, there providence is, in its effective reality; and as the whole office of such a science of humanity as Vico conceives would be, in its positive character, to document such a movement, and in its speculative character, to establish its ideal principles, it would by this fact constitute a substantial demonstration of the idea and the fact of providence. In its concreteness, the science of humanity is a supreme theodicy of providence.

It is, consequently, this operative and essentially dramatic conception of providence which is essential to the theoretical structure of the Vichian conception of history and to the methodological integrity of the 'New Science'. Providence, in this view, is essentially a soteric principle. Its function, or the term of its operation, is the restoration of the movement of human history deflected from its ideal term. Or again, it is a principle of conversion, in the fundamentally religious sense of that term. It restores to integrity that 'broken world', as it has been called, into the presence of which the awakening self-consciousness of man introduces him. That broken world, on Vico's account, is not the result of a diremption between man and nature, but of a constitutive contradiction within man himself. His insight into the internal and constitutive fracture of the human spirit coincides perfectly with the Christian insight and finds its inevitable expression in the Christian image of that plight, the

[1] SNS, 343, 136; DU, I, 44.　　　　[2] SNS, 342.

image of fallen man. For this reason, Vico establishes the dualism between sacred and profane history which pervades his theory.[1] Sacred history is the image of the unbroken movement of the human spirit toward its ideal supposition; in this movement it is sustained by a power which, in its pure otherness, mends that fracture. Sacred history is, therefore, normative with respect of the movement of profane or gentile history; it describes the movement which gentile or profane history might traverse were it transmuted into sacred history. But in itself, gentile history is the movement of the human history toward its ideality by way of the excursion through that broken world. In this movement it, too, is sustained by a power which does not, however, appear as pure otherness, but, in some manner, as intimate to that hazardous movement. This power is providence in its operative and dramatic character; and it is this conception of providence which must be kept in mind in addressing the inevitable question concerning the ultimate character of this power, or as it might be called the ontological implication of the operative conception of providence.

This question, formulated in its most unambiguous terms, is the question whether this operative conception of providence implies a transcendent divine principle, or whether it must be identified as a dramatization of the inward and constitutive movement of the human spirit itself in its self-rectifying or autosoteric action. The one and the other of these alternatives has formidable advocacy; as a consequence, neither can be dealt with cavalierly. Again, it is necessary to draw the distinction between the question of this implication as it involves Vico's own position and as it involves a purely logical issue, that is, the logical implications of this operative character itself. And finally, it is necessary to ask in what manner the decision in favour of one or the other of these alternatives must affect the theory of history itself.

Although a distinction is drawn between Vico's own position and the question of the logical implications of the operative concept of providence, it must be recognized at once that his own position is the source of not a little of the ambiguity which envelops the problem. The most truculent of the immanentists have recognized, without hesitation, that it is Vico's intention and opinion that his doctrine of providence in the theory of history both conforms to and by its own power sustains an unequivocal theism. Nevertheless, the emphasis which he places upon the 'naturalness' of the mode of

[1] SNS, 9, 53, 166, 172, 313; SNP, pp. 19–20.

operation of providence throws into great relief the inwardness, the immanence of its process to the movement of history itself. This opposition is strengthened by Vico's conception of the effect which he hoped to achieve by means of the 'New Science'; this was not merely to trace out, as an object of contemplation, the ideal history of the nations through time, as he calls it, but even more to place in man's hands power over that movement, and an essentially rectifying power. This observation is in its turn to be complemented by another, that the very ideal process of which the 'New Science' itself would be a supreme example, the process by which man enters into the total presence or idea of himself, involves his entering by the same process into the knowledge of that inner and constitutive fracture of his nature, and the further question whether such knowledge does not itself resolve that fracture. In a word, it raises the classical question whether virtue is not knowledge and whether the knowledge and the power with which the 'New Science' would endow man is not itself the resolution of the puzzle of providence and the dissolution of the concept of providence by the fulfilment of the providential operation. This problem of transcendence and immanence which the Vichian description of providence evokes is one of the points of greatest obscurity in Vico's own doctrine and one in which Croce's assertion that the celebrated Vichian obscurity resides in a failure to grasp the inner, logical relations between certain problems and concepts would seem to be completely confirmed.

The issue between transcendence and immanence as the alternate implications of the Vichian doctrine of providence turns about the interpretation of the phenomenon designated as the 'heterogeneity of ends'. This term, it is necessary to note, is not Vico's; it would seem to have originated at a much later date and in a context which does not entirely coincide with that of Vico's thought. The phenomenon within his thought which it has been employed to identify, however, is not ambiguous and has already been indicated earlier in these paragraphs. It is precisely that movement whereby the deflected force of the human subject of history is redirected toward its ideality, the essential moment, without question, of the concept of providence. The crucial question is the quality of the 'otherness' involved.

The most forceful statement of the thesis of transcendence translates the entire process into the naturalistic terms of causality. The phenomenon of the heterogeneity of ends essentially reflects the disequilibrium of causes operative in the realization of the values of history. These values, even when they are present totally to human consciousness, in moments, that is, of geniune philosophical reflection, still lie outside the pale of human efficient causality in history. As a consequence, the essential fracture of the human world is conceived to reside precisely in this disequilibrium between the discernible ideality of history and the efficiency available to man as the creator of history. But this disequilibrium receives its major emphasis in the fact that the ideality of history, its values, are, as a matter of fact, achieved in history. To the first disequilibrium between the ideality and the human efficiency in history, there is added this further, and even more intriguing disequilibrium between the actual value of history and that human efficiency in history. In a word, man, in addressing history, is confronted by an order of achievement of which he stands as ostensible centre and subject, but which bears no direct proportion to the efficiency at his command. In the simplest formulation, the effects in history, that is, the very structures of human civility and society, technic and culture, in which man's intimate and constitutive idea of his nature is realized, exceed any efficiency which man might assign to himself. Into this picture the principle of providence is introduced as the rectifier of this disequilibrium. It is that alternate causality, adequate to the magnitude of the actual effects and achievements of history which is operative there and of which these effects are the works. That this power is essentially a transcendent power, first with respect to man, conceived as an efficient principle in history, and secondly to the total process of history itself, would follow simply and directly from the concept of causality. For the efficient cause is essentially transcendent to its effect. The actuality of causation is the reduction of a potency or potentiality to its corresponding and defining act or perfection; but this reduction is effectible only through the agency of a principle which is itself in act, that is, in actual possession of the perfection which is effected. This actuality of the effecting agent with respect to the perfection effected is itself the most adequate conception of transcendence which may be formulated. And in this most adequate of senses, providence is transcendent to the order of effects which it produces in history and to man as the ostensible centre and subject of history. The principle of providence is transcendent to the order of its epiphany, so to say, and from this transcendence, which is a relative thing, to its absolute transcendence as a subsistent principle the way lies by a continuation of the same reasoning by which this 'relative' transcendence has been established. It is to these conclusions that the logical implications of his thought would seem to commit Vico to the extent to which the order of history can be conceived as an order of cause and effect.

This same concept of the heterogeneity of ends is the point of departure, in turn, of the interpretation of providence as a principle immanent alike to history and to the human spirit as its centre and source. In this sense, providence has been called variously the rationality of history, its logicity, or the astuteness of reason.[1] Its essentially rectifying or soteric function remains intact; providence is that principle by which the movement of history is effectively ordered to its ideality even by way of deflections of spirit from that ideality. But the question arises, in what way does this rectifying action of providence differ from the constitutive activity of reason, of thought, of effective will itself? For if the human spirit be dialecticized, as it must, into its constitutive moments must not these moments, at least in their abstractness, appear precisely in this opposition to and deflection from each other? If, in its theoretical moments, the spirit be dialecticized into the moments of spontaneity and reflection, must not spontaneity, in its abstraction at least, be set in opposition to reflection and conceived as moving away from it, toward other 'ends' of its own? Or, in its moments of 'praxis', must not effective will, as permeated by reason, appear in similar dialectical opposition to impulse, to the forces of self-interest and cupidity, which, in turn, would seem to pursue ends of their own? But when this is recognized, is it not at once imperative to recognize that in such a dialectical scheme the whole reality alike of reason and effective will can be conceived only as the rectification of the movements of spontaneity, of phantasy and impulse, in the direction of that ideality of which reason is the vehicle and voice? What can the actuality of reason be but the evocation of such a movement toward the idea in the very heart of the movement of the phantasy? And so of effective will with respect to impulse and appetite. In a word, the drama which lies at the heart of history is seen to reside within the spirit of man itself. The soteric function is that of reason itself and, indeed, in the perspective of history, defines and exhausts the character of reason. But to speak of transcendence in this context is to mistake the process of the dialectic of spirit for its actuality. For transcendence can have reference only to that abstract opposition in which the moments of human awareness and activity appear to each other in the structure of that dialectic. In the concreteness of history, of mind or spirit this

[1] Croce, *La Filosofia di G. B. Vico*, pp. 115 et seq.

abstract opposition is seen to give way to a synthesis whose inner structure is precisely that resolution of contradiction which is recognized as the especial office of providence. The doctrine of providence in Vico, consequently, is thought rather to bear the burden of the whole sense of the drama and the tragic and comic character of human history. Of implications of transcendence, it supports no trace; indeed, these are against its inner movement and genius.

The resolution of this controversy in unequivocal favour of one or the other of the contending interpretations would surely alter the quality of Vico's doctrine. In the case of the first, it would dissolve his thought into a form of naturalism and threaten that freedom of man in history, freedom in the sense of non-determination and of creative activity, upon which he places so much stress. Again, the naturalistic transformation of his thought would introduce a principle which appears particularly alien in the context of his ideas, namely, the conception of history as an order of cause and effect. On the differentiation between the orders of nature and history Vico would, on the contrary, appear to be particular emphatic. Nature is opaque to human science precisely because it can be known only as an order of cause and effect. Knowledge in these terms yields not science but awareness. The transformation of history into a causal system would consequently threaten its intelligibility, its aptitude to become the object of genuine science. While he admits the concept cause into his analysis of the process of history, he does so in a radically altered form; cause becomes for him, the appearance in time according to determined conditions of a positive structure of reality. The concept, in a word, is made equivalent to the actuality of that time-ideal order of which he is seeking the principles. The concept of science as knowledge by causes he also retains, but with a similar alteration of sense. To know by cause can be only to know the ideal and eternal principles of temporal order and appearance, to know, that is, that ideal and eternal history which is the object of his 'New Science'. A transcendence established on these principles of cause and effect understood in a naturalistic manner would, consequently, be alien to the spirit of his thought and would radically alter the quality of his theory.

The transformation in the quality of his thought and doctrine effected by the total immanentization of the principle of providence and by its identification with the rationality of history is equally radical. In the first place it renders the principle of providence a pure tautology in the theory, and not a principle of explanation. For if providence be but that movement of the human spirit between its own dialectical moments, it is but the tautological designation of that dialectic. But it is obvious that in the actual structure of the Vichian theory of history the value assigned to the concept of providence is not conceived by its author in this manner. On the contrary, it is evident at every point that providence appears to him as a principle of scientific explanation. In its weakest form, it is an hypothesis, which, as he remarks in one place, is converted into certitude by the normative power of sacred history and, implicitly, of revelation. In its strongest form, it is a first principle, in a classic sense, that is, as a principle beyond which it is irrational to demand another. A reduction of this principle to tautology, consequently, assumes a burden of proof which, it is safe to predict, it cannot redeem. In the second place, the immanentization of providence replaces the actual movement of history toward its ideal term by another, a movement of contradiction by a dialectical movement of opposition or distinction. It is clear, however, that such a substitution, while it may constitute a fresh and even genial analysis of the structure of the human spirit and of history, cannot function as an interpretation of Vico's thought, nor as its logical extension. To Vico, as it has been suggested before, the movement of the finite spirit back upon itself and away from the ideal term which is the supposition of its movement constitutes an irreducible contradiction. Finite and infinite are not for him terms of a dialectical opposition or distinction, but of a pure contradiction. Providence, consequently, as a resolution of this predicament of spirit, appears as the resolution of a contradiction, and not of a dialectical opposition. Neither a method of synthesis nor a method of approximation suffices to close this contradiction; on the contrary, each in its own way exacerbates the dilemma of spirit, and condemns it to an utopianism to which it is particularly resistant. The reduction of this contradiction imposes conditions which the immanentization of providence cannot meet. These are that the reduction be, on the one hand, without residue and, on the other, definitive in principle; that is to say, the movement of the finite principle toward its infinite term, the idea, must become a pervasive movement of the spirit, so that spirit in none of its moments may persist in a movement opposed to the ideal direction. Again it means that the principle must provide for the reduction of all possible appearances of spirit in time. But in either case, the immanentization of providence falls short of these conditions. To illustrate concretely, in the Crocian analysis, the poetic and the economic moments retain an anarchic freedom and opposition to the general movement of spirit toward ideality; the actual process of the idealization of history is accidental and unpredictable. For this reason, there is an unbridgeable gulf between the Crocian and the Vichian aesthetic, the Crocian and the Vichian ethics. For this same reason, the resolution of the inner contradiction of spirit by the immanentization of providence is not definitive in principle; on the contrary, it implies the retention of this contradiction, on principle, as the sole evidence of the freedom and hence of the spirituality of spirit.

In a word, the unambiguous identification of providence as a principle either of transcendence or of immanentization does not conform to the characteristics of the operative concept of providence which controls Vico's thought; as a consequence, neither can advance itself as the development of the logical implication of Vico's thought. It is necessary, consequently, to develop these logical implications in a manner consonant with this operative character of the concept, for this last alone, to borrow a term of Vico's, constitutes the 'certum' of the problem, and, in line with this certitude of his thought, to abandon the rigid alternality of these conceptions, transcendence and immanence as inconsonant with that certitude. More positively, it is necessary to determine accurately the root idea of his thought of which the notion of providence is the flower.

An indication, fruitful though negative, of this seminal idea is offered by Vico in the pages of the *Autobiography*. Discussing his early philosophical studies (from the point of view, however, which included the first *Scienza Nuova*) he remarks[1] that an unalterable preference for Plato over Aristotle was determined by the reflection that the latter's metaphysics led to the conception of God as a 'potter, fashioning things outside himself' and therefore could not furnish the principle of a moral philosophy. Plato's metaphysics, by contrast, indicated as the ultimate principle of reality an idea which generated and sustained the world of time within itself. The preference indicated here is fortified by the character of his polemic against the jusnaturalists and their exclusion, even by way of hypothesis, of the principle of providence from the basic science of political humanism. The position of the jusnaturalists, as Vico understood it, might be conceived as the logical outcome of the deism which was part of the pattern of jusnaturalism and whose effect was in fact precisely to exclude that immediacy of presence between the ultimate metaphysical principle and the temporal process of finite being which

[1] *Auto*, p. 11.

106

preoccupied him. As a consequence, the emphasis of his thought lay in the direction of that immediacy; the power he sought to designate by the term providence was before all else an immanent power, in the sense that its activity formed an integral motif in that temporal process. Any conception of the ontological implications of providence which might lead to any doubt concerning the actuality or the possibility of such immediate activity and presence of the ultimate ideal principle in the temporal process must stand in immedicable opposition to Vico's fundamental insight into the meaning of providence.

At the same time, there is no indication in Vico's thought of the radical immanentism of historicism, for he nowhere indicates that the presence which he denominated by the term providence is such that it exhausts itself in the temporal process of which it is the principle. Even less does he suggest that the temporal process is the process of the self-generation of that principle, as an immanentistic historicism must conclude. What is generated in that temporal process of history is the presence and the idea of man in his social or political essence. To the extent, consequently, that this presence of man to himself in history embraces a principle of alternality, of otherness, that principle of alternality must be characterized as transcendent within the process of history itself and with respect to that process conceived as a whole. But providence, as it is a principle of political humanism and a science of humanity, and as it may be demonstrated by that science is such a principle of alternality and must, therefore, within the terms of the 'New Science' be recognized as transcendent.

The terms transcendent and immanent cannot, therefore, be taken as defining a radical and irreducible alternality in Vico's thought. On the contrary, at the risk of paradox it must be asserted that the immanence of the transcendent is the central principle of his historicism and the whole meaning of his doctrine of providence. In its most concrete sense, and in terms closest to those of his own 'New Science', the ontological reference of the concept of providence is to man's presence to himself in history and not primarily to a principle beyond history. As such, providence is a principle of alternality in history; that is, it is a dimension of presence in history which cannot be reduced without residue to man's presence to himself. And as such, providence can only be characterized as transcendent, within the terms of history.

This quality of transcendence within the framework of history alone is consonant with the operative character of the concept of providence in the Vichian theory of history. For, as it has been seen, man's presence to himself in history is contradiction; that is to say, man is present to himself in history as a finite principle orientated toward the absolute, but deflected in his movement toward that term by the recessive dynamism of his own finiteness. The actuality of the movement of history toward an ideal term, which to Vico is indisputable, cannot be for man a principle of his presence to himself in history. On the contrary, such movement must appear to him basically as alternality, the presence of an 'other'. The rectification of the movement of history in the direction of the ideal must always be to man the clearest evidence of this alternate presence in history. And this rectifying activity wholly defines the character of that alternate presence, and is itself, therefore, the concept of providence as an operative conception.

As a consequence, it ought to be recognized that the concept of providence as an operative principle in history is not a concept which demands justification from another source. Rather, it constitutes an original and self sustaining insight into the meaning and the reality of God and of at least one primary dimension of his nature, that of his immanence to man's presence to himself in history as the irreducible alternality of historical process. The concept of God as providence in human history in its turn renders the alternality of immanence and transcendence, from the point of view of human history, less rigid than it would at first appear. For the God whose being and activity is recognized in providence is immanent and transcendent in history at once; manifesting, by the naturalness of his operations and their rectifying force the concrete synthesis of these characters.

For the integrity of the Vichian theory of history itself it is necessary, above all, to place emphasis on the central operative force of this concept of providence. This is, as we have suggested, the synthesis of time and idea. The first principle of this synthesis, as we have seen, is human presence itself, the modifications of the human mind in history. The synthesis achieved in these terms was marred by a radical trauma in human presence: the contradiction involved in the structure of a finite presence whose term is the infinite. Providence appears as the rectifying principle of this trauma and at the same time, in virtue of this very rectifying force, as the ultimate and determinate principle of the synthesis of time and idea, the ultimate metaphysical principle of history conceived as temporal-ideal process.

VI

IDEAL ETERNAL HISTORY AND THE COURSE OF THE NATIONS IN TIME

THE determination of the dual principles of the synthesis of time and idea, the modifications of the human mind and Providence, establishes the basic dimensions of the science of humanity, the 'two histories' which define its form and substance. These Vico calls respectively ideal and eternal history and the course of the nations in time. In reality, these are not two, but one. For the course of the nations in time fulfils within the limits of the time-forms of human culture the eternal and ideal history, while the latter, in turn, defines the immanent ideality of all time process. Their distinction can be only formal and dialectical. The science which embraces them does so in their unity and distinction and must be, consequently, philosophy and history at once; or more truly, since philosophy and history have always, in western tradition, stood in dialectical opposition to each other, a 'New Science' indeed. The principles of the synthesis of time and idea establish these histories alike in their distinction and their unity. On the one hand, from these principles are drawn the properties which define the ideal and eternal history and which are the unchanging structural principles of all ideal movement in time. On the other, from these same principles are drawn the dynamic patterns of the course of the individual nations in time and of the course of humanity itself in its movement toward total presence in concrete time-forms of culture. To fix the sense of these two histories, consequently, is to transpose those elemental principles of synthesis into the proper matter of the science of humanity.

The clarification of the concept of the ideal and eternal history demands first of all that it be dissociated from all forms of eternism, of whatever provenance. The characteristic of eternism in all its forms is that, seeking the eternal principles of things, it becomes nihilistic toward their temporal processes, dissolving the latter into the former and nullifying the relationship between them which experience indicates. To eternism, in this sense, Vico is adamantly opposed. The 'storia ideale eterna' is not, for him, a technique for the dissolution of time-process, of reducing it to appearance and absurdity, but of determining its constitutive ideality and necessity. It is not, therefore, a transcendent history in any sense, but a history which transpires in time and which accounts for the form of temporal events.

In their failure to grasp this radical opposition to eternism the modern interpreters of Vico have displayed an insensitivity perhaps fatal to their otherwise rich and responsive penetration of his thought, and Croce and Gentile alike give evidence of this insensitivity. Croce makes light of the 'storia ideale eterna' in Vico. He finds the phrase susceptible of a diversity of interpretations only one of which he judges acceptable, and this only in an eternistic sense. In one sense, he writes, Vico intends by the ideal and eternal history the determination of the forms, categories or ideal moments of spirit in their necessary (or purely logical) succession, and in this sense alone does it merit serious attention. Concurrently, he accuses Vico of various obscurities in the employment of the phrase, chief among which is the tendency to identify it with the actual temporal order of events, the 'empirical' order of history. From this identity a double ambiguity seems, for Croce, to arise; the empirical is made absolute, the eternal order temporalized. 'And in the same act of making absolute the empirical movement the ideal course is veiled in an empirical shade because, made identical with that other, it takes on its empirical character and, from that eternal and extratemporal character which it possesses in the initial conception, is made temporal.'[1] The necessary context for the interpretation of this statement is the analysis which Croce has previously offered of the internal structure of the 'New Science'. In this analysis, the 'New Science' is resolved into three distinct elements, each of which is capable of being established and developed independently: a philosophy of spirit, an 'empirical' science of society, and certain actual histories.[2] It is the first distinction of this analysis, between the philosophy of spirit and the 'empirical' science of society, which opens the way to the charge that Vico confuses the temporal and the ideal orders in his account of the 'storia ideale eterna'. Such distinction is, of course, eternism in its essence. More importantly, it directly contravenes Vico's own intention, which is precisely that unification of the ideal and temporal

[1] Croce, *La Filosofia di G. B. Vico*, p. 41.   [2] Ibid., p. 37.

against which Croce, in the name, ironically enough, of the coherence of Vico's own thought, rebels. The actual effect of his criticism of Vico is not to render suspect Vico's account of his own insight, but to arouse a certain scepticism toward Croce's analysis of the structure of the 'New Science'. The one canon for the interpretation of the 'storia ideale eterna' which may be accepted absolutely, and which is a canon also for the interpretation of the whole *Scienza Nuova*, is Vico's own assertion that this eternal history transpires in time.[1] For Vico, the whole problem of history, as we have suggested, is precisely the union of these processes, temporal and eternal, ideal and logical. The diremption of these terms, which is the effect of eternism, is to destroy for Vico the possibility of intelligible history and scientific historiography.

Gentile is even more imperious in the manner in which he seeks to impose an eternistic interpretation on the ideal and eternal history. As always, his expression is even more trenchant than that of Croce. The 'New Science' is intrinsically and wholly a 'philosophy of spirit', a 'metaphysics of the human mind'. Whoever would taste the meat of the 'New Science' must first break the thick, hard shell of inedible matter which encases it.[2] That meat is nothing but the 'philosophy of spirit'; the hard, encasing shell, the whole apparatus and the whole argument by which Vico seeks to demonstrate that humanity enacts and re-enacts in time an ideal and eternal history. The effort to bring together these two orders, the ideal and the temporal constitutes, as a matter of fact, 'quell' errore capitale della sua costruzione', which renders Vico the most inept interpreter of his own insight. With the structure of the philosophy of the spirit and the metaphysics of the human mind the temporal is absorbed, assimilated, swallowed up in the eternal, and time is seen to be a veil which matter and sense draws between the human mind and its own eternal and supratemporal reality.

The dangers of interpretation of this type, which substitute for the insight of Vico and his own account of it a reconstructed and rectified account, need scarcely be mentioned. Independent of the violence done to Vico's thought, and more important from the philosophical point of view, is the shadow thrown upon the crucial exegetical question. This is the question of determining in what manner Vico conceived the synthesis of these orders of time and idea under the rubric of the ideal and eternal history. It is sobering, consequently, to turn to Vico's own words.

[1] SNP, p. 66; SNS, passim. [2] Giovanni Gentile, *Studi Vichiani*, p. 115.

How far Vico is from conceiving these two processes as distinct and independent of each other, how far, that is, from his intention are the abstract and methodological philosophy of spirit and the 'empirical' science of society, which Croce evokes, is illustrated by his own definition of the 'storia ideale eterna'. From Vico's point of view, the 'New Science' must eventuate at once, 'ad un fiato', and on the *same principles*, in the philosophy and the history of human institutions; such are the two parts of the 'universal jurisprudence' of the human race which will be realized in that science. These two parts are so closely correlated that while the one, philosophy, expounds a concatenated series of 'ragioni', the other, history, narrates a continuous and uninterrupted series of facts or events in conformity with those 'ragioni'. It is this absolute co-ordination of the one and the other, the 'ragioni' and the facts or events, which constitutes the material dimension of the ideal and eternal history; its formal dimension, clearly, can reside only in those common principles which unite the two orders. It is these common principles which must be determined as the answer to the question of the Vichian sense of the ideal and eternal history. These principles Vico compendiously summarizes in the following manner: 'with the establishment of the eternity and the universality of the natural law of the nations . . . and since that law arises with the customs of the peoples, and since the customs of the peoples are made constant by the nations and at the same time, human customs are practices or usages of human nature . . . and since human nature does not change all at once but always retains an impression of earlier or first usage . . . this Science ought to achieve by one act both the philosophy and the history of human customs. . . .'[1] The primary and common principles which establish the ideal and eternal history would seem, consequently, to be those properties of the natural law of the nations which constitutes the object of universal jurisprudence: eternity and universality.

The eternity which adheres to the natural law of the nations as its property is in turn equated with immutability. The concept of this immutability is developed against the foil of another concept of eternity and immutability which he has already found reprehensible in the position of jusnaturalism. The jusnaturalists, he asserts, due to their neglect of the principle of providence had fallen into three profound, indeed fatal, errors. 'And of these the first is that that natural law which they establish on the basis of the reasoned maxims of the moral philosophers, of the theologians and, in part, of the juriscon-

[1] SNP, p. 66.

sults, as it is in its idea eternal, so they suppose that it must always have been practised in the customs of the nations. And they do not perceive that the natural law, of which the Roman jurisconsults reasoned better than they in that principle division which they recognize as ruled by divine providence, is a natural law which has arisen with those customs of the nations and is eternal among all of them in this that . . . through certain "divisions of the times" and through the same gradations in every case it moves toward and arrives at a certain term of clarity. . . .'[1]

There are clearly opposed in this context two conceptions of eternal. The one is the eternity of the philosophers, which is illustrated or exemplified for Vico by the thought of the jusnaturalists; the central note of this eternity also is immutability, but an immutability which is nothing other than the self-coherence of the idea. This is clearly a logical property of the idea and looks only to its internal perfection, so to say, the law of which is an absolute law of identity. It is this conception of eternity which lies at the root of all eternism and is to be observed in every system in which emphasis is placed upon the logical necessity constitutive of the idea and not upon its existential force. In Vico's own terms, this is fundamentally an error of perspective; it is the 'boria dei dotti' who judge everything from the level of this logical and formal necessity and are led thence to the fallacies of atemporalism and antihistoricism. To this conception of 'eternity' he opposes another, which might well be called the process by which the idea reaches its logical clarity à travers the existential conditions which evoke it. This is the eternity which 'corre in tempo' and which Vico illustrates by the Augustinian similitude of the seminal truths: 'but as there are buried in us certain eternal seeds of truth which by degrees from infancy are cultivated until with maturity and by means of the disciplines they become the clearest cognitions of science, so in the human race by sin there were buried the eternal seeds of the just which by degrees from the infancy of the world have been explicated into the demonstrated maxims of justice. . . .'[2], and exemplifies by the diverse modes of obtaining proprietorship. In the final analysis, it is clear that these two kinds of eternity are not, in Vico's mind, in conflict. On the contrary, they stand in a positive relationship, which in its turn may be illustrated by reference to the opinions of the jusnaturalists. What for them is initial, the point of departure, is for Vico terminal: namely, the idea, in its internal logical coherence. For Vico the idea is something to-

[1] SNP, p. 15.   [2] SNP, p. 41.

ward which human history moves with labour; it is the idea that alone makes the historical process intelligible, but which apart from that process is itself unintelligible. His science, as much as any that jusnaturalism could advance, moves toward an idea eternal in this formal, logical sense; but that idea is the term toward which that science moves, not its point of departure. The very formal properties of the eternal idea are themselves, however, dependent upon the terminal position of the idea in the historical process. If, on the contrary, the idea appears as the apodictic principle of the science, there is called into question, on the one hand, the reality of the positive historical and temporal process and, on the other, that formal perfection of the idea. The apodictic idea must always be in partial contradiction, at least, to existential process; but being this, it is also in partial contradiction to itself, for it is, in principle, the ideal and defining principle of that positive process and not a pure tautology. This contradiction can be overcome, both from the part of temporal, positive process and from the part of the idea, if that process be conceived as process toward the idea, the idea as the constitutive term of temporal process. This concept implies in turn a transformation of the conception of immutability which has functioned as the defining term of eternity. This immutability can consist, as Vico has suggested, only in the uniformity of the temporal process. It is in this sense that the 'New Science' exemplifies an eternal, ideal history; that history exhibits the law of the uniform temporal process of the idea. Comprehended in this eternity, that history yields principles of a genuine science of social process.

The second property of the 'storia ideale eterna', or, more precisely, the second property of natural law which is incorporated into the conception of the ideal eternal history, is 'universality'.[1] In this case also it is necessary to distinguish the sense in which the term is employed by Vico from the sense in which it is excluded from his thought. There is intended by Vico nothing of that abstract, logical universality which gives rise to the conception of law prevalent in some theories of the natural science. The later universality is indistinguishable from generality, and logically confounded with it. Like the abstract and negative eternity of the idea, it looks only to its internal structure and stands in contradiction to its existential dimension. Vico's rejection of this abstract kind of universality, it may be remarked parenthetically, is the reason why it is impossible to say, with Croce, that one dimension of the 'New Science' is the establish-

[1] SNP, pp. 40-2.

ment of the 'empirical' science of society. There is entirely lacking, from the formal structure of the 'New Science', the type of universality, which, on Croce's own recognizance,[1] lies at the basis of empirical generalizations. This statement, on the contrary, is the evidence of Croce's insensitivity to the sense of the temporal in Vico; for the temporality which Croce, ambiguously, assigns to the empirical, for Vico is an intrinsic and unalterable dimension of the formal structure of the 'New Science'. Croce's concern to protect the ideal categories or forms of spirit from the shadow of time is directly in opposition to Vico's robust desire to grasp the idea as it is immersed, breathing and living, in temporal process. The universality proper to the 'storia ideale eterna' is quite distinct from this abstract generality and in its turn exhibits two characteristics.

In the first place, this universality signifies the uniqueness of origin, not to be sure in time and place, but in principle, of that entire process of the existential actualization of the idea which constitutes the 'storia ideale eterna'. This universality, or uniqueness, consists in the assertion that wherever, and whenever, and however, that existential process, according to the immutability already assigned to the ideal eternal history as the mark of its eternity, is initiated, it has its beginnings in identical 'connatural' necessities of the human spirit. This necessity is nothing general; in every case, it is concrete and specific and draws its concrete conformation from the determining and limiting factors of history and nature. Its universality is purely ideal and pertains to its essence, so to say. It is not an empirical law of the origins of human community, but the ideal principle, wholly incorporated in every instance, and in every instance wholly and entirely illustrating that necessity in its ideality. 'Just as there is asserted one of its two most important properties, that is, immutability, so by the same means there is established the other, that is, universality, by the consideration that the progress of human ideas concerning natural justice cannot be understood to have come about otherwise than that in a solitary state, that is, in the solitary, weak and needy man of Grotius, the man bereft of all help from others of Pufendorf . . . it must have begun by the most connatural necessity. . . .'[2]

The second characteristic of this universality is that it is marked by a uniformity of 'ragioni' wherever and in whatever circumstances the process of incivilment, or humanity, begins. The multiplicity and

---

[1] Benedetto Croce, *Logica*, Bari, G. Laterza (7a ed., 1947), pp. 212 et seq.
[2] SNP, p. 44.

the diversity of these beginnings in time and space are no deterrent to their ideal unity, for wherever and whenever the process of incivilment begins, it is moved by identical causes uniformly distributed. This principle is illustrated by specific reference to the origins of civil law. The illustration is especially apt because the mark of civil law is diversity. Civil law, according to the definition of the two laws, civil and natural, by the process of exclusion, is that dimension of universal law proper to specific peoples or communities and in which they differ from others. Nevertheless, according to Vico, this difference of material reference, traceable to diversity of utility and civil necessity, 'd'intorno alle civili necessità o utilità di ciascuno', far from contradicting, actually illustrates the ideal unity of the source of all civil law. This utility or necessity can ultimately be only one; all civil law emerges from the movement of the law of the 'gentes majores' toward its elevation to a law of the 'gentes minores', that is from a law of privilege, based on the asserted diversities among men, to a law of universal right, founded on the idea of a common human nature shared by all men, the universality of an ideal principle throughout the diversity of its material content in time and place of origin.

This description of the universality of natural law clarifies the sense of the 'storia ideale eterna'. It is the ideal principle of human incivilment not only in time-depth, so to say, but in breadth and diversity of quality as well. The concept of justice, for example, defines the ideal term of all processes of legislation, whatever be the material conditions under which the forms of positive law may be determined. As such, it is a constitutive element of the ideal and eternal history and a dimension of its universality. For the universality of the natural law consists, not in the fact that in all times and in all places identical positive law should prevail, but that in all the forms of positive law, despite the diversity of material circumstances which dictate the immediate form of the law, the same ideal principle is at work. And what is thus true in the area of law, is true also, and in a larger sense commensurate with the greater magnitude of the enterprise, in the whole process of culture. The ideal, universal principle operative throughout the process is the idea of man, of humanity, moving toward its total actual and existential presence in institutions which actualize that idea in its fullness.

Nevertheless, it is counter to Vico's insight to suppose that this ideal and eternal history can be determined abstractly or independently of the positive processes of that other history, the course of the nations in time, in the form, for example, of an abstract philosophy of the human spirit which should operate only as the methodological moment of that second history. This possibility is precluded by the fact that the ideal principles which are the components of that eternal history are the terminal points of that course of the nations in time. They can, therefore, be fixed and established only in and through that second history. There can be no science of those pure forms which should fix and determine them in their transcendent self-identity, as *a priori* principles of the synthetic process of human culture, any more than there might be a science only of the positive forms of human culture, independently of the establishment of the ideal principle which defines the positive movement. The one and the other science, as it has been suggested, would eventuate in pseudomyths; on the one hand, the pure ideas of the Platonic heaven of ideas, on the other the generalizations of the positivist or the 'empiricist'. The one and the other of the two histories can be the object only of a single science in which the unity of these two dimensions of the historical order is realized. The principle of this unity must, consequently, be the most radical principle of the entire science; and this principle, as has been seen, is providence, whose whole function is to guarantee the ideality of the temporal process of the formation of the positive forms of sociality. When, consequently, Vico assures us that one chief fruit of the 'New Science' must be the ideal and eternal history upon which are patterned the courses of the nations in time, he assures this fruit only as an integral part of that science and not as an apodictic structure whose relations to the second history should be wholly extraneous and formal.

It is, finally, counter to Vico's insight to derive the one or the other of these two histories, separately or together, from the structure of human nature as antecedent, even logically, from the form and content of the two histories. This is made clear by the clause by which, in the passage quoted, Vico immediately qualifies his reference to human nature 'and since the nature of men does not change all at once but always retains an impression of the . . . first usage. . . .'[1] Human nature does not, therefore, stand over against the historical process; it does not fall outside the scope of the two histories, but is rather the final subject and reality of those histories. There is, consequently, no philosophy of man apart from the history of man. Rather the idea of human nature represents the final product of the 'New Science', in its two dimensions of the ideal eternal history and

[1] SNP, p. 66.

the course of the nations in time; it is the idea which emerges only after the entire course of the 'New Science' has been run. If the philosophy of man were presumed to be antecedent to the 'New Science', its metaphysical presupposition as it were, there would recur the whole fallacy which had been observed with respect to the relationship of the natural and the positive law. This dualism can be healed only when the fundamental integrity and unity of the temporal and ideal processes is recognized; then human nature is seen to be the actuality of the two histories and not their *a priori* ground.

The ideal and eternal history, consequently, is not, by its eternity and its ideality, set in contradiction to the temporal process of historical culture, but rather wears that process as a garment or, by a more intimate figure, as its own incorporation. All of the positive forms of the human spirit are time-forms, that is structures of the synthesis in time of finite and infinite. Such forms are all the multitudinous forms of human social activity which through symbolic processes crystallize into institutions, traditions, styles, arts, philosophies. These forms are not, however, in Vico's view, autonomous; rather, they enter into complex relations by which they tend to generate ever fuller expressions of the inexhaustible power of the human spirit. The web of relationships which weaves itself about all of these separate, or at least distinguishable, forms of the synthesis of finite and infinite, of temporal and ideal, works a transformation in each at the same time that it receives from each its peculiar impress. In this way there is generated a fresh synthesis which constitutes a wider time-form in the context of which all elements may be viewed in their relations to all others. This fresh and wider synthesis is itself a superior time-form, and is defined by Vico as the 'nation'. The nation is, therefore, for Vico, an ideal-temporal unity within the human spirit, in which the synthesis of the finite and the infinite is achieved according to a certain modality and with a certain correspondence to the ideal plenitude of the life of the human spirit.

The nation, understood in this sense, is for Vico the natural unit of historical life. In it are present the principles both of the unity and of the inexhaustibility of the historical process. The nation reflects in its structure all of the elements or dimensions of the human spirit in their unity and distinction. At the same time it embodies the essential finitude of the human subject and hence its essential historicity. It is the nation which runs its course through time according to the interior, dynamical historical principle of the human subject, which realizes in its form the synthesis of finite and infinite.

While the nation is thus, for Vico, the effective unit of history, it is still not the ultimate principle of unity in history. This is rather humanity itself, in its idea and in its existence. Humanity itself is not, however, the subject of concrete history, but rather of an ideal history of infinite perspective. It is true that in principle the exhaustive realization of the programme of the 'storia ideale eterna' might with plausibility be thought to have humanity and not the nations as subject; and Vico indeed speaks in this fashion. The plausibility of this notion rests upon the assumption or presumption that humanity might have a reality distinct from and terminally transcendent to its own historical process. This presumption is specifically rejected by Vico.[1] The essential being of humanity is historical; the idea, consequently, of its eluding history, of its possessing a transcendent reality in the same terms in which it possesses historical reality is contradictory. The nation is the authentic term of man's historical life because it preserves the elements of universality and particularity, of finite and infinite in the peculiar synthesis which is proper to history, the time-form. Both the individual and humanity in its ultimate unity tend to escape this form; in doing so, however, they escape into the realm of abstractions.

The time-structure of history is not simple, but complex, not linear, but contrapuntal. It must be traced along a number of lines of development, nor is it possible to establish an unequivocal coherence among these. Vico discusses the problem of the time structure of history against two diverse backgrounds, between which he moves according to the demands of the immediate problem. The first of these is the internal life of the nation, in accordance with which the nation is conceived as an autonomous unity. The other is the idea of the universality of humanity, in the concrete form of the interrelation of the nations as time-forms; in this context, the life of humanity takes on the stature of a superior time-form. This dualism is of basic importance, especially with reference to the significance of the doctrine of 'ricorsi'.

The inner time structure of the nation in its pure idea is defined by the theory of the 'tre sette dei tempi', or three supreme divisions of the times according to the modality of the synthesis of finite and infinite. These divisions he characterizes as religious, punctilious and civil times,[2] a characterization somewhat unexpected after the analysis of the modifications of the human mind. For this, it would seem, must furnish the immediate principles of any qualitative distinctions

[1] SNS, 147. [2] SNS, 975-9.

119

of the historical process. The expected balance is, however, quickly restored; the first designation, as a matter of fact, constitutes a kind of figure of speech whereby a part or a quality is substituted for the whole and for its principle. The religious character is ascribed to times dominated, from the point of view of the modifications of the human mind, by the senses and the phantasy, and by the passionate and impulsive character of action which is the reflection of that domination in the area of 'praxis'. It is the state of the finite subject in which its infinite term appears to it in the dim, rude impressions of sense and images of sensuous phantasy, as subjective transformations of the forces of nature to which it responds with mingled and conflicting attitudes of fear and adulation, of defiance and abject submission. Amid these reactions and images there is born that first sense of finite subjectivity under the overspreading presence of the infinite 'other' which imparts its basic religious tonality to human life and correctly and faithfully reflects that intimate 'broken' world of the human spirit conceived as finite principle which tends to the infinite. In the same manner, and by the same figure of speech, punctiliousness is employed to designate the division of the life of the human spirit in time in which the phantasy has achieved a certain sovereignty over the senses, but no genuine freedom from them (a shift of the seat of power, as it were, in what Amerio calls the 'fantastic complex'). Here, at the gnoseological level, in the order, that is, of the *nosse* of the human subject, the image of phantasy has taken dominance over the direct and rude impression of sense; at the level of the will, the *velle*, pride and a rude sense of elemental equity, based on an equally elemental egotism, over the movements of fear and adulation, of defiance and abject subjection. Punctiliousness is the character attaching to spirit in its first elemental spiritual advances, attached with all the power of a rude and passional nature to the few, obscure ideal principles which it has conquered. It is a spiritual state in which these ideal values hang precariously by a thread, as it were, from the scarcely conquered passions. Finally, civil times, by the same figure of speech, designates the reflective moment of spirit, the state of the human subject in which reflection has gained a substantial dominion over all of the spontaneous movements of life. The quality of this moment of spirit is a suave movement within an area of ideas securely conquered and a spiritual discipline of the passions and the will to the formalities of these ideas. In this state of spirit, man has overcome the basic trauma of his nature and entered into possession of his own idea, the idea, that is, of his own humanity. Finally, by a second figure of speech, these divisions of times are characterized as divine, heroic and civil, and Vico employs these alternative designations with literary freedom, according to the preoccupation of the moment.

Essential to the comprehension of either mode of designation, however, is their common dependence on the previous analysis of the modifications of the human mind. The actual force of these triadic divisions, as Vico employs them, derives from this more radical analysis; and the movement of the life of the nation in time reflects the latter without ambiguity. That analysis of the modifications of the human mind has been seen to possess the complexity of a tri-dimensional division articulated within a more radical division in two terms. The more radical distinction is spontaneity and reflection; within this, the tri-dimensional distinction of sense-phantasy-reflection appears as an attempt to create a certain tension within the moment of spontaneity. The divisions of the times in the life of the nations reflects this inner and more highly articulated structure of spirit. At the same time, it was noted that the triadic analysis of the modifications of the human mind is not of the same force or character as the diadic. The distinction or opposition between sense and phantasy is diverse from the distinction between spontaneity and reflection; the first is a distinction of emphasis. As a result, the relation between sense and phantasy, even in their distinction, is closer than the relation between spontaneity and reflection. This, too, is faithfully translated into the time-structure of the nation; for the relation between religious and punctilious, divine and heroic times is closer by far than their mutual relation to civil times; indeed, together, the earlier form a unity opposed to the later. Thus the two-dimensional analysis tends to assert itself and the three dimensional to appear more as a distribution of emphasis within the former. In similar manner, the three-fold division of the times tends to give way to a diadic, an age of spontaneity set over against an age or time of reflection within which the narrower divisions again appear as distributions of emphasis.

Finally, it must be recalled that the whole force of these distinctions is historical-social. The divisions of the times designate before all else the qualitative principles of social organization at the diverse stages of the movement of the subject of history, that is the nation, toward its ideality. Spontaneity and reflection, sense, phantasy, reason, designate, therefore, not primarily and functionally modes of human consciousness in the abstract, but principles of organization and coherence in social institutions, in the complex ligatures of community. The full force of these characterizations is not, consequently, to be read back into the abstract structure of the human spirit, but forward and outward, as it were, into the social structure of historical process. As the nation designates just such an articulation of the social consciousness of man, so the divisions of the times, predicated on the modifications of the human mind, designate such qualitative diversity in the principles of social life and organization. For this reason, the abstract division of the time structure must, for Vico, be translated immediately into terms of the qualitative diversity of the structures of group life. The whole economy of group life is thus transposed; the three-fold division of the times appears as the distinction in turn of the three-fold division of languages, of economy, of polity, of jurisprudence, and so forth through the full range of the bonds of community. These divisions first in terms of the modifications of the human mind, later in terms of the time-structure of the nations, have all a common final force as principles of the analysis of historical social process. This in turn is reflected in the positive structure of the 'New Science'; for what it attempts in the most extended application of its own principles is a reconstruction of the poetic structure of society, that is of the institutions of a society which is dominated by the complex of spontaneity, and to discover here the seeds of the reflective structures of civil life.

This reference to the social and historical force of these divisions and distinctions and to the positive service to which Vico puts them recalls attention to the central problem of the time-structure of the nations, that is to the *course* of the nations in time, or the inner dynamic of the divisions of the time. For it is clear that the purpose of Vico, in the distinction whether of the modifications of the human mind or of the time-structure of the nation, is not to establish these in their counterdistinctions, but rather as moments in the inward movement of history, of the nation within history, and finally of man in the life of the nation, toward ideality. That is to say, this is a dynamic and not a static analysis. The problem of this movement is reflected also in the total life of humanity which ideally should find its record in universal history.

It would seem, at first glance, that the movement of the nation, its 'corso', must be linear, direct, and determined along the line described in the first instance by the modifications of the human mind and later by the divisions of the times. In one very important sense this is so. There does appear to Vico to be overall, general movement between the extremes these divisions separate, that is, from spontaneity to reflection, from religiosity to civility, and this with a certain determination and necessity. As a result, there are, undoubtedly, optimistic and progressivistic elements in his theory of history, though these terms are not his and though the full weight of the theory is against the full implication these terms must bear. Frustration awaits anyone, however, who would seek the principle of this overall movement in the analysis of the time-structure of history, in an inner law of development after the pattern of the 'laws of nature'. This principle is to be found rather in the Vichian conception of providence. Providence, it was suggested, is for Vico a term wholly immanent to the historical process; for this reason, the law of progress must in its turn be an immanent principle. It was also suggested that the specific mode of the operation of providence in history is time; for this reason, further, time must be recognized as the vehicle of the Vichian optimism. Time is for Vico, in a certain sense, the vehicle of progress and of ideality. Nevertheless, the actual time-structure of the life or 'corso' of the nation, is not drawn from the principle of providence itself, but from the dynamic structure of the human mind, its modifications, which are not transcendent to the historical process (so as to constitute a 'nature' of man distinct from his history) any more than is providence. Consequently, within the time-structure of the life of the nation, the distinction between this time-structure and the principle of providence must be maintained. Reference must be made to the radical contradiction involved in the definition of man as finite principle which tends to the infinite. Of this contradiction providence is the ultimate rectifying force. It is here, therefore, that the principle of progress in Vico is to be found. For providence, while guaranteeing the overall movement of history toward ideality, does not cancel the deviations, the contradictions, the oscillations, the retrogressive and paralogical movements of the human spirit in history; rather, working in and through all these, it bends that course in the direction of the idea. Progress, in Vico's theory, is part of that wider conception of providence in which the radical trauma of human history is healed. And the sense of progress is balanced, indeed at times very nearly outweighed, by the sense of the imminent tragic element or potentiality of history; this latter, in its turn, to be traced to that contradiction implicit in the human spirit in its distention between the terms of finitude and infinite.

This tragic sense of history, or sense of the tragic element in history, is reflected in the time-structure of the 'corso' of the nation.

It finds validation in the tendency to effect a total transvaluation of the moments of spirit, that is, to lift the principles of its finiteness into absolutes. And as this transvaluation can be the work only of reflection, it must properly be viewed as a perversion within the life of spirit and not as a simple deviation or lapse. There is, for example, a direct and native sensism of the human spirit which, at a certain level of its cultural movement, is the positive principle of its forms of expression. There is also a sophisticated sensism, which Vico condemns in Locke and in others whom he calls the modern followers of the classical Epicureans. This sensism is far more subtle than that previous native form; it is the product of reflection and, considered in itself as an act of the spirit, is seen to consist in the elevation into an absolute of a principle of the contradiction in the life of spirit. Its result can be only an ideal and temporal perversion of the life of spirit. In the ideal order, this perversion consists precisely in the elevation by spirit of a principle of contradiction into a principle of its own life; the self-denial of spirit which is the full burden of a philosophical sensism, for example, is nothing less than cultural suicide and can lead only to barbaric recursion. In the temporal order it results in a number of interesting aspects of the time-form structure of the nation.

The first of these may be called the residual penetration of time-forms, or the phenomenon of historical residues. Vico symbolizes this phenomenon in an image which for its magnificence and sweep has been called Homeric, the image of a great river, which, by reason of its great momentum and the force of its current tends to preserve the identity and the sweetness of its own waters long after they have entered into the sea.[1] The elemental moments of the life of spirit tend to persist into later moments; and this persistence is not merely passive, as the remains of a temple may persist in a landscape which has changed character, but active, as laws which remain in vigour against the changing character of a civil code, of modes of speech which endure and determine modes and habits of thought long after there has ceased to be any authentic consonance between the word and the idea struggling for expression. The peculiar temporal structure resulting from this phenomenon of persistence might well be called pseudo-contemporaneity; a pseudo-contemporaneity, because based not on the enunciation but on the deletion of ideal lines. The actual structure of every culture or society, of every nation, at any given moment of its life, must present such a profile of pseudo-

[1] SNS, 412.

contemporaneities; its institutions, its laws, its language, are woven of such texture. Needless to say, these persistences or residues, being active, must become centres of tension and contradiction within that society or nation, tensions and contradictions not always clearly understood even by the most vigilant critical minds within a culture. Nevertheless, it must be said that in all its moments of movement toward the realization of the idea the course of the nation in time consists to a great extent in the vanquishing of such pseudo-contemporaneous elements within its own structure, a task which is essentially critical and hence the work of reflection. Since, however, the critical or reflective moment is not itself immune from the tendency toward false absolutes, as Vico remarks in the axioms concerning the conceits of the nations and of the learned, criticism in a simplicistic, rationalistic and illuministic sense is clearly not the instrument of this progress.

If there is a pseudo-contemporaneity, which threatens the time-form structure of the nation, there is also an authentic form of contemporaneity which is the guarantor of its vigour and health. A great part of the ideal movement of the nation in its temporal course is expended in the elimination of the past from the present, not in a revolutionary sense necessarily, but in a liberal sense, by which the present is delivered from the tyranny of the past, and in a progressive sense, in which the present finds in the past its own roots and authentification. At the same time, there is a sense in which the past constitutes a genuine dimension of the present and hence is not a principle to be exorcised or eliminated, but an element to be made a positive dimension of the presence to self in which the present of the nation consists. It is in this sense that every nation seeks to be wholly contemporaneous to itself, and not the nation only, but the human spirit itself, as it seeks its idea in its history. This genuine contemporaneity, which is, clearly, the basis of that plenitude of presence toward which the human spirit moves as toward its idea, is possible precisely because the moments of spirit, the modifications of the human mind, are not autonomous, but imply each other in a definite order. Pseudo-contemporaneity violates this order of ideality and presence. The movement from spontaneity to reflection, described above as the basic movement of the life of spirit, is a movement of implication and presupposition. The moment of spontaneity is the moment of minimal presupposition, or of its total absence; at the same time it is the presupposition of all other ideally and temporally subsequent and dependent moments. As the nation moves, ideally and in time, from its spontaneous to its reflective moment, it does not shed its past in a kind of historical amnesia; on the contrary, it assumes its past as the irreducible presupposition of its present. Only as the elements of the past become dimensions of the present has the present structure, form and content. To this effect, however, the mode of presence in which the past enters the structure of the present must be a genuine contemporaneity—one, that is, which is ideally ordered to the present. In passing to the state of civility the nation sheds nothing of its heroic and barbaric past, which is after all the seed-plot of its vitality; rather, it carries this with it into a critical perspective, transposing the mode of presence of the past. In this way, the springs of its vitality are not closed, but are open and abundant even within its reflective and civil life. The errors of pseudo-contemporaneity (which are, clearly, not academic errors, but vital, which in history may cost a nation its identity by paralysing its powers of judgment and of action, by distorting its own presence to itself and causing it to entertain an entirely delusive and historically fatal conception or image of itself) are avoided when the elements of its past, those passional and poetic moments in which it was conceived and which still enclose the secret vital forces of its life are present to it, but now ideally and temporally ordered to its reflective and civil consciousness. Thus the time-structure of the nation is revealed as a multidimensional present of which the past is a constitutive element, rather than a progress, which can only be, so far as it involves the renunciation of the past rather than its constant recall, a movement toward oblivion.

The contrast between genuine and pseudo-contemporaneity within the time-structure of the life of the nation makes it possible to form a more nearly accurate conception of the course of the nation in time in the sense of a law of its inward process. Basically, this law would seem to be a law of linear progress through the stages of consciousness or presence distinguished as the modifications of the human mind. From the nature of the case, however, it appears at once that such linear progress is contradicted or opposed by the movement of the distinguishable stages of consciousness or presence and their correlative time components toward a pseudo-autonomy, a movement which has its roots ultimately in that basic tension between finite and infinite which constitutes the most intimate structure of the human spirit. The progress involved in the time-ideal movement of the life of the nation cannot, therefore, be a linear movement, but an ultimate progress which passes through, or includes, the contradictions inherent in this finite-infinite structure of the human spirit. The first result of this movement toward autonomy is to induce a pseudo-contemporaneity; the ideal movement of history involves before all else the correction of this distortion of presence. This in turn is achieved by the nation when its past is ideally ordered to its present; when, that is, its past is made constitutive of its present and an element of its presence to itself in a perspective of time and idea which conforms to its ideal movement. Essential to this ideal perspective, is the eternal moment of providence; in this moment, spirit grasps the root of its ideality, its orientation toward the infinite. In so far, consequently, as a nation achieves a genuine historical consciousness, its time-structure will always present the character of a multidimensional present, whose dimensions reach, on the one hand, into the dark recesses of its own pre-reflective past and, on the other, into the eternal present of providence, but whose actuality is always the synthesis of these dimensions in the immediacy of its total presence to itself.

The individual nation, as defined earlier, is for Vico the normal illustration of the time-structure of history. Nevertheless, there is present in his thought a further dimension or aspect of the process of time and idea, namely that in which history transcends the limited presence of the nation to become the history of man, of humanity. The first hint of this time-structure of history which is at once immanent to the life of the nations and transcendent to it, appears in the concept of the universal jurisprudence. In this context it is Vico's purpose to derive a universal jurisprudence of the human race through the analogy with the jurisprudence of the individual nations; such a universal jurisprudence would exhibit a natural law which is immanent to the process of the formation of the structures of law in individual nations but which has as its ultimate reference mankind, or humanity. Universal history is the exact correlative, on the level of the general problem of history, of this concept of universal jurisprudence at the level of the problem of natural law. The universal history of mankind is a history which arises with and is lived in and through the histories of the nations.

The analysis of the time-form structure of universal history is based on the triadic division of the times encountered in the life of the individual nation, a division which, as we have pointed out, has its roots in the distinction of the modifications of the human mind. The phases of universal history, as immanent to but transcending the histories of the individual nations, are again those of spontaneity and reflection, of sense, phantasy and reason. Nevertheless, it is clear that the time structure of universal history cannot be simply the synthesis of the histories of the individual nations in an order of linear process; that is to say, it is impossible to suppose that certain nations in their character as nations, are to be assigned to one moment of presence rather than another, and hence to one place rather than another, in the total history of mankind. No nation stands to humanity as its moment of childhood. Every nation runs the full course of humanity. The ascription of mono-qualitative structure to any nation or to individual nations would alter the entire conception of the time-structure of the nation and of universal history itself. It is obvious, consequently, that the relationship between the time-structure of the life of the nation and that of universal history is to be conceived in a more complex manner. It consists, precisely, in a counterpuntal relationship between the triadic division of the times in these respective contexts; and as such it leads directly to the problem underlying the Vichian doctrine of 'ricorsi'.

It is possible, however, before addressing the doctrine of 'ricorsi' directly, to indicate the general character of the time-structure of universal history as it is immanent yet transcendent, to the time-forms of the individual nations. The clue to this structure is to be found in the problem of contemporaneity already encountered at the level of the life of the individual nation. False or pseudo-contemporaneity appears in opposition to genuine contemporaneity at this level also, with differences induced by the special character and quality of universal history. It appears as the simple parallelism of the time-structures of the individual nations. Nations may be thought to be contemporaneous in two ways, first as chronologically at the same stage of internal time-ideal development; secondly, as qualitatively contemporaneous despite chronological distance. Both are forms of pseudo-contemporaneity, because they destroy the time-structure of universal history while they pretend to define it. In the first instance, two 'nations' chronologically and qualitatively contemporaneous would not appear in universal history as nations, in the Vichian sense, at all; the lines which would define them as nations are, by these qualifications, deleted. In the second case, the contemporaneity involved is, from the point of view of universal history, sterile; it can be viewed metaphysically as recurrence, which would make a universal history a pure tautology, or positivistically, as the basis of abstract 'laws' of historical becoming which are pure description. On the other hand, it is evident that in some sense all the time-forms of the individual nations must be contemporaneous in universal history. This follows from the fact, already established with respect to the unity of the life of the individual nation, that only contemporaneity can establish the identity of the nation; in like manner, only contemporaneity can establish the unity of the life of humanity. The contemporaneity of universal history can be conceived only when that universal history is thought of, not as the transcendent history of the race beyond the life of the individual nations, but as the lives of these nations viewed from the standpoint of the absolute ideality revealed in them. Only in this way may the time-ideal order both of the individual nation and of the history of mankind be preserved. The individual nations become contemporary in virtue of their relationship to this idea, which is the total presence to itself toward which humanity moves. For this reason, the supreme problem of universal history must be the problem of chronology, as Vico remarks. Chronology is the form of the total presence of mankind to itself in universal history; that is, it is the form under which that presence is actualized. But again, the problem leads directly to the doctrine of 'ricorso'; for without 'ricorsi' chronology on Vichian principles is impossible.

VII

'RICORSI'

THE doctrine of 'ricorsi' is, without doubt, the most celebrated thesis in the entire Vichian theory of history. As is apt to be the case with such doctrines, it has also been the centre of the greatest obscurity, misunderstanding and controversy. Vico himself is not without blame for this state of affairs. Nowhere, it is safe to say, is the obscurity for which he is famous better exemplified. From the interpretative aspect, however, the source of confusion lies elsewhere. The doctrine of 'ricorsi' has seldom been addressed in the context of the integral theory of history. It has, rather, been endowed with a certain autonomy. But the sense and force of the doctrine can be discerned only from its function within the entire economy of the theory of history. Apart from this context it can be made to sustain the most contradictory interpretations.

The most common interpretation of 'ricorsi' is that it illustrates a recurrence theory of history. As a consequence, it has been thought that Vico reduced history to a 'statuesque' immobility [1] and denied it all genuine and significant movement. It is most difficult, however, to see in what sense recurrence can be admitted into Vico's theory; there would seem to be no point at which it can be introduced with logical force. The ideal and eternal history is not a principle of recurrence; it defines the eternal principles of historical becoming, which themselves do not become, but are. What does not become, clearly, cannot recur; the notion of recurrence, consequently, can have no reference here. Nor can the concept of recurrence be admitted at the level of the course of the nations through time. The fact that the essential time-structure of the nation, as we have suggested, is contemporaneous would seem to preclude the notion of recurrence. Finally, the orientation of Vico's theory of history toward universal history makes recurrence without meaning in his thought; universal history is open and inexhaustible; above all, it is unique.

---

[1] The adjective is that of Lorenzo Giusso, *La Filosofia di G. B. Vico e L'Eta' Barocca*, Roma, Perrella, 1943, Avvertenza.

As open, it is the realm of limitless possibility; as inexhaustible, of endless novelty; as unique, without reduplication in any dimension. On every score, consequently, the notion of recurrence must be alien to universal history.

A second interpretation of 'ricorsi' is that which sees in it the prime evidence for the circularity of spirit.[1] This interpretation is, obviously, predicated on the idea that the Vichian theory of history is, in its authentic speculative character, a metaphysic of mind or spirit. 'Ricorsi' appears as the dynamic and dialectical law of the inner life of spirit. This interpretation of 'ricorsi' is invalidated, in the first place, by the evidence which denies that the Vichian theory of history can be conceived fundamentally as a philosophy of spirit or metaphysic of mind. The historical structure of spirit, implicit in the definition of man which Vico advances, excludes such a metaphysic and above all repudiates the elements of eternism which such a metaphysic harbours. 'Ricorsi' as the law of the circularity of spirit lacks authentic Vichian flavour and is without relevance to the discernible structure of Vico's conception of historical movement.

What is necessary, for the clarification of this concept, is a return to the total context of the Vichian theory of history. In that context it is possible to put two meaningful questions with reference to 'ricorsi'. What are the concrete employments of the term? What is the function of the concept of 'ricorsi' in the full economy of the theory of history?

'Ricorsi' appears in Vico, in the first instance, as a methodological notion. It designates a methodological device for making effective his discovery of the primacy of poetry and, with this, of the genuine time-structure and movement of history. It consists in the employment of the categories of poetic wisdom for the interpretation of the cultural and social structures of post-poetic times. By this employment there is determined abstract contemporaneity between time-form structures. This abstract contemporaneity, in turn, is nothing more, concretely, than the very possibility of employing these same categories with respect to temporally distant historical contents. In this manner Vico employs the term and concept 'ricorsi' with respect to the 'Middle Ages', in which he sees a returned heroic age.[2] The 'Middle Ages' are a returned barbarism in the strictly methodological sense that to their concrete structures and documents there are

---

[1] Croce, *La Filosofia di G. B. Vico*, pp. 127–8.
[2] SNS, 1047 et seq.

applicable, with certain modifications, those canons of interpretation which he has discovered to be valid with respect to the heroic times of the human race. And in the long run this is, perhaps, the most important sense which the term 'ricorsi' is called upon to bear in Vico's thought, for it is the final historiographic value of the term.

Vico's methodology is not, however, suspended in mid-air; it is his boast that his method rests upon elements of genuinely speculative force. It is, therefore, imperative to ask in virtue of what character of the historical process this methodological employment of 'ricorsi' is possible. This question throws into relief the genuine principle of 'ricorsi', that is, the function which this concept exercises in the economy of the theory of history.

The speculative root of the concept of 'ricorsi' is the complex contemporaneity of history, the contemporaneity, that is, which relates, in the first instance, the unit time-forms of history, the nations, and, in the second, the nations and the time-structure of universal history. The function of the concept is to resolve the dualism between the course of the nations through time and the ideal movement of universal history. 'Ricorsi' describes the path which history traverses between the pluralism of the life of the nations and the absolute ideal unity of universal history. The fact that universal history cannot, in the strict sense of Vico's theory of history, sustain an existential being, does not render this sense of 'ricorsi' implausible; on the contrary, it makes this interpretation of the concept inevitable. It is 'ricorsi' which, within the orbit of providence, sustains the movement of history from finite to infinite, resolving those contradictions which impede this movement, while resisting the dissolution of the dynamic finite into the immobility of the infinite.

From this conception of the function of 'ricorsi' it is clear that the concept has in fact two theatres of operation or reference. It refers, in the first place, to the internal time-structure of the nation, in the second, to the movement of the plurality of nations toward the unity of universal history. It is necessary, consequently, to examine its operation in each of these frames of reference and also in the context of their relationship to each other. Finally, it will be necessary to inquire in which area its primary application is to be found, in which the secondary and derivative.

Early in this formulation of the theory of history Vico tends to centre attention on the significance of the concept of 'ricorsi' in the life of the individual nation. It is the purpose of the 'New Science' to discover the law of the origin, growth, and decline of the social economy, that is, of the complex of institutions in which the social consciousness of humanity is incorporated and effected; even more, the 'New Science' seeks, through the determination of this law, to place in the hands of the nations, so to say, the power of recapturing the sources of their life and, even in the moment of decline, of initiating anew their movement toward ideality and vigorous life. This must be recognized, without doubt, as the protoform of the concept of 'ricorsi', and it is, clearly, thoroughly moralistic in character.

This moralistic quality of the concept of 'ricorsi' in its protoform removes it, more perhaps than any other factor, from all reference to recurrence. In virtue of this moralism, the process of 'ricorsi', here the rejuvenation and revitalization of the life form of the nation, is referred wholly to the free and reflective moment of the nation's life. 'Ricorso' is a movement of and within the free, reflective life of spirit. For this reason, it can imply no recurrence to the spontaneous, prereflective or prelogical moment. If the vital sources of the nation's strength and civil growth are recovered by 'ricorso', they may be recovered in their pristine force, but not in their pristine form. There can be no recurrence to the prereflective springs of life; in such a notion there is to be found only the most illusory form of romanticism. For this reason 'ricorsi' must be conceived not as recurrence, but as an advance which is yet a return upon itself, a movement which is possible only on the reflective plane of spiritual life. 'Ricorsi' transpires wholly on the plane of reflection; the characteristic of its action, however, is that the principle of vitality of life on quite another plane, namely the prereflective or spontaneous, is recaptured, not, obviously, in its immediacy, but in its idea. 'Ricorsi', in this protoform of the concept, is a reflective process or movement by which the spontaneous life of spirit is assumed and re-lived on the level of reflection and freedom.

For this reason, it is clear, neither in a formal nor in a material sense can recurrence attach to the concept of 'ricorsi'. It denominates, rather, a movement within the life of the nation by which that life is lifted and advanced in ideality at the same time that it retreats upon itself. Material recurrence is, in this context, without meaning. Restored institutions can never be, in even a material sense, identical with the institutions which they imitate. Examples of Vico's intent may with profit be sought in areas far removed from his own purview; their appositeness may throw the force of his own theory into greater relief than examples of his own choosing. The primitivistic movement within the Church of England in the nineteenth century may serve as such an example, as may also certain aspects of primitivism in modern art. Keble, Pusey, Newman perceived in the apostolic church the first, pure and unreflective movement of the Christian life; it was this life, in the first instance, which they sought to recapture. Yet how deep in them, and above all in Newman, was the sense of the historical distance, so to say, which separated them from that life. No movement back through time, however ardent its inspiration, could recapture that lost life. Least of all could that life be repossessed by the return to its material forms; its ritual, its practices, even its formulae, repeated in the new historical moment, became empty gestures and hollow-sounding words. It was Newman who sensed most clearly the impossibility of this movement back to spontaneity and the necessity of recapturing that pristine life of the church in idea. The whole sense of his essay on the *Development of Christian Doctrine* may be read as the record of his discovery of this historical principle, a discovery which made possible his recognition in an historical institution of the Christian life he was seeking. Similarly, certain primitivistic movements in modern art may exemplify the same idea. Much modern art is born of the malaise of reflection; it seeks to recapture the unburdened and untroubled moment of spontaneity, the spontaneity of sense, of impulse, of action. Yet within the patterns of the psyche, how impossible this movement is. The simple forms of spontaneous awareness and action elude all capture. Imitated, they wear a garment of sophistication which is the clearest mark of their origin, reflection, and the unambiguous measure of their distance from that spontaneity they would recapture. Material recurrence, in a word, is precluded from the life of spirit.

It is precluded, however, only because formal recurrence is impossible. In this context it is clear that the unity of form and content in history is complete; the mind, or spirit, according to the modalities of its modifications, is the formal and creative principle both of itself and of its total content so that any distinction between them is necessarily abstract. A formal recurrence in the life of spirit and in the life of the nation would, consequently, not only make possible but would directly produce a material recurrence. A formal recurrence is, however, impossible, because the movement of 'ricorsi' transpires wholly on the level of reflection. The formal principle of 'ricorsi' is and can be only the idea, never the spontaneous forms of the phantasy. The reality which 'ricorsi' generates is a mediate, not an immediate, reality; the structures of 'ricorsi', i.e. the structures of a 'returned barbarism', are never recurrences in either a formal or a material sense. The picture which has been painted, in profoundly romantic terms, of a nation's return to its origins, that is to the pristine moment of spontaneity and passion, of myth and blood unity, of mystical and ritualistic oneness, is in Vico's terms an illusion, and a fatal illusion. The products or expressions of 'ricorsi' are qualitatively different from the products of spontaneity; they are clearly products of reflection, even when they wear the mask of the prelogical moment. As a result, they cannot work the works of spontaneity and are entirely lacking in that character of truth which is, to Vico, the genuine mark of spontaneity.

The actual function of 'ricorsi' in the life of the nation cannot, however, be grasped until a fallacy concerning Vico's conception of the human spirit is examined. It is the fallacy that Vico conceived the reflective moment as a moment of instability, of moral malice, even of essential perversion and of the moment of spontaneity, by contrast, as possessing a monolithic integrity; in a word, that Vico is at once anti-intellectual and romantic. It is true, indeed, that Vico is a relentless critic of abstract intellectualism; his critique is not advanced, however, in the name of a romantic faith in the veridical quality of spontaneity or in its moral integrity; it is advanced wholly in the interests of the integrity of the life of spirit. He is entirely innocent of the romanticism which certain critics and interpreters impute to him, for the most part on the basis of the distinction between the barbarism of sense and the barbarism of reflection. It is true that Vico speaks of the barbarism of reflection as 'worse' than that of the senses;[1] it is clear, however, from the total context of his theory whence this pejorative character springs. The barbarism of reflection is essentially intellectualism; it resides in the failure of presence, or the absence, which intellectualism induces in the spirit; it is, therefore, in itself essentially a fracture of the integrity of spirit, whose total presence must embrace sense and intellect, image and idea at once. Neither phantasy nor intellect, spontaneity or reflection possesses any autonomy; they achieve reality only in the integrity of spirit.

It is in the context of the integrity of spirit that the actual function of 'ricorsi' is to be recognized. 'Ricorsi' lifts the time-form of the life of the nation to a higher stage of ideality by putting it in

[1] SNS, 1105–6.

reflective, or ideal, possession of principles and sources of power and strength which it had previously possessed only on a spontaneous basis. In this way, there accrues to spirit by 'ricorsi' an authentic increment of wisdom, for the unity of thought and action, in which wisdom consists, is greater when its formal principle is the idea. The 'ricorsi' implies a return only in the sense that the powers now possessed in idea where before possessed unreflectively. The time-form of the nation is advanced toward its own ideality, not by an abstract gesture of the detached intellect, but by an ideal penetration of its own historical character and integrity. Vico at no point appears to countenance, on philosophical principles, the logically absurd conception of a recurrence from the reflective to the pre-reflective levels of presence.

The determination of the actual function of 'ricorsi' in the life of the nation induces the problem of the mechanism of this function. This is dual, involving both spirit and providence. And, as in a former confrontation, spirit and providence appeared in a certain contradictory relation to each other, so here a similar contradiction,. not readily resolved, appears again.

The effort which can send a nation back upon its origins to grasp anew, in idea, the principles of its own spontaneous life and power is the greatest spiritual effort a nation can make. It is criticism in its purest, that is, its most concrete, and historical, form. It is closely akin to the effort which Vico describes himself as putting forth in the composition of his 'New Science', an effort which encloses the whole gnoseology of the 'New Science'. It implies before all else a rejection of the notion of intellectual contemplation, that is, the notion that the intellect apprehends universal first principles intuitively, without reference to its concrete historical experience and that it can, from the vantage point of these principles, approach with confidence the task of categorizing the concrete content of history; in a word, it embraces the Vichian critique of intellectualism as it was directed both against Cartesianism and against jusnaturalism. By contrast, the intellect is conceived to act in a manner diametrically opposed to intuition. The universal is indeed its term, but it comes to this term only by a movement back upon the whole of its concrete experience. This power of so directing itself is the essence of intellect and provides the denomination of its essential operation, reflection. By this movement, the intellect does not impose an abstract or *a priori* categorization upon the content of that experience, but educes the immanent ideality of the process of historical movement. Nor does the intellect stand outside of the process which is the object of this redirection; if this were so, there would be but a recurrence of the attitude of naturalism. The process of intellect is immanent to the total process toward which it is directed; intellect, reflection, is itself historical and, concretely, is identified with that immanent ideality which it educes. Reflection, however, as it has been suggested, is the principle of 'ricorsi'; conversely it must now be said, 'ricorsi' is the pure form of reflection. That is, the essential operation of reflection in spirit is itself the purest type of 'ricorso'. As a consequence, 'ricorso' is seen to be, not an accidental movement of the spirit, but its most intimate and constitutive movement. The mechanism of 'ricorso' is identical with the reflective movement of spirit or mind.

This process of the intellect, it is clear, is wholly a time-process, or, more accurately perhaps, is the process most clearly constitutive of historical time. It is the process by which the true contemporaneity of the time-structure of the nation is revealed. This contemporaneity consists precisely in the approach of spirit to ideality by the reassimilation of its total process or movement into the life of the idea. Or, stated conversely and again, perhaps, more accurately, it is the movement of the total historical process toward its total presence in the idea. The fact that this is an infinite process and hence intrinsically incapable of being closed introduces no contradiction but rather emphasizes the essential historical structure of spirit itself. And since it has been shown that, in Vico's view, the operation of reflection is the essential movement of 'ricorsi', contemporaneity may be defined as the form induced by 'ricorsi' in the time-structure of the nation; it is that state of ideality in which the nation possesses as presence and in idea all of the principles of its life. It is identical with philosophical wisdom.

'Ricorsi', it must follow, is not a single or isolated episode in the life of the nation. Rather, it is a process through which the nation must pass many times, indeed continuously, when once it has achieved an initial reflective stage. For the nation lives only by seeking its own total presence and ideality. This, in turn, it may do only by the construction of that 'true' contemporaneity in which the full resources of its life are available to it at the highest level of presence, as a wisdom whose formal principle is the idea. 'Ricorso', it has been established, is the process by which this contemporaneity is induced. This is its function within the time-structure of the nation. As a consequence, the nation must recur to the sources of its power and strength as often as alienation from these sources threatens it; and, indeed, the power so to recur is the accurate measure of its will to life, of its central vitality.

The process of 'ricorsi' does not, however, even within the life of the nation take place wholly through the effort of the human principle; it demands the complement of the principle of providence. Even 'ricorso' is providential and is to be read ultimately only in providential terms. As the principle which induces 'ricorsi' in the time-structure of the nation, providence operates in its general pattern, that is, as a principle for the resolution of contradictions. In the present instance, the contradiction is between the time-form moments of the life of the nation and that absolute self-identity or presence toward which the nation moves. As finite, these moments tend toward exclusiveness and autonomy. The principle which can rectify this tendency in the direction of the ideality of the nation can only be the infinite. It is as providence, as we have suggested, that the infinite appears operative in history. 'Ricorso', in the function which it fulfils in the life of the nation, is a specialized movement of providence. The final presence before which the contradictions of history are resolved is not that of the human spirit to itself, but providence.

'Ricorso', as it is operative within the ambit of the life of the individual nation, is thus seen to be a genuine principle of ideality, a process in line with the original and constitutive movement of the human spirit toward its own ideality. The spirit in history retreats only to advance; it is like a great hound circling to pick up the trace which it has lost for the moment. This conception of 'ricorso' is also consonant with the Vichian contrast between the barbarism of sense and the barbarism of reflection. The latter, in his account, is more terrible than the former. The barbarism of sense is characterized by a limited but undeviating truth character; the phantasy, because it is wholly immediate, bears always a direct relationship to truth; the impulsive action of the heroic barbarian, though it be cruel and insensate, is without guile or malice. But the barbarism of reflection is marked by the possibility of both the lie and deceit. This possibility inheres in it precisely because it is the product of reflection. Reflection and reason, while they open the spirit to the infinite horizons of truth, at the same time remove it from the truth. Its relationship to that wider truth is not spontaneous and immediate but mediate and reduplicative. It is at the level of this mediacy that the lie may enter. By reflection, man is not so much in the power of truth, as truth is in his power. For this reason the 'Middle Ages' may not appear as the clearest example of a returned barbarism; a clearer might be found in the very age in which Vico lived, in the 'Enlightenment' in which reason was raised to such heights and in which it reveals its inner contradictions so clearly. Voltaire, or even more, a Helvetius or a Condillac, is more the type of the barbarian of reflection than the bear-limbed barons of the Anjou dynasty in Naples or the subtle masters of the schools. The barbarism of reflection is the risk involved in the process of 'ricorso', which as an existential undertaking cannot be immune from its peculiar perils.

The function of 'ricorso' remains essentially the same when the concept is projected into its second theatre: that dimension of history which transcends the life of the individual nation and is orientated toward the unitary life of humanity, the area of the relationship between the history of the nations and universal history. Its function is to induce an increment in ideality by the creation of a mode of contemporaneity in which the total presence of humanity to itself is achieved. The ultimate point of reference of the 'science of humanity' and of the theory of history which is its speculative frame is clearly, for Vico, universal history. Between this notion of universal history, however, and that of the course of the nations in time there recurs the basic Vichian problem, which gives form to his inquiry into the theory of natural law and the project of the 'science of humanity', the problem of the immanence of the ideal to concrete process. Universal history cannot be a history which transcends the history of the nations, any more than the natural law can be a principle which transcends the process of the formation of the structures of positive law. Universal history, like the 'natural law of the nations', must be immanent to the processes of positive law to the history of the nations. It must arise in and with that history as the natural law of the nations arises in and with the laws and customs of the nations. Mankind, humanity, does not traverse two histories, but one: its universal history in and with the history of the nations.

Two alternatives present themselves as to the manner in which universal history may emerge from the histories of the individual nations in time. It is conceivable, in the first place, that a linear progression might prevail among the nations in time. Each, in traversing its individual course, might at the same time constitute a stage in the emerging and advancing ideality of mankind. If this were conceived to be the case, certain nations, in their relation to universal history, must occupy time-ideal positions corresponding to the time-form structure of the life of the individual nations. Certain nations, that is to say, would belong to the 'infancy' of the world and of the race of men, as certain institutions, because of the time-ideal structure of the nation, must belong to the nation's infancy. This linear progression would find its complete reflective expression in a universal chronology in which the nations should appear in the time-ideal order of their relation to the universal history of humanity. The notion of such a chronology is not altogether foreign to the 'New Science'. It would, however, appear to be in intimate contradiction to its speculative principles and an insuperable impediment to its positive programme. Specifically, such a universal chronology is in contradiction to the complex and contemporaneous time-structure of history, as exemplified in the history of the nations. The notion of a linear time-ideal process, it has been suggested, is inapplicable to the individual nation, whose true time-structure is contemporaneous. The nation does not 'lose' its past, as it traverses the time-ideal moments differentiated on the basis of the modifications of the human mind. On the contrary, it moves constantly to 'recover' its past and to render that past present and available in the structure of the higher and more complex form of consciousness. By this movement it generates its true time-structure, which is a present in which the elements of its past are contained, though in a mode diverse from that in which they were initially traversed. The supposition that the relationship of the history of the nations to the universal history of mankind, or humanity is one of linear progress is in contradiction to this established contemporaneity of the nation, because such linear process would imply that certain nations are arrested at the pre-reflective stage of the time-idea movement. It is indeed conceivable that one nation or another should be so arrested; but this must appear only as a 'sport' of historical process; indeed, it is even questionable that the notion of such an arrested process is significant and meaningful in the context of Vico's thought, since he must, by the force of his own terms, be led to deny the denomination of nation to it. The nation, by definition, traverses the entire time-form movement; as a consequence, its true time-structure is contemporaneous; as a further consequence, no nation can stand to another as one time-form moment to another in a linear progress to the universal history of mankind.

The rejection of this notion of a linear time-ideal process between the history of the nations and the universal history of mankind indicates its own alternative. Universal history must represent a time-structure in which the individual nations, as traversing their particular histories, are absolutely present. In a word, the time-form of universal history must be contemporaneity, strictly analogous to the true contemporaneity of the individual nation. Only in this way can the notion of a universal history be sustained, because only in this way is universal history compatible with the established time-structure of the history of the nation. Universal history must be the total presence of humanity, or the human spirit, to itself in the absolute contemporaneity of the nations, in their particular histories, to that spirit. Even more, universal history must be essentially that moment in which the human spirit grasps the contemporaneity of the nations to itself and its own identity in the identity of the time-form structure of the individual nations. That is to say, the essential contemporaneity of the histories of the individual nations to universal history and, consequently, the essence and reality of universal history itself must consist precisely in the perception by the human spirit of the ideal identity of the time-form structure of the nations in the perception that the ideal and eternal history is realized in each. Universal history, in a word, can be only the universal contemporaneity of all history to the human spirit in virtue of that ideal and eternal history which is the common principle of all particular histories.

The problem of universal history, consequently, is simply the problem of the construction of such contemporaneity in the human spirit. Here the analogy with the contemporaneous structure of the history of the individual reasserts itself. That contemporaneity within the life of the individual nation is the product of 'ricorso'; so, too, is it in the life of humanity. 'Ricorso' in universal history and as the principle of universal history is the act by which the human spirit renders present and contemporaneous to itself the life of all the individual nations in their eternal and ideal principles. This act of 'ricorso' is the supreme and constitutive act of humanity in its own ideas and presence. By this act, the human spirit reaches, so to say, back through all time, that is the time of the life of the individual nations, and down into the depths of consciousness to bring the entire content of history before itself in a single and total act of presence. It is a supreme act of reflection, moreover, for it achieves this 'ricorso' not by advertence to the infinite and tedious detail of life of the nations, but by advertence to the eternal and ideal history. This act of 'ricorso', it is almost needless to indicate, is the best possible definition of the historiographic act and is clearly identical with Vico's conception of the actual method of the 'New Science'. For this reason, the notion of universal history is the culmination of the 'New Science' as the theory of poetry on Vico's own statement, is its key.

There occurs at once, however, a serious objection which would seem to threaten this whole speculative structure. Is not such an act of supreme 'ricorso' in intimate contradiction to the whole conception of the human spirit implicit in the Vichian theory? For in that theory, as we have suggested many times, the structure of the human spirit is itself historical, that is, immanent to its own phenomenology. Would not such an act of 'ricorso' constitute a self-transcendence of the human spirit which would destroy its own idea and immobilize that very movement in which its life and actuality consist? For the act by which the human spirit could thus render itself totally present to itself in universal history would be the act by which it destroyed itself in its existential dimension and reduced itself to its own transcendent idea.[1]

But the reply to this objection or difficulty is not far to seek in Vico. Indeed, it has been unambiguously indicated by him from the very outside of the enterprise of the 'New Science'. It is to be found in the concept of providence, which in the final analysis is the supreme principle of the 'New Science'. It is by its perception of the principle and the actuality of providence that the human spirit achieves the supreme act of 'ricorso' which establishes universal history and not by any contradictory and self-annihilating act of transcendence. The establishment of providence establishes universal history, the total presence of the human spirit to itself in idea. In this principle, the supreme 'ricorso' is achieved by the human spirit in idea, and it possesses itself, past, present, and future, in an act which is wholly consonant with its own historicity. For the determination of the principle of providence, as we have suggested, is, for Vico, possible wholly within the structure of history itself. The circularity of his 'New Science' is complete in that, as he asserts, it is itself the demonstration of its own first principle, providence.

Providence renders the supreme 'ricorso' of universal history possible and free of contradiction because it is the principle by which the essential and constitutive, so to say, contradiction of the human

---

[1] The objection is Croce's and the basis, in part at least, for his constant opposition to the concept of universal history. Cf. *Teoria e storia della storiografia*, Bari, Laterza, 6a ed., 1948.

spirit is closed. To say that the spirit, by the 'ricorso' of universal history, would transcend itself is to say that from its finite character it would pass to infinite. This is exactly what does transpire in universal history, in Vico's theory. But the passage is not contradictory. Rather its principle, providence, whose mode of operation has already been examined, has been laid down as the first principle of the 'New Science' and as the first principle of the historical career of the human spirit itself.

VIII

PHILOSOPHY AND PHILOLOGY

THE concepts which have been considered to this point: the modifications of the human mind, the time structure of the life of the nation, Providence, 'ricorsi', develop what Vico calls the ideal, philosophical or metaphysical dimension of the theory of history. By these concepts the speculative problem underlying or informing the concept of a 'science of humanity' would seem to be resolved in its principal aspects. That speculative problem, as has been seen, was the synthesis of time and idea or the establishment of the intrinsic possibility of a temporal process which would be at the same time ideal. The diremption of these processes, temporal and ideal, in western thought had seemed to Vico the fundamental reason why that tradition, although demanding by its internal logic and as the answer to its most intimate theoretical and practical needs a science such as he conceived had been unable to develop its principles, but had fallen into those 'borie' or conceits which precluded any genuine approach to the problem of history. The closing of this diremption, consequently, constituted the first and, at the same time, the most intimate speculative problem of the science of humanity. This purpose is achieved, in Vico's theory of history, first by the discovery that the process which he proposes to examine, namely, that of human incivilment, is essentially a process of the human subject itself, 'that this world of the nations was made by man';[1] secondly, that the internal and constitutive structure of the human subject could be defined only as the kind of time-ideal process whose possibility was at stake or in question.

Man is essentially and constitutively a finite principle which strives toward the infinite: *finitum quod tendit ad infinitum*; the distention of his being between the terms of this 'tendency' is the very substance of time and temporal process. At the same time, this whole movement of the human subject is ideal, for it is a movement in terms of presence. The movement of the human subject is toward the

[1] SNP, p. 29; SNS, 331.

144

totality of its own presence to itself, toward its own idea; it strives to become itself, to realize in its own actuality the ultimate ideal implications of its open or 'indefinite' nature. This is essentially the meaning of that 'humanity' which forms the object of Vico's 'New Science': the idea, or presence of itself to itself, toward which the human subject moves in history. The 'modifications of the human mind' in turn constitute a pure phenomenology of the human subject in its time-ideal structure; that is, a descriptive and logical distinction and characterization of the moments of its time-ideal process. That these moments are, in their intrinsic character, at once temporal and ideal must be apparent; so, too, must be the fact that in their inter-relations they must constitute a temporal, ideal process whose terms are, on the one hand, the absence, and, on the other, the total presence, of the human subject to itself. But Vico discovers an intimate contradiction in this conception of the human subject; there is a contradiction in the idea of a finite subject whose tendency is toward the infinite. The actuality of the movement of such a principle toward its term cannot, in his view, be ascribed wholly or principally to that subject; it demands, rather, the presence of an 'other', a principle which should not be subject to this contradiction but whose action, within the process of history, should be precisely the rectification of the movement of the finite subject toward its infinite term. This principle Vico denominates providence, and by it establishes that the presence of the human subject to itself in history must include the presence of this 'other' which stands to it as the rectifying principle of its own constitutive contradiction. The exploration of the time-structure of history reveals its complex character, the elements of residual, abstract, and true contemporaneity, while the concept of 'ricorso' identifies the specific activity of providence and the human spirit in the construction of the true contemporaneity of universal history.

The establishment of the possibility of the time-ideal process, even in this abstract manner, is a significant achievement; significant enough, one is tempted to say, to establish its author in the first ranks of the philosophers. In itself, however, it constitutes but half Vico's task. Were his effort to arrest itself at this point, he would himself exhibit that dimidial character which he imputes alike to the philosophers and the philologians who had preceded him.[1] For his object is the actuality of that science of humanity of which he speaks, and not merely the establishment of its speculative basis. The science of

[1] SNS, 140.

humanity must be, in his own words, at once philosophy and history; it must, in other words, establish the time-ideal process of human culture in its actual, concrete terms, as well as in its abstract possibility. It must establish that the course of human incivilment has indeed been such as the schematic structure of the human spirit might lead us to expect. Nor is this establishment of the concrete actuality of the process of human civilization a mere derivation from that abstract structure of possibility; it is, rather, the ultimate ground of that speculative structure itself. For should that concrete process resist formulation in these speculative terms, it is the speculative structure which must give way. In other words, Vico envisages a complete circularity between the speculative and the programmatic dimensions of the 'New Science'. The speculative structure and the factual or philological structure are completely interdependent, so that each is the ground, and the ultimate ground, of the other. The whole elaborate speculative structure is without value save as it makes possible the penetration and the ideal ordering of the actual, concrete processes of the formations of the structures of human society and civility; these, in the last analysis, constitute the sole frame of reference of these abstract principles. The historical process, on the other hand, remains opaque until the illumination of the speculative principles falls upon it, and it is an illumination which comes to that process not as an external adjunct but as the revelation of its inner ideality.

This circularity of the structure of the science of humanity is what Vico intends by the concept of the unity of philosophy and philology. By philology he intends, in the widest signification of the term, the science of the 'certum'. The 'certum', it has been seen, is a term which Vico draws from the nomenclature of jurisprudence and which he projects, as he projects the whole speculative problem of jurisprudence, onto the wider plane of human culture. It serves in the first, restricted context, to designate the law under the aspect of its authority or mere givenness; in the second, it serves, by strict analogy, to indicate the whole body of the residua of the historical process in its awesome complexity: from the written documents of literate history, through the vestigial institutional remains, which constitute the pseudo-contemporaneity of cultural structures, back into the legendary and fabulous echoes which come down to us from the obscure ages of pre-history. Philology, in its character as a learned discipline, addresses these residua with the intention, at the very least, of fixing them in their certitude, and ultimately, of grasping them in their ideality; under the aspect of their certitude, to fix their external characteristics, under that of ideality, to grasp them as vehicles as the human spirit itself. When the latter intention is brought to the fore, the continuity of philology with philosophy is made clear. But without this intention, even the earlier, and seemingly more modest, purpose of philology must remain without hope of success. For the very externality of the documents of history is determined by the breath of the human spirit which they carry or express. The concept of the circularity, or dialectical unity, of philosophy and philology, consequently, raises the final speculative question of the Vichian theory of history, the speculative question which is most intimately associated with the 'arte critica'[1] in which the actual method of the positive science of humanity will consist. It is the speculative problem of the intrinsic principle and possibility of this circularity itself.

For the principles of the solution of this speculative issue Vico does not need to go beyond the circle of the principles he has already established. This fact already constitutes the kind of reciprocal evidence upon which he will want the science to rest. The concepts by means of which he has already resolved the problem of time-ideal process now enable him to resolve the problem of the unity or circularity of philosophy and philology which constitutes the essence of his 'arte critica', or the method of the 'New Science'. They do this by stripping the residua or documents of history, the whole content of philology that is to say, of all character of 'externality' to the human spirit and by revealing them to be the expressive forms of that spirit in which it finds actuality and existence. As a consequence, it becomes apparent that philology and philosophy address not two processes, but diverse dimensions of one. This it is which Vico calls the reduction of philology to a science[2] and which might as well and as aptly be called the recovery of the 'certum' from nature and its reunion to spirit as the expressive structure of its time-ideal process.

The recovery of the 'certum' from nature, that is from its externality or abstract opposition to spirit, and its identification as a moment of spirit itself is accomplished in two stages. These are indicated by Vico under the two rubrics of the convertibility of the 'certum' and the 'factum' and of the 'factum' with the 'verum'.[3] The recurrence to the terms of the jurisprudential form of the general problem is not without significance. As the whole reality of the

---

[1] *Auto.*, p. 49; SNP, p. 67; SNS, 348, 392.
[2] SNS, 390; cf. also SNP, p. 16; DU, II, 268, 308.　　　　[3] DIS, p. 140, 131.

jurisprudential process depended upon the discovery of the term which might convert 'certum' and 'verum', so the whole of Vico's theory of history might be conceived as the discovery and elaboration of that conception 'factum' which here appears as the mediatorial term of the conversion. And this dual conversion is effected, as we have suggested, by means of principles already established in the process of healing the diremption of time and idea.

The 'certum', that is the cultural residuum, the documents to which philology addresses itself, appears in the first instance as nature. Nature, for Vico, is reality in its irreducible otherness to the human spirit; and this otherness must indeed, for him, appear as the ultimate character of the real. In its totality and in its ultimate character the real is the product, not of the human spirit, but of an absolute spirit. To that spirit or principle, in a word to God, nature is an open book because it is His product. Man, however, must toward nature assume a saving agnosticism; for him it can be the object not of 'scienza' but only of 'coscienza', not of genuine science, that is, but of mere awareness.[1] The documents of his own history, in the first instance, impose themselves upon man as he seeks his identity in history in this manner: as products of alien spirit, perhaps, but as none of his own; as apparent to that alternate spirit, but closed to his own and no part of its presence to itself. Thus the papyrus, the runic stone, the inscription on an ancient tomb; the monolithic or pyramidic structure of that tomb itself; the customary or the legal structure of another, older society, as we may laboriously reconstruct it from the forms of the documents; the legendary and the fabulous wisdom of a half-forgotten people and age. Before these the spirit seeking itself in history stands as before the alien, the unknown and the unknowable. It assumes a posture of historical and spiritual alienation.

The 'certum' is recovered from nature by the perception that it is not 'certum' but 'factum'; that is, not an alien given or imposition, but the term of the active and creative process of spirit itself. This perception is made possible by the concept of the human spirit as activity, indeed, as pure activity, contained in the definition of man as *posse finitum*. The sense of 'factum' here is almost diametrically opposed to that carried by the term 'fact' in empirical contexts. The 'fact' is precisely this given from which all experience must take its point of departure and to which it must return; and this sense clings to the term despite the activistic echoes which its etymology should evoke. The 'factum', on the contrary, in Vico's sense, derives directly

[1] DIS, p. 138.

from the activistic root and reflects its primitive significance. It is that which completes and, completing, embodies a generative and creative process and one to which the principle of that process is immanent. It is the 'factum' of the artifact; even more intimately, the term of the artistic process, for the completed work of art is indeed the 'factum', the deed, of the creative activity which brought it forth and which it, in turn, embodies; finally, and most intimately of all, it is the 'factum' of the living spiritual principle itself in which the immanence of the process and the embodying term is complete, so complete that any distinction between them must appear abstract and nihilistic. Before the historical document conceived thus as its own 'factum', the human spirit cannot assume a posture of alienation. Rather the document so conceived elicits an act of recognition, of self-recognition, however rudimentary, on the part of spirit. Between spirit and the terms of products of its own historical creative activity there can be, not alienation, but only recognition and identity. The human spirit, as *posse finitum*, is wholly, in its actuality, the actuality of the production of the 'facta' of history. Moreover, because of its 'indefinite', that is finite, character, it has no life apart from the activity of this production and is wholly immanent to the works which it creates. This immanence is its most intimate nexus with its own concreteness, and nothing of that concreteness, which it has made, and in making, made itself, can be alien to it. This would seem to be the basic significance of Vico's dictum that there is no better basis for the knowledge of a thing than to have made it.[1] The spirit is never alien to the forms of its own creativity and the products which this creativity has brought forth. Thus is established the first conversion, that of the 'certum' with the 'factum', and by this conversion, the reunion of spirit with itself in its documents.

Vico takes care, in the exposition of this concept of the 'factum' with which the 'certum' of history is convertible, to distinguish it from another kind of 'factum' toward which the human spirit must, in his view, assume an attitude of immedicable scepticism. This is the 'factum' which, with great acumen, he perceives to take place in the mathematical sciences, and which, as a consequence, is characteristic of the empirico-mathematical sciences [2] which may be developed by the union of mathematics and sensible experience. The nature of geometry, he observes, is to establish its postulates, and the operative laws which govern them, by convention. The world of geometry, consequently, might appear to exemplify in the very purest

[1] DIS, pp. 134-5.　　　　[2] DIS, p. 144.

form the law of the conversion of the made and the knowable, for what is here produced is the purest product of the free movement of mind. This is, in Vico's view, illusion. Toward the world of mathematical forms the human spirit must ultimately assume an attitude of complete scepticism because there transpires in that theatre a pseudocreation. By that conventional act which establishes the mathematical realm, spirit does not constitute or call into itself being; it is not immanent in that process as it is in the process of the formation of the structures of culture. The point of departure of the process of mathematical creation is a moment of the self-alienation of spirit; it is, as he says, those points and lines in which spirit can discover no element of its own presence. The activity by which the order of cultural time-forms is established is an activity by which the human spirit itself is established together with its actual world. By comparison, that other mode of creation by convention is a moment of the absence of spirit to itself. As a consequence, spirit cannot discover itself in the world thus called into being any more than it can discover itself in the world of nature. The one and the other are alien and 'other' to spirit. The world of mathematics, while it is a world which spirit makes, is not the world in which spirit creates itself. Toward that world of mathematics, consequently, spirit cannot take but a posture of alienation and scepticism. The difference is that between the act of blowing bubbles of soap and the vital act of drawing breath; by the one there is called into being an ephemeral appearance, by the other the concrete life of the organism.

It is not, however, the mere 'factive' character which Vico discovers in the 'certum' which restores the historical document to the life of spirit and dissolves that first alienation which arises between spirit and its own past. It is rather a *quality* of the 'factum', its expressive and symbolic force. The life of spirit is essentially an expressive and symbolic process. Its products, its 'facta', consequently, are not *things* but *words*, interior words by which spirit expresses and gives form to its own being.

How this must be, is readily apparent when the life of finite spirit, or mind, is examined in its intimate and constitutive activity. Spirit is wholly presence. Infinite spirit must be total and absolute presence. Finite spirit, which is open in the dimension of being, which *becomes*, becomes only as it generates concrete and specified forms of presence out of the open or indeterminate presence which is its *posse*. This open or indeterminate presence, the indefinite nature of man, in Vico's words, is not to be thought of as in any way actual or preexistent with reference to the concrete process of the life of finite spirit; it is wholly immanent to that concrete process and, in itself, without form. Under this aspect, it bears the character of absence rather than of presence, but absence which is pregnant with presence. Of this indeterminate presence, so near to absence, are generated the forms of concrete presence. Prior to the formation of the concrete modes of presence, finite spirit *is* not; it achieves its being and its existence only in those concrete forms. Its constitutive activity, that which endows finite spirit with being and existence, is the activity by which these modes of spirit are generated. This activity, in its most intimate character, is thought and speech. It is not a physical or mechanical process, such as may be discovered in physical nature, but a creative and self-generative process by which spirit comes to be in its own character. Thought is the active generation of presence; it is speech, because by this process the being and the existence of spirit itself is enunciated and formed. The product of this activity is the word. Not, clearly, the word as external and conventional sign; rather the word as the constitute form of the concrete being of finite spirit. In the word thus generated, it is not something other than spirit which is produced; the activity of spirit is not transitive. It is spirit itself which is thus generated, in the concrete modalities of its presence. Spirit itself, consequently, in its concrete being and existence is word, is expression and symbol.

For this reason, spirit, in the historiographic act, addressing itself to the documents of its history or transpired life, finds itself confronted, not by an order of things, but of words. These residua of its departed life are not alien to it but are the transcended modes of its own being and existence. They are not objects of nature, projected into existence by some power before which spirit must remain alienated. They are forms of itself which it has left behind, in one sense, but which, in another, are instinct with its own life. The whole order of these residua is to be referred, not outward to some alien principle, but inward, back upon spirit itself. Philology, as the science of the 'certum', is clearly not a science of objects; it is a science of spirit itself under its expressive character. The crudest violation of these *residua* is to consider them as objects of nature. The first step toward the total self-recognition of spirit is its recognition of these documents as its own words.

Thus the conversion of the 'certum' with the 'factum' is completed in the perception of the 'factum' as the symbol and the word of spirit, instinct with its presence. To these words spirit can never be external nor alien save as it becomes external and alien to itself. It cannot become alien to them because they are itself. As it recognizes them at all, it recognizes them as integral to its own being. As it fails to recognize them, it becomes absent from itself, passes into non-being, and is annihilated in one whole dimension of itself. Philology, consequently, even in its most material sense, as the gathering of these dry bones of spirit's past, is essentially the inchoate science of spirit or of humanity. Its most rudimentary task ministers directly to the actuality of spirit because it restores to the presence of spirit, though in a rude and yet unexpressive manner, a dimension of that presence itself.

Since the 'facta' of spirit, the documents of history to which philology addresses itself, are the word of spirit, expressive and symbolic, it must be asked of what are they the expression, the symbol? In a sense, this question has already been answered. The word of spirit, in the first instance, expresses spirit itself. Even more, it constitutes spirit, so that outside of that word spirit is not. The initial act of spirit and the act which constitutes it in being and existence is the word by which it speaks itself to itself. The fundamental being and actuality of spirit is its *dirsi a se stesso* in the words of a modern writer.[1] But this *dirsi a se stesso*, Vico perceives, is not an abstract word. Spirit is not present to itself as mere *posse*; such presence, it has been noted, is indistinguishable from absence. Spirit is present to itself in terms of the concrete factors which determined the immediate and concrete form of the word. Every word that spirit utters, so to say, every concrete form of historical social consciousness which it evokes and projects, expresses spirit seeking to define itself consonantly with the whole range of limiting and shaping factors of its life both internal and external. Its every word, consequently, is a highly complex symbol or sign, of which Vico clearly distinguishes the two basic dimensions, in the dictum: 'the order of ideas follows the order of (human) things'.[2] The basic significance of this 'axiom' of the 'New Science' is that every word of spirit, every document of history, is symbolic both of the inward and constitutive modality of the presence of spirit to itself and of the external order of 'events' through which history transpires. That word expresses spirit as it defines its being and reality under specific conditions. Concretely, a document of the law, for instance, or the vestigial form of a political institution, is the expression of spirit defining and establishing itself in the presence of certain factors, external

[1] Guido Calogero, *Logica*, Einaudi, 1948.   [2] SNS, 238.

and natural, as well as interior and spiritual. From that document, consequently, correctly read or interpreted may be gathered an episode at once of the history of human events and of the inward history of spirit itself; of ideas and of things, in Vico's words. By the penetration of those documents, spirit narrates to itself its total history; if the penetration be deep enough, it narrates even that ideal and eternal history which is its highest and its most profound life.[1]

 The sense in which a science of humanity, in one dimension, must be identical with philology is thus made clear. If the end of that science be, as Vico asserts, the total presence of man to himself, not in abstract idea, as in the naturalistic definition, but in the eternal and ideal principles which govern the appearance of the time-forms of his concrete historical existence, philology is the indispensable basis of such presence. Philology restores to the presence of the human spirit the symbolic basis of its transpired life, that is, its documents. These straitly define the form of the life of the spirit, even as it seeks to define its total presence to itself. For the total presence of spirit which will be actual and genuine, and not illusory, will be the life actually traversed through the expressive moments represented in those documents. It is according to these, and according to these alone, that spirit can define itself to itself. Its history is the basis of its total presence to itself even in idea.

If, consequently, by contrast to philology, philosophy be conceived as the act of spirit by which it renders itself totally present to itself in idea, spirit speaking, as it were, its absolute and final word, its true *logos*, it appears readily in what sense philosophy and philology are one. They are one, because the idea of humanity which philosophy may speak is confined within and arises from the documents which philology provides and cannot fall outside those documents. These documents, consequently, and not that sense experience with which naturalistic theory seeks to circumscribe the movement of mind represent that periphery of 'experience' within which the life of spirit moves. Philosophy, in the sense in which it may minister to a science of humanity, and by this fact, establish the presence of humanity to itself in its idea, arises within philology as an ulterior movement of the human spirit to render itself present to itself in terms of the documents of philology, or, in a word, to read those documents. Philosophy, in this sense, is the act whereby spirit reads the documents of its own history to draw thence that idea of itself in which its total presence and its actuality must consist.

[1] SNS, 393.

This is not, however, a relation of simple identity. Philosophy arises within philology, but it is not for that reason reducible to philosophy. It is not, in a word, an imitative act whereby the life which spirit has traversed in the forms represented by the documents is simply repeated, like a lesson learned by rote. Philosophy arises within the matrix of philology in response to a distinctive exigency of the spirit, the exigency, as has been suggested, of rendering itself present to itself totally and in idea. The totality and the idea here indicated are not inertly equivalent to the sum of the documents; they represent rather the significance of those documents and of the order of those documents, the relation, that is, of the limited and specific words of spirit to its final and definitive word or idea. The task of philosophy is to discover and to formulate the law according to which the specific, concrete, and limited words of the documents of history are related to the total idea of man, the law, consequently, which would establish the supreme interpretative canon of the documents of human history. Read in isolation, the documents of history can generate but fragmentary and chaotic pictures of the human spirit. Before the documents can be made to yield the idea, the law or rule of the specific to the total must be discovered and formulated.

In substance, this is precisely what Vico has attempted in the principles which he has advanced on the 'metaphysical' plane, and which we have considered one by one. The concepts of the modifications of the human mind, of providence, of the time-structure of the nations and of universal history, of 'ricorso', these are, in their ultimate character, as they are operative within the structure of a science of humanity, rules for the interpretation of the documents of history. They define the manner and the order in which those documents must be read. In their most intimate character they are, not metaphysical, but methodological. They enter into the constitution of the final presence of the human spirit to itself not as transcendent, *a priori* structures, but as immanent and dynamic rules of its life and above all of the act by which the total presence to itself is generated. In this way again, the unity of philosophy and philology within the science of humanity is established and illuminated. Vico is not, as some would suggest, seeking to replace abstract metaphysical cosmology by an equally abstract metaphysical psychology or philosophy of spirit or mind. He is seeking to establish the concrete laws of spirit in history, in this special context of its supreme act the constitution of itself, concretely, according to its idea or total presence. The entire metaphysical or ideal dimension, as Vico calls it somewhat indifferently, of the 'New Science' is an attempt to carry out the programme of philosophy within the concept of a science of humanity, that is, to discover the laws by which the universal significance for spirit of the documents of its historical life might be determined.

Nevertheless, this task of philosophy may be conceived in a more abstract manner and Vico does, as a matter of fact, consider it in this way. It appears, in this guise, as the establishment of the law of the conversion of the 'factum' with the 'verum'; or, more concretely, of the manner in which the isolated documents of history may be read not merely with reference to the immediate conditions which they reflect, but also with reference to that ultimate term of historical movement, the idea or the total presence of spirit to itself. Read in this first manner, that is, in terms of the conditions which they immediately reflect and express, the documents of history lead to what is generally called historical relativism; but this, from Vico's point of view, can be only the absence, the partial absence at least, of spirit from itself. Historical relativism may be identified, from a spiritualistic point of view, as the notion that the documents of spirit, its historical words, can be read only in terms of the immediate conditions they reflect. This restriction is wholly against the spirit of the 'New Science'. The avowed purpose of the 'New Science' is to read out of those documents the ideal and eternal principles of historical process and not merely the character of its isolated and positive moments. The conversion of the 'factum' with the 'verum' is, consequently, its most important interpretative canon.

This conversion is established, in the first instance, on the principle of common sense. Common sense is the first rule of the conversion of the 'factum' and the 'verum', or, more concretely, the first rule of arriving at the ideal and universal significance of the isolated symbols or documents of history. The form of the rule of common sense is, for Vico, regularity or uniformity; the human mind delights, he remarks, in the uniform.[1] The actual operation of this principle follows closely the pattern of Roman jurisprudence in the establishment, in the first place, of the 'jus gentium' and, in the second, of the natural law. This is the method which Donati [2] has called exclusion, and which might with greater clarity be called the method of residue. For Roman jurisprudence, the 'jus gentium', was established by

[1] SNS, 204.
[2] Benvenuto Donati, *Nuovi Studi sulla Filosofia Civile di G. B. Vico*, Firenze, Le Monnier, 1936, pp. 105 et seq.

155

the exclusion of the proper or peculiar laws of communities; the residue of this process of exclusion, in its positive character, was the 'jus gentium'. Similarly, the law of nature was established by exclusion and residue from the 'jus gentium'. This procedure is also the background for the phrase peculiar to himself by which Vico ordinarily designates the natural law—'giure naturale delle nazioni'. The operation of common sense, in the Vichian scheme, is precisely analogous to this operation by exclusion and residue; but he assigns to the residual factor an ideal, and not merely a positive, value. The 'verum' appears in this first instance as the common significance of the 'facta' conceived in their character as the word. Whatever, amid the diversity and variety of the special and immediate circumstances reflected in the documents, is found to be common is to be ascribed to the 'common sense' of mankind and has this ideal and universal character and value. The three 'first principles' of the 'New Science' are established primarily in this way and illustrate concretely the conversion of the 'factum' and the 'verum' as effected by the principle of common sense; these principles are religion, marriage, burial. These, Vico asserts, will be found to be the most fundamental uniformities of human society and constitute its essential ligature.[1] On the basis of this uniform character these principles are assigned an ideal value. And he is at pains to refute the evidence adduced in his day of 'atheistic' peoples discovered in far places of the globe. Providence, he declares, leads the gentile nations to civility by a common wisdom, which is summed up in these fundamental principles, and which may be established philologically by address to the uniformities of the documents, which uniformities consist always in the exclusive residue of their intention or significance. In this way the conversion of 'factum' and 'verum' is established in the sense that the documents, the 'facta', are now read, not in the limited terms of the immediate situation, needs, conditions which they reflect, but in universal and ideal terms, which have the element of necessity required by the most rigorous science.

The conversion of 'factum' and 'verum' as established by common sense is a limited conversion. It establishes merely the material or contentual universality of the symbols or the documents and of the principles derived from them; or, to put it in terms closer to Vico's own distinctions, the principle of common sense establishes merely 'coscienza' and not 'scienza' of those uniformities and of the 'verum', or the universal and ideal significance and term of human

[1] SNS, 330 et seq.

historical process. These uniformities appear, on the principle of common sense, as mere positivities or as mere generalizations and reveal nothing of the ideal principle which links them to the isolated and particular documents. The human spirit, confronting itself in these uniformities, discerns its universality but not its ideality. There is needed a principle which will establish the convertibility of the 'factum' and the 'verum' in the more radical sense that every document, even in its particularity and isolation, reveals directly, and not merely by the residual indirection of common sense, its ideal and universal dimension, its own character as a vehicle of the 'verum' of human nature.

This second and more radical principle for the conversion of the 'factum' and the 'verum' is to be found within the Vichian doctrine of the modifications of the human mind. Specifically, it is to be found in his conception of the reflective process which constitutes the second of these moments or modifications, that is to say, in the Vichian concept of thought itself. This concept of reflection may profitably be contrasted with the notion of common sense which has effected the first conversion of these terms. Common sense, Vico writes, is judgment without reflection, shared by an entire class, nation, people, or the human race.[1] He is speaking, it is clear, of common sense in its hidden and operative character as determining, without prescience, the uniformities of human civility. It is equally clear, however, that the determination of the uniformities established by common sense in its operation is itself a work of reflection. In this sense, common sense may also be viewed as a dimension of reflection, and the first operation of reflection itself is seen to be that generalizing activity of which the uniformities of common sense are the product. Yet this operation cannot, within the Vichian context, exhaust the activity of reflection; on the contrary, it cannot constitute its most characteristic transaction. For this generalizing power or operation takes account, as it were, only of a superficial character of the relationship between the two great moments of the modifications of the human mind, spontaneity and reflection; it adverts only to the continuity which Vico discerns between them; it does not advert to the deeper contradiction which they exhibit. As a result, the generalizing process of reflection yields not the idea, but the universalized image and achieves, therefore, as has been suggested, a merely material universality or uniformity.

The second, more characteristic and constitutive operation of

[1] SNS, 142.

reflection is predicated, by contrast, upon the contradiction which must necessarily exist between the modifications of the human mind and, consequently, between their respective products, the image and the idea. That spontaneity and its expressions must inevitably stand in contradiction, as well as in continuity, to reflection, the image to the idea, impulse to will, has emerged clearly from the consideration of the general doctrine of the modifications of the human mind. This contradiction, it has been seen, derived from the definition of man as a finite principle which tends to the infinite, and image and idea, impulse and will, stand within the human spirit as finite to infinite. The 'facta', the documents of history, share this character. Where they are the expressive symbols of spontaneity they stand in inevitable contradiction to the 'verum' which the 'New Science' would educe from them; where, on the other hand, they are the expressions of reflection itself, access to them by reflection would be immediate and free of contradiction. To illustrate this concretely, where a political constitution is a reflective document, establishing government on reflective and ideal principles, the penetration of that constitution by reflective principles should offer no difficulties. The difficulties arise, on the contrary, with the discovery that every such purportedly reflective document contains residual and perhaps inevitable spontaneous elements; the resolution of these present the obstacles to interpretation of the document. This difficulty is multiplied a thousandfold when the document is without reflective character but represents the direct expression of a spontaneous response to historical needs and conditions. In this case, the immediate form of the document must appear in direct contradiction to its latent ideality and wholly identical with those immediate conditions which it reflects. The operation of reflection here is called upon clearly to resolve this contradiction, as the price of the conversion of the 'factum' with the 'verum' and, consequently, of that presence of spirit to itself in its idea which is the term of the historiographical movement.

Reflection recovers the 'verum' from the 'factum', as the 'factum' itself was recovered from the 'certum' by an act of the self-recognition of the human spirit; it is in this self-recognition, precisely, that reflection consists. This act of self-recognition by the human spirit is not simple and intuitive or inspective like the generalizing operation mentioned earlier. It is complex because it embraces the contradictory terms of image and idea, of 'factum' and 'verum' in one act, which transcends them even as it affirms them. The spirit, in the first place, recognizes itself in the image, in the 'factum', as both present and absent to itself. The conditions reflected or expressed in that 'factum', that image or limited word, certainly define its presence to itself according to specific factors; but, as clearly, they alienate spirit from itself, because the factors which condition that expression cannot conceivably exhaust its presence to itself. That it cannot so exhaust the presence of spirit follows directly from spirit's discernment of presence and absence in the 'factum' or the image. If spirit saw there only presence, it would conceivably identify presence wholly with the positivity of that 'factum'. Such an identification is impossible, however, because the very act by which spirit has recognized its presence in that 'factum' has already placed it as a distance, as absent to that document. The 'factum' is transcendent in the very act in which it is taken up into spirit by the act of self-recognition. By the same act, also, a new mode of presence is generated by spirit, the mode of presence which is, in principle, the idea. This new mode of presence arises, in its turn, directly from the discernment of absence and presence in the 'factum'; it is a presence which affirms the 'factum' at the same instant and in the same act by which it denies it. The 'factum' is affirmed as a positive moment and denied as the definitive form of presence. Even more, the act of reflection establishes that the 'factum' in its positive and limited character is the vehicle not only of presence, but also of that absence which is the first shadow of the idea. The idea arises, through reflection, as an absence, an 'otherness' of spirit from its presence to itself in the expressive form of the 'factum'. The idea does not arise as an alternate positive moment, but as an absence, to be converted in its turn into positive presence by a positive act of spirit. To illustrate by an idea much cherished by Vico and which is the culmination of his own political theory, the natural equality of men, the foundation of civil government, arises historically in the first instance as a mode of absence. In the historical circumstances to which he himself refers, the revolt of the 'gentes minores' against the 'gentes majores' transpired in the name of this idea discerned as an absence, the denial of the privilege of 'connubium' to the 'gentes minores'; the idea of their humanity presented itself to the 'gentes minores' in the first instance as the absence of this privilege, in the second, as presence, as its extension. The act by which the 'gentes minores' were brought to the point of violent revolt must be considered an act of reflection, however rudimentary, which is typical of the transaction of reflection in all its reaches.[1] It is thus that the act of reflection is seen in turn

[1] SNS, 1006 et seq.

to illustrate and to incorporate the historical structure of man's being. Ideas are not born by an abstract act of intuition, full-grown, as it were, from the head of Jove, but by this laborious process of historical reflection. Thought itself, human thought, has its history, which when conceived clearly is the history of the recovery of its own idea, or better the generation of its own idea, by reflection, by presence and absence, from the documents of its own past.

This conception of reflection, while it is clearly diverse from the type of reflection seen operative in the recovery of the principles of common sense, still is not in contradiction to that operation. It arises rather most readily within the area of the principles of common sense, and for this reason Vico considers both dimensions of reflection as essential to the 'arte critica' of the 'New Science'. But this fact should not obscure the more important consideration that the second characterization of reflection derives from the more profound character of his own teaching, that is, from the notion of man as *finitum quod tendit ad infinitum* and reflects directly the insight into the historical structure of human nature itself. The act of reflection in its second character is readily recognized to be the genuine dynamic principle of historical movement; it identifies the specific act by which the human spirit recovers its past, converts the 'factum' and the 'verum', and constructs, laboriously enough, that total presence toward which, Vico believes, history moves.

By this same token, the concept of reflection as self-recognition of spirit by presence and absence completes the justification of the circularity of philosophy and philology. This justification is established by the conversion of the 'factum' and the 'verum', which identifies both moments of the 'arte critica' of the 'New Science' in their diversity and in their unity. Philology, taken in distinction from philosophy, addresses itself to the positive character of the 'certum'. It can, however, maintain itself only precariously for it is open to the risk of assuming the 'certum' to be mere nature. It is rescued from this danger by the discovery of the 'certum' as 'factum', as the word, as spirit. This act of recognition is already an act of reflection and therefore advances spirit to the philosophical level. Philosophy, in its own positive character and as abstractly opposed to philology, is precisely that act of reflection, by presence and absence, of which the idea is born. Its abstraction from the process of philology, however, is clearly arbitrary. It is rather to be conceived as the clarification and continuation of the same movement of self-recognition initiated by spirit in philology. Philosophy cannot, for Vico, transpire outside of philology, no more than philology, without the inception within it of the movement of philosophy, can advance one step toward its term. Their circularity is complete even though, in the expository scheme of the 'New Science', they may appear as successive, philosophy preceding philology in the determination of the elements, the principles and the method. The full importance of the concept of the circularity of philosophy and philology appears only when it is recognized that its first, methodological reference leads inevitably to its further ontological reference. The method of the 'New Science' reflects faithfully the ontological structure of the human spirit itself, the method of history the historical structure of human social reality. It is not only philology and philosophy but the 'New Science', or the science of humanity as historiography, and humanity itself, as historical or time-ideal process, which are demonstrated to be circular.

There is, however, a further quality or character of the 'certum' which must be brought into the movement of its final conversion with the 'verum' before the Vichian notion of the unity of philosophy and philology may be understood completely. For Vico speaks, in an axiom which is, perhaps, the most fundamental of all those adduced in the book of the elements, of philology as 'observing the authority of human choice'.[1] In this phrase, since he has already identified philology as the science of the 'certum', Vico draws into relief the character of the 'certum' as the creation and the sign of the human *arbitrium*. This quality may be most clearly recognized in the primary instance, the 'certum' of the law; for every positive law, toward the interpretation of which the jurisprudential process is directed, represents, as Vico indicates in his characterization of Roman jurisprudence, a decision, according to the divisions of the times, concerning human utility and necessity.[2] It is, indeed, in its character as decision, as an act of the 'arbitrium', that the 'certum' appears most clearly as the 'given', as imposed. The question necessarily arises whether the 'certum' in this quality or character can be drawn into the circle of the unity of philosophy and philology by the same ideal process by which the 'certum' as word, symbol, or sign had been.

Vico, as the elaboration of the axiom cited above clearly indicates, asserts this possibility, and on grounds which he had already indicated, and again with reference to the 'certum' in its primary context, the law. For he has pointed out, in distinguishing the levels of the 'certum' of the law, that the reality or actuality of the law cannot

[1] SNS, 138.   [2] SNP, pp. 14 et seq.

be identified unambiguously with its positivity, either as the will or the intention of the legislator. Before jurisprudence the law appears as the vehicle of an ideality, and ideal discernment, which while immanent to the 'certum' as an act of decision, of the will, and indeed the informing principle of that decision, nevertheless cannot be reduced without residue to the immediate character of that act. This is the 'ratio' of the law, and it is to the 'ratio', in the last analysis, that jurisprudence addresses itself as to the only dimension of the positive law which makes its interpretation and its translation into the theatre of judgment viable. This 'ratio' of the law is never for Vico reducible to the intention of the law; it must transcend that intention, and even, on occasion, stand in contradiction to it, as he is prepared to assert that the whole movement of history, of the civil life of man transcends and stands in contradiction to the intentions and the decisions of the immediate agents of history.[1] As a consequence, he sees the 'certum' as decision essentially as the vehicle of an ideality; an ideality, it is true, which is not or may not be wholly its own but which is, nevertheless, immanent to it. No opposition arises in Vico's thought between the character of the 'certum' as decision and its character as word and sign. Indeed, the unity of these dimensions of the 'certum' is already indicated in its conversion with the 'factum'; for the human act is always decision informed by ideality, ideality of a degree to be sure, but never absent wholly, so long as the act is genuinely the human act. The conversion of the 'certum' as decision with the 'verum' is effected, consequently, by way of the immanent ideality of which human decision is seen to be the vehicle. Vico's vindication of authority is effected wholly in the name of the idea. The validity and the self-imposing character of authority derive wholly from the fact that authority is the vehicle, and the necessary vehicle, of the historical ideality of the race and of society. The arbitrariness, the imposition and the sheer force of authority is dissolved in the same manner as the positivity of the law, that is, by revealing both as vehicles of the idea in its temporal process. Philology is the science of authority and the 'New Science', in its integral character, a philosophy of authority, as Vico asserts.[2] Both assertions are true wholly in conformity with and on the basis of the circularity of philosophy and philology. This circular movement transpires in an identical manner whether the point of departure be the 'certum' as decision or as word, because the unity of the word and the will in the human act is complete.

[1] SNS, 342.　　　　　　[2] SNS, 386.

The thesis concerning the circularity of philosophy and philology in the method of the 'New Science' also brings to full cycle the movement of Vico's thought. The *De Antiquissima Italorum Sapientia*, as we have already noted, is based on the thesis that the philosophical concepts of the antique Italic peoples might be reconstructed on the basis of the etymology of the Latin language. The attempt, in its immediate character, is a failure. In that treatise Vico imputes to those mythical Italics a metaphysics of 'Zenonic' points of his own fabrication. In its final import, however, the attempt of the *De Antiquissima* is no failure; it marks the first movement of Vico's thought toward its authentic problem and its authentic method. The fundamental insight of the treatise, the evocation of history by way of language, remains constant in Vico's thought. What is lacking in the *De Antiquissima* is any genuine perception as to the character of the linguistic process itself. Concretely, Vico exhibits in the method of the treatise the fallacy of supposition and of method which he later formulates as the 'boria dei dotti'; he conceives language wholly as a reflective process and thus violates the whole structure of historical movement in the same manner which later he condemns in Grotius and the other 'princes' of jurisprudence. The insight itself was sound; it needed only that penetration into the true character of language as the ultimate form of the time-ideal process of history to which Vico came, in his own words, only after twenty years of rude and unrelenting meditation. The fruit of this meditation was precisely the unity or circularity of philology and philosophy as it is sustained by the insights into the process of the human subject. The thesis of the circularity and unity of philosophy and philology may, therefore, be correctly considered as the final fulfilment of the insight of the *De Antiquissima Italorum Sapientia*. In a complementary manner, the whole of the 'New Science' may be thought of as the transcendence and, at the same time, the realization of the project of the *De Antiquissima* effected, not in the narrow theatre of an Italic culture of a shadowy antiquity, but in the universal theatre of humanity itself.

IX

POETRY, MYTH, AND LANGUAGE

POETRY, Vico writes, is the key to the 'New Science',[1] and his discovery of the true character of poetry is the discovery beyond all others on which he would rest the case for the originality of the new discipline. He assigns this paramount place to the theory of poetry because it was his sensitivity to the problems of poetics which afforded the first glimpse into the qualitative and dynamic structure of the primordial moment of the temporal-ideal process of history and thus effectively opened to him the positive programme of the 'New Science'. The theoretical considerations which he had traversed had made clear, in general outline, what that positive programme must be. The doctrine of the modifications of the human mind, with the ancillary notions of providence and 'ricorso', had established the intrinsic possibility of time-ideal process; this possibility derives from the structure of the human subject as finite principle which tends to the infinite. The doctrine of the unity, or circularity, of philosophy and philology had further established the most general and basic methodological principle of the science; the process of the subject has been demonstrated to be essentially symbolic and expressive. From these considerations the positive programme of the science emerges. It is the ideal repossession and assimilation by the human spirit of its past. More concretely, the 'New Science' must reconstruct, through the penetration of the documents, the total movement of history in its temporal-ideal stages. More concretely still, and in conformity with the basic methodological 'axiom' of the 'Elements'[2] that doctrines must take their beginning from that of the matter of which they treat, the 'New Science' must descend or return to the moment of inception of the temporal-ideal movement of history and thence take its departure in the work of reconstruction. Since the beginnings of the historical process lie in the depths of the spontaneous moment of the human spirit, it is this moment which must be restored to spirit in idea. The

[1] SNS, 34. [2] SNS, 314; DU, I, 7.

spirit is confronted by the documents of that time-moment, but only in their immediacy, their 'certitude'. In order to penetrate them truly it must possess in idea the reality of that spontaneity of which those documents are the expression and the historical substance. The positive programme of the 'New Science' is, in fact, the supreme 'ricorso' of the human spirit; it is the descent into the inferno of its own beginnings, thence to reascend, laden with the reality of its own past, to the light of its own idea. And to Vico this descent appeared as laborious and dolorous as the Dantean journey; the jungle, the 'ingens sylva' of the first moments of the human mind as horrendous as the 'selva selvaggia'. In this descent, the theory of poetry is his Virgil.

The heart of the Vichian conception of poetry, and his great discovery, is its 'necessity'.[1] This notion of the necessity of poetry is complex. It is developed against the notions, on the one hand, that the function of poetry is to delight and, on the other, that it is the work of the artifact of reflection. Both of these notions are present in that network of ideas concerning art and poetry which is loosely denominated neo-classicism and which, in a wide sense, forms the environment or climate of Vico's speculations on the poetic activity. The notion that the function of poetry is to delight or to beguile had been impeccably expressed by Horace as one member of his celebrated dictum: 'Aut prodesse aut delectare poetas.' The notion becomes associated in Vico's thought with the conviction, synthesized in another axiom of the elements, that men seek first the necessary, then the commodious, thirdly the useful, and only finally that which delights.[2] Projected against the historical movement of mankind or humanity, this would lead to the association of poetry, not with its primitive, inceptive and spontaneous moment, but with a temporally advanced and reflectively developed stage of its life. This association is in turn fortified by the general persuasion, from which Vico is not wholly free, that the poetic activity is susceptible of control by rule and law and that it is, therefore, a reflective operation based on that perception of universal principles which is the hallmark of reflection and reason. The one notion and the other, moreover, are plausibly radicated in the general theory of art, and indeed, of the whole theoretic life of the human spirit as the 'imitation of nature'. For that imitation implies both a reflective posture of the spirit

[1] DU, II, 313, 379; SNP, pp. 147 et seq.; SNS, 181, 186, 213, 236, 374 et seq., 412.
[2] SNS, 241.

toward nature and ultimately an otiose of 'aesthetic' and contemplative attitude, as Plato had long since suggested. In sum, the whole tendency of this complex of ideas is to assign art to the periphery of the life of spirit.[1]

Against this tendency Vico adduces two circumstances or, as he would say, a philological and philosophical proof. The first is the philological argument that the earliest documents are almost without exception poetic, at least in external structure; the earliest legislative documents, for example, and the earliest records of cosmological and anthropological speculation are in verse.[2] This phenomenon can be explained within the complex of ideas which we have called neo-classic only on the assumption of a sophistication in early man sufficient to make a radical distinction between the content and the form of the document. Further, this philological circumstance imposes the problem, ultimately insoluble in Vico's view, of determining why the poetic form should have been chosen to express a content in itself reflective. There appears between the content and the form of the document a purely external relation for which some practicalistic explanation, such as the didactic or hedonic relation suggested by the Horatian dictum, must be advanced. Such a sophistication as must here be assumed is untenable on the philosophical grounds which Vico has established, namely, the constitutive time-structure of the human subject and its intimately symbolic character. These philosophical conceptions suggest, if they do not dictate, a contrary view, the intimate unity, indeed the complete identity, between the time-form moment of spirit and its expressive vehicle.

On this view, consequently, it must be concluded that the philological circumstance noted finds its true explanation in an intimate 'necessity' of the human subject of history. Early documents are poetic in form, even in the most external sense of the term, because the consciousness of early man was itself intimately and constitutively poetic. Poetry, consequently, becomes the defining term of the inner quality of that first time-form moment which he has to this point characterized as spontaneous and which he has further analysed into the sense-phantasy complex.[3] And poetic becomes the adjective by which he designates and describes the whole pre-reflective life of man, comprising both its gnoseological and its volitive movements,

[1] SNP, p. 147.
[2] DU, II, 380; SNP, pp. 147, 169; SNS, 7, 199, 412.
[3] Franco Amerio, *Introduzione allo Studio di G. B. Vico*, p. 171.

and becomes, most properly of all, the designation of that wisdom which is the concrete synthesis and expression of that pre-reflective life. The forms of poetry are not the external encasement of the movements of unreflective life; they are its genuine incorporation and articulation and spring with complete necessity from the internal character of the movement of spontaneous consciousness.

For this same reason, it is impossible to consider seriously any 'external', transitive end, as the purpose or function of poetry, such as the Horatian dictum suggests. These may indeed be the case in decadent and sophisticated epochs, when the practice of poetry has become an exercise of reflection. In its initial form, the whole function of poetry can be only the expression of the pre-reflective or spontaneous consciousness of man; nor can there be any but a reflective and formal distinction between expression and state of consciousness; expression is the state of consciousness in its concrete actuality. The characteristics of poetry must themselves, consequently, derive from and perfectly reflect the inner structure of the spontaneous consciousness.

If such is the case, Vico has discovered the royal road, so to say, by which the consciousness of primitive man may be penetrated and the principle by which the positive programme of the 'New Science' may be set in motion. The documents of early history must be read, not as skilfully contrived expressions of ideas which are essentially in contrast with the structure of the expressive media, but as direct records. Further, it is a mistake, at the philological level, to identify those first documents of the poetic consciousness with the linguistic structures of poetry, with written verse-records. The latter clearly have undergone the transforming action of reflection. It is necessary to discover the cellular form, so to say, of poetic consciousness; the minimal whole, that is, in which that consciousness is expressed. This Vico discovers in the myth.[1] Poetry in its essence, the poetic consciousness in its constitutive gnoseological or theoretical activity, is the making of the myth. Mythopoeia is the pure form of the poetic consciousness. It is the myth which the poetic activity initially generates and it is the myth which later becomes the argument of the more reflective and self-conscious modes of poetic expression. The spontaneous consciousness is essentially mythical in structure in that it realizes itself and indeed exhausts itself in the creation of the myth. The Vichian poetics, as it provides the instrument for the penetration of the spontaneous consciousness and for the inception

[1] SNP, p. 146; SNS, 186.

of the positive programme of the 'New Science' is a theory of myth.

The essential note of the Vichian conception of myth is its verediciousness, its truth-bearing power.[1] This character of the myth is thrown into greater relief by the rationalistic tendency to establish a linkage between myth and illusion, myth and error, even myth and delusion. For Vico the myth is wholly a vehicle of truth, a veredicious structure of consciousness. Indeed, to the degree to which he tends to oppose spontaneity and reflection it may even be said that he would assign the higher truth value to the symbolic products of spontaneous consciousness. It is necessary, however, to avoid any exaggeration of this tendency in Vico. The Vichian cult of the spontaneous, unlike its romantic counterpart, is strictly limited by a radical attachment to reason and reflection which assigns an ultimately transcendent truth-value to the idea. The point which Vico seeks to establish above all is a movement in degree of verediciousness between spontaneity and reflection limited only by the inevitable contradiction which must exist between all finite symbols and the infinite truth toward which the human consciousness tends.

The truth-value of the myth in Vico's theory derives from its participation in the classical, Platonic quality, universality.[2] The absolute, the universal is the presupposition, and not merely the product, of human inquiry and thought. It is the presence of the universal, however dimly perceived, which releases the movement of human consciousness and imparts its fundamental direction. At the same time, he rejects the notion, imposed on his attention by the dominant Cartesianism of his environment, that the universal in question must be a *primum verum*, a first truth immediately intuited from which successive truths of narrower extension may be reached by a concatenation of dependent intuitions. With this fallacy of the *primum verum* there is associated in his thought the hyper-evaluation of the clear and distinct idea and the correlative devaluation of the 'lower' forms of awareness, the image or the phantasm. In Vico's view, the universality of the intuited first truth must prove an immobilizing factor in human awareness; it can yield at best, to his mind, that paradoxical world of mathematical construction in which the 'verum-factum' relation is ostensibly realized but actually negated.[3] In opposition both to Cartesianism and to Platonism, which have in common this attempt to make the intuited universal the point of departure of human thought and share a common

[1] SNP, p. 146; SNS, 401.   [2] SNS, 209, 403.   [3] DIS, p. 138.

168

apprehensiveness toward the 'lower' forms of human awareness, the senses and the imagination, Vico establishes the universal as the implicit term of the historical movement of human consciousness through its time-moments. The universal is not the point of departure, but the point of arrival of human awareness, the term toward which the human mind, however obscurely, and with however many cross-movements and retrogressions advances through all its phases, moments, and modifications. The human mind, he states in a basic axiom of the 'elements',[1] first senses without advertence, adverts then with passion and commotion, and finally reflects with clarity and serenity. Advertence here is the symbol of universality. In this manner he would avert the fallacy alike of Cartesianism and Platonism, which tend to evoke a radical dualism, in psycho-gnoseological terms, between the spontaneous and the reflective moments of human awareness, and, in historical terms, between the primitive and civil moments of history—a fallacy which both seek to rectify by the introjection of a spurious spontaneity 'intellectual intuition'. Instead, Vico would restore the unity and integrity alike of the psycho-gnoseological and the historical processes of human consciousness by insisting that the unifying and integrating principle is a movement toward universality at the gnoseological level, the idea.

It is within the framework of the terminal theory of universality that the verediciousness character of the Vichian myth becomes intelligible. The myth is a vehicle of truth because it is an elementary form of universality, the form in which the human mind expresses its first, limited advertence of the universal and absolute idea which is its term.[2]

The relationship in which the universality and the truth-character of the myth stand to its spontaneity is complex. Under one aspect, an aspect upon which Vico lays considerable stress, the truth-value of the myth is fortified by its spontaneous origin. Where there is but a simple and direct movement of consciousness, uncomplicated by any counter-movement of reflection, the springs of error are closed. However strait the limits of awareness in the myth, this awareness, within those limits, must have the positive character of truth since the myth can never be nor signify other than that which it is and which it signifies. At the same time, however, and in contrast to the plentitude of the truth of the idea, the limits of the truth of the myth become so pronounced as to take on the semblance of a form of error.[3]

[1] SNS, 218. [2] SNS, 205, 209, 401–3. [3] SNS, 205.

To say that the formal principle of truth, universality, is constant in the myth and the idea, in spontaneity and in reflection, is not, however, to take the further step of asserting that myth is but a rudimentary form of the idea. There is in Vico's theory of myth none of those elements of the Leibnizian 'petites perceptions', or of any similar doctrine in which the attempt has been made to establish a continuum of degrees between the rudimentary and the explicated forms of consciousness. The universality of the myth and the universality of the idea, in Vico's thought, stand in a complex and counterpuntal relation. The key to this relationship is again to be sought in the essential structure of human consciousness according to Vico: its finitude, its orientation to the infinite, and the contradiction which attends this character. The distance which separates myth from idea is the same that separates finite and infinite; they are incommensurate and exhibit a radical contradiction. Therefore, under this aspect, myth and idea are essentially autonomous; neither may be reductively equated with the other. Myth is not mere rudimentary idea; idea is not merely explicated, 'rationalized' myth. They are two distinct attitudes of the human consciousness toward truth, toward the idea. The presence of the one, in the human subject, is the absence of the other; presence and absence to be understood, of course, in terms of a specific content. The emergence of the idea in a like material necessarily involves the eclipse of myth. The persistence of myth, with equal necessity, aborts the idea. Nevertheless, they are linked within the structure of human consciousness by the closest affinity, an affinity which is complex and which in no wise minimizes the contradiction, the distinction, the distance which exists between them. In the first place, myth is the seed-bed of idea; ideas arise only through the corrosion and the decay of myth under the action of reflection and criticism. The dissolution of myth, in one sense at least, is the whole office and actuality of criticism. Ideas are not born full grown from a spontaneous, transcendent insight; they are hammered out, to change the metaphor, between the anvil of the implicit universality of all truth and the sledge of criticism which seeks to disengage that universality from the limits of the myth. At the same time, the corrosive force of criticism and reflection, far from destroying the myth, actually releases its innermost reality, the universal idea, which is, in a sense, imprisoned within it. As it contradicts and destroys the myth in its limits and restrictions, criticism releases and realizes myth in its human essence. Myth and idea stand in a relationship of tension and dialectic, which is the most intimate and self-generative process of the human subject.[1]

An example of this process which Vico develops with considerable force and profound conviction is the concept of freedom. Unlike the doctrinaire libertarianism of the illumination which was to overrun Europe within a generation of his death, Vico saw liberty, the idea of liberty, as the slowly won prize of the unceasing criticism of all myths of political and social power, of all attempts, that is, to fix social and political power in certain forms, in certain areas of incidence, upon phantastic and uncritical bases and, on the same grounds, to identify it with certain limited aspects of its full character. At the same time, he discovers in the core of those myths the seed of the idea of freedom itself. The seed of liberty is law. Law, in its mythical form, is always power and, in the rudest instances, naked power. It is not, however, in the abolition of power that the idea of liberty is born or its actuality realized. Rather it is in the release of the idea of power and law from the limits imposed upon it by the myth. The act of power by which the first law was imposed was indeed the first liberation of man. It rescued him, above all, from that spurious freedom with which libertarianism would endow him, and endows him instead with the first actuality of liberty, freedom under law. As restricted within the hard crust of the myths of power, this liberty becomes readily identical with bondage. It is released by the critical activity which discovers the universality of that idea within the limits that the myth would impose upon it. To revert to Vico's own example: the harsh law of the aristocratic proto-states was genuine liberty; it was cruelly limited, and the idea of liberty aborted, by its mythical imprisonment within the aristocratic structure based upon the 'eternal enmity' which the patricians, as Aristotle observes, swore against the plebs. It was released by the critical action which discovered the true basis of law to be, not that mythical divine nature of the aristocratic order, but the common human nature of all men; and which compelled, by the laborious decrees and stages which history records, the extension of law, the vehicle of true freedom, to all men in virtue of this common nature. In this latter form the notion of liberty as life under law approached the form of the idea. In this form it is the negation of the myth of aristocratic power. Yet that myth is not unconditionally condemned as false. It is rather discerned to be the idea, standing in a certain contradictory relationship to itself.

[1] DU, II, 373; SNS, 185.

The economy of the mythical or poetic order of consciousness is summarized in a rubric of the 'New Science': the first nations thought in heroic (poetic) characters, spoke in fables, wrote in hieroglyphics.[1] The concept of the heroic or poetic character reveals the structure and the dynamics of the first, constitutive act of human consciousness and of the world which it invokes and in which it dwells; it establishes, as it were, the ontology of that world. The notion of speech in fable establishes the significative operation of the world evoked or created in the poetic character, first in its internal, mental, or expressive dimension, then in its communicative function. The hieroglyphic origin of scripture, finally, establishes the economic structure of the world of communication. Upon this basis, in turn, are erected the canons of mythology which constitute the first methodological principles of the 'New Science'. The force which establishes this economy in its unity is the concept of the 'necessary' and creative character of poetry; for this reason, Vico speaks of this economy as poetic wisdom, the synthesis of human life in all its dimensions by the poetic principle.

The inceptive universality of the myth and of the poetic act, which has been shown to be the basis of its truth-value, furnishes the clue to the heroic character. For the heroic or poetic character, in its essence, is the first attempt of the human mind to evoke the world of idea; that is, to render present to itself the totality, the universality of its own being. The normative conception of the idea, of total presence, which Vico employs (not without the introduction, it must be remarked, of some ambiguity or 'obscurity' into the general line of his thought) is the general class-concept of classical logic.[2] The ambiguity arises from the fact that this is not, in fact, the notion of the concept of reflection, of the idea, or of total presence implied in his general theory of the modifications of the human mind. But the function of this class-concept is to serve as foil for the notion of the poetic character and it stands, therefore, only in a dialectical relation to the latter. Vico is not committed, by its normative and dialectical employment, to the theoretical acceptance of the class-concept as the form of the reflective moment of consciousness. The heroic or poetic character does not, as a matter of fact, foreshadow the universality attributed to the class-concept by classical logic; it adumbrates rather the quality of universality which characterizes the total presence of the subject. The normative employment of the class-concept serves to throw into relief the basic

[1] SNS, 429. [2] SNS, 209.

direction of the poetic character in a manner oblique. It is the inability of the primitive mind, the human mind in its first time-form moment, to abstract the class-universal which drives it to the formation of the mode of universality proper to it, the universality, that is, of the poetic character. Incapable of reflection, it creates or evokes the universal of the imagination, the phantastic universal.

In the formation of this universal of phantasy, the imagination follows, not the laws of reflection, but its own native dynamics. And as its power is limited wholly to the order of the immediate, the particular and the concrete, its universal is before all else an image, concrete and particular, displaying all the limits of the image and moving within these limits. The image (as we have already noted) is not, for Vico, the passive reflection of an alien form imposed by the senses; the passive moment of 'pure' sensation, which is the presupposition of this conception of the image, is wholly lacking in the life of the human spirit as he conceives it. The image is rather the imposition by the mind or spirit of its own form, as this is present in the first time-form of its consciousness, upon the object to which the senses direct its attention.[1] The image is, therefore, an image, not of an alien object, of an external world, but of the spirit itself. It is, consequently, a mode of the presence of spirit to itself. It signifies, when it shall prove the moment to speak of its significance, the human spirit itself. Whatever universality this image may possess, consequently, must be the universality proper to, or characteristic of, the internal structure of the presence of spirit and not the universality which might characterize its moment of alienation. This quality of the image is exhibited by all the examples of the poetic character adduced by Vico; it is especially evident and cogent, perhaps, in the supreme heroic figure, that of Jove. Jove is, by Vico's account, the heroic character of the universe of the heavens conceived as a vast animate and sensate body, incorporating a principle of consciousness, and speaking to man; or again, in a more developed social context, he is the heroic character of the auspices by which the first founders of the nations ruled the body politic. In either instance, it is immediately evident that the reference of the image is to the human spirit itself, according to the conditions of its initial time-form. Jove as the animate principle of the heavens is the investment of nature with the sensate form of human consciousness; the Jove of the auspices reflects the first moment of human political authority, namely, that it draws jurisdictional sanction from the

[1] SNS, 374-9, 401-2.

name of the divine.[1] What is, therefore, the quality of universality which may inform the structure of presence of spirit?

It is the universality, to revert to a term already employed, of contemporaneity; or, more concretely, it is universality in and through time, the universality by which the human spirit closes up the distention of its own presence in time. The human spirit achieves universality when its presence, which is deployed through time, is synthesized into a moment of relative or absolute totality. This notion of universality defines the universality of the idea. It is with reference to this notion of universality, that the image is the inception of ideal process. And that this is the universality which Vico intends is demonstrated by his account of the formation and the mode of operation of the poetic character. The poetic character is formed by time process and operates to create a relatively total presence of the spirit to itself through time.

This account is presented in two *loci classici*, from the first and the second form of the 'New Science' respectively, although, like the whole of the 'New Science' it is adumbrated in the *Diritto Universale* as well.[2] In the *Scienza Nuova Prima* Vico writes: '(The poetic characters are found to be the elements of the languages by which the first gentile nations spoke) . . . because when a nation, by reason of being of most limited intelligence, is unable to name an abstract or generic property, and having, on its first advertence of that property denominated specifically the name of the man who had come to its attention in the first instance under the aspect of the property . . . that nation, certainly, by reason of all the achievements of that same property which it adverts to have been effected by other men in later times, will endow these later men with the name of that first man with whom that property was first associated. . . .'[3] This statement is exemplified by the name and character of Hercules, who is, for Vico, the heroic or poetic character of all the labours associated with the first founding of the familial economy and polity. The *locus* from the second *Scienza Nuova* is, of course, the forty-ninth 'Degnità', which is, in its substance, a recapitulation of the three preceding 'axioms': 'These three axioms give us the origin of the poetic characters that constitute the essence of the fables. The first of the three shows the natural inclination of the vulgar to invent them, and to invent them appropriately. The second shows that the first men, the children, as it were, of the human race not being able to form intelligible class-concepts of things, had a natural need to

[1] SNS, 379, 380, 381.   [2] DU, II, 363.   [3] SNP, p. 150.

create poetic characters, that is imaginative class-concepts or universals, by reducing to them as to certain models or ideal portraits all the particular species which resembled them.'[1]

What is revealed by the common element in these two passages is the internal time-structure of the poetic character, and with this time-structure, the quality of universality proper to it. For the poetic character is generated not by a process of abstraction, but by a process of associative memory. And it is to memory, in the axiom immediately following, that Vico reduces imagination.[2] Memory is precisely that dimension of consciousness which reveals its distention between finite and infinite, its indefinite character, its time-structure. As a result, the quality which accrues to the poetic character from its origin in memory (as imagination and not as simple recall) is precisely its own time-structure. The distribution of the poetic character (to maintain for the time being its analogy to the logical term) is not, in the first place, to abstract instances, but to the temporal dimension of the consciousness of the human spirit. The poetic character is the first form under which the human spirit glimpses the ideality of its process through time. This time-perception is effected, it is true, through a kind of rudimentary abstraction, which is expressed in the first passage quoted precisely by the term advertence, which, as we have noted, is the proper Vichian symbol for the presence of reflection in any context. This abstract element is represented as the property common to the temporally distributed acts which enter into the structure of the poetic character. But what the poetic character yields to the human spirit is not the abstract concept of that property but its own self-identity or presence through the temporally distributed moments in which that property is glimpsed. This fact is recognized by Vico and is expressed in the statement that the poetic character is in fact a history;[3] and it is, further, the only possible basis for the second assertion, of the rubric quoted above, namely, that the first nations spoke in fable. The universality, consequently, which inheres in the poetic character is the universality of the identity and presence of the spirit to itself in time, the same quality of universality, it may be emphasized, which characterizes the idea in Vico.

A certain ambiguity or obscurity adheres, in both these passages, to the origin of the image which is the nucleus of the poetic character. Vico speaks as though this nucleus is itself a simple datum of memory, that is, an historical personage who becomes, by reason of his

[1] SNS, 209.　　　[2] SNS, 211.　　　[3] SNS, 379, 381, 414-17.

association with the 'property' in question, the hard core about which the poetic character is formed. Thus, in another passage,[1] he speaks of another poetic character, Solon, as one who must have been a party leader of the Athenian plebs in their struggle against the optimates for a share in the civil status. He immediately qualifies this observation, however, by an alternate possibility; Solon may be but the figure of the Athenian plebs themselves, under this particular aspect of the struggle for civil rights and status. What underlies this obscurity is the fact that the process of the formation of the poetic myth may begin in the idealization of an historical figure. What must be observed immediately, however, is that the actuality of this figure is of indifference both to the form and to the operation of the poetic character and cannot, in the last analysis, explain the process of its formation or its properties. The human mind creates, not merely the complex structure of the poetic character, but its nucleus or core as well. This is proven by the example of the poetic character of Jove;[2] for Jove is a character created, as it were, from the whole cloth of the human mind and stands as an instance, indeed as the supreme instance, of the formation of the poetic character in its purity. When, moreover, the nucleus of the poetic character may be an historical datum, some figure who might actually have existed, the distinction, for the purposes of the poetic character, between his private or physical existence and his status in the heroic character must be made. For the operation by which the poetic character is created dissolves in the very process of creation the physical or natural existence of that nucleus; that is to say, the natural existence becomes a matter of indifference for historiographic purposes and is replaced wholly by the poetic character itself. This is illustrated most concretely of all, perhaps, by Vico's treatment of Homer.[3]

The poetic character, finally, is an ontological structure. This is the force of Vico's assertion that the first nations *thought* in poetic characters and his distinction of this moment of thought from the moment of speech with which it is, under another aspect, identical. It is an ontological structure because it is an act by which the human spirit generates or creates its own being. This being is presence, and presence is the whole being of the human spirit. Thought is not, for Vico, the activity by which the human spirit reproduces in itself the form and the ideality of an alien or alternate actuality; it is the act by which it generates its own presence to itself, and in that presence, its

[1] SNS, 414.   [2] SNS, 401–2.   [3] Cf. Chapter X.

176

whole being as spirit. It is for this reason that the moment of spontaneity, of the poetic character, of the imagination, is genuinely a moment of spirit, because, in that moment, however dimly, there is evoked the actuality of presence. This is the final significance of the Vichian thesis of the modifications of the human mind. These modifications designate not the abstract formalities according to which spirit assimilates an alien or external world of nature, but those formalities under which it generates its own being, which is wholly presence. This is also the force of the Vichian statement, repeated many times, that the reference of metaphysics is not to nature but to the human mind itself, and the sense in which, if it is possible at all, the 'New Science' may be thought of as a metaphysics of mind.[1] This admission is not, however, to forget the objection raised elsewhere against this conception of the 'New Science'. The force of that objection was that the statements of the 'New Science' are all statements within the science, while the conception of it as a metaphysics of mind implies an abstract formalism which, we believe, is wholly foreign to its character. This ontological status of the poetic character (and of the idea also, as would appear, were it possible to follow the implications of Vico's theory into the problem of the structures of reflective consciousness) accounts ultimately for the reality of the historical process of spirit. It is here that the full force of Vico's criticism of the method of the mathematical sciences is felt. The synthetic transaction of those sciences generates an alien world because it effects no ontological result. The world which is generated in history is real because it is the being of the human spirit itself which informs that world.[2]

As the first nations thought in poetic characters, so they spoke in fables; this is the second member of the rubric cited above. The sense in which the term 'spoke' is to be accepted here is clearly indicated by Vico. The term denotes, in the first instance, the mental word; for speech, he writes, was born in mute times as mental language, which existed before vocal or articulate language.[3] It is the 'logos', the intimate, significative transaction of the human consciousness. This 'logos' or mental word, at the level of the poetic form of consciousness, is none other than the heroic or poetic character. The poetic character, as seen above, is in the first instance an ontological, a metaphysical principle; it establishes the human spirit in the first mode of being proper to itself. But the mode of being proper to spirit is, for Vico, presence. The 'logos' is but the being established

[1] SNS, 374.   [2] DIS, p. 132.   [3] SNS, 401.

by and in the poetic character addressed specifically under its quality as presence, and hence as signification. The 'logos' or the mental word, at the poetic level, is the poetic character grasped in its significative quality. At this level the poetic character induces a certain alienation from itself in the human spirit. To reflection, it is apparent that the presence generated by the poetic character is the presence of the human spirit to itself because reflection recognizes that the form imposed in the poetic character is always the form of the human spirit itself. At the level of poetic or spontaneous consciousness this is not apparent. The poetic character is accepted rather in its 'objectivity'. The poetic consciousness does not recognize the figure of Jove as its own translated formality; it accepts that figure as simply other to itself. The transaction is analogous when the character is grasped in its significative quality. The ultimate reference of the mental word, the 'logos' at the poetic level, is to the human spirit itself; but this is apparent to reflection, and not to spontaneous awareness. The poetic character as the word is taken to signify the poetic character in its objectivity. Inwardly enunciating the mental word, the poetic consciousness interprets it as signifying not the act by which it translates its own form into the world of nature, but that form as enjoying a specious natural character. The speech to which Vico here refers, consequently, is the mental word, the 'logos' of the imagination, by which the human spirit signifies or indicates, as a transcendent form of nature, the poetic character which the imagination has evoked and which is the image of the spirit itself. It is the transaction which Tacitus recorded in the aphorism 'simul fingunt creduntque'.[1]

The fable is the inner and constitutive form of the poetic 'logos' and it derives from the time structure of the poetic character. Indeed, the basic sense of 'logos', Vico suggests, is fable or myth, while fable, in turn, is properly defined as 'true narration'.[2] By the fable, as the inner or mental word, the poetic consciousness recounts to itself the significance of the poetic character which it has evoked or created. The essence of this mode of recounting, the narrative, is its time-structure. The basic 'logos' is a narrative exhibiting a time-structure, the before and after of the events which it recounts, because the poetic character is a time-structure. It is only thus, consequently, that its significance can be indicated. The significance of the figure of Jove, for example, in its first reference as the poetic character of the heavens imagined as a vast body incorporating sensate spirit is to

[1] Tacitus, *Annales*, V, 10; SNS, 376. [2] SNS, 401.

recount the actions of that principle. The significance of Jove is thus indicated by the narration of the acts attributed to him and Jove becomes the protagonist of fables narrated of him. Similarly, the significance of Hercules, who is, for Vico, the poetic character of the familial form of society, can be indicated only by the recounting of the deed ascribed to him in the fables of Hercules. These deeds comprise all the labours entailed in the passage from the stage of feral wandering to that of settled domicile, from that of promiscuous intercourse of the sexes to that of established unions in marriage. Again, the significance of Solon as the figure of the Athenian plebs in their struggle for civil status can be established only by narration attributing to him all of the actions involved in that struggle. The fables, consequently, Vico says, in their collectivity constitute the vocabulary of the first nations, the repertory, that is to say, of their mental words by which they were able to indicate the significance of the poetic characters in which they thought.[1]

The fables are therefore, as Vico says again and again, histories. They are histories, however, only because the poetic characters which they signify are themselves time-structures. As histories, the fables are vehicles of different import, now metaphysical, now physical, now civil. Thus the poetic character of Jove supports fables at all three levels, that of Hercules at two, the physical and the civil, that of Solon, finally, at one only, the civil. Ultimately, however, as the reality of the fable and of the whole poetic moment of consciousness becomes apparent to reflection, all levels of significance tend to converge on one, which must properly be called the historical. All, that is to say, narrate in the final analysis the reality of the human spirit to itself in its time-ideal process and reality. But this convergence takes place only at the level of reflection, when the fabric of the fables is in process of dissolution by that criticism from which the idea will arise.

As the vocabulary of the first nations, that is, as the repertory of their mental words, the fables constitute the first language, the first significative process of human consciousness. The statement, consequently, that the first nations spoke in fables, constitutes further a proof, indeed, *the* proof of the Vichian thesis that the origin of language is in poetry.[2] This thesis, in the light of the relationship indicated between the poetic character and the fable, can mean only that the one and the other are born of a single transaction of the

[1] SNP, p. 145.   [2] SNS, 428 et seq.

spirit. This transaction is that synthesis of time in the image by which the poetic character is first created and then explicated. This is the true, the nuclear reality of poetry and of language. The origins of language, therefore, must be as natural and necessary as those of poetry itself. From this necessity Vico is led back to the insight into the radical truth of the fable. Every fable, every poetic character contains some public truth, which is guaranteed by the necessary and spontaneous character of the act by which the one and the other are generated. The development of language from the vocabulary of the fables to the reflective nomenclature of the philosophical sciences must traverse the same stages as the human spirit itself in the movement toward its total or ideal presence. Even more, the two movements are identical, for it is in the 'logos', the mental word, whether poetic or reflective, that the presence of spirit consists most formally.

The first nations which thought in poetic characters and spoke in fables, wrote in hieroglyphics; thus the general rubric of the poetic consciousness concludes. Scripture arises in the impulse and the necessity to communicate. This impulse and necessity is native to every moment of human consciousness; indeed it springs from the profoundest dimension of human presence. This is the perception of the human spirit of its social or political character, the perception that the fullness of its reality and its presence to itself lies in the structures of community. Its impulse to communicate, consequently, is one with the basic movement of humanity and civility, namely, to overcome the limits which natural existence imposes upon man and to enter into the social communion with his kind in which humanity and civility consists. In this effort the structures of communication become the strongest ligatures of community. They establish community effectively within any specific society. They create the forms of community which achieve a kind of natural existence and which thus become the documents upon which historical community rests. Finally, it is clear that communication is the means by which the human spirit achieves that being for another which is the fullest mode of its being and presence to itself.

As it informs the whole of the life of spirit, the impulse to communicate originates in the poetic moment of consciousness. At this level communication is effected according to the general form and movement of the poetic consciousness; in other words, communication is a poetic activity. For this reason, the channel which this impulse takes is identical with the basic movement of the poetic consciousness: it moves to appropriate nature to the form of its own presence or, expressed conversely, to invest nature with that presence. The fundamental process by which the poetic character was evoked is the process by which the poetic forms of scripture are determined. The poetic character of Jove, was created or evoked by the investment of the natural phenomena of the heavens with the sensate form of human consciousness. The forms of poetic scripture are created by an exactly parallel movement: a natural form is invested with the formality of the poetic consciousness. In this latter case, however, the form of consciousness with which the natural object is invested is the mental word, the poetic 'logos', the basic significative structure of the poetic consciousness. In Vico's words, the first men expressed themselves by gestures or by physical objects which had natural relations with the ideas (i.e. the mental 'logoi').[1]

The crucial term in this statement is clearly the term 'natural'. The crucial moment of poetic communication and the creation of the first scripture is the moment of the selection of the 'natural' gesture or object to be invested with communicative office. At first glance, the 'naturalness' at stake might appear to be a property of the object in its objectivity, its purely natural character. This view would eventuate in the notion that natural objects, or natural postures and movements of the human body, or its natural members, in and of themselves possess some correspondence to the idea or the poetic 'logos'. Such a notion, it very easily appears, is fundamentally opposed to all that Vico has said about the movement of the poetic consciousness. The term 'natural' here is deceptive; the expressive relation proceeds in this case, as in the case of the poetic character, not from the object, but from the human spirit. The 'natural' relation between gesture and object, of which communication avails itself, is itself created by the spirit by a poetic act; and every such form is itself a poem, a poetic character, in this new context of communication.

This truth may be illustrated by the hieroglyphic examples which Vico himself adduces in both the orders he has suggested, gesture and object. The hieroglyphic of gesture is exemplified by the heroic gesture of the Spartan; when the latter was asked why his city, unlike the other cities of the world, was without walls, his response was simply to expose his chest. The impact upon the imagination is direct and forceful. The essence of the gesture is the metaphor between the bared chest and the city wall of mud or stone; but this

[1] SNS, 428, 434.

similitude is a poetic creation, not the recognition of an antecedent, 'natural' relation; the imagination of the Spartan had invested the member of his body and its peculiar exposed posture with the civil and the physical properties of the city wall. The same is true of the object-hieroglyphic which Vico adduces: the use of three grains of wheat, or of corn, with the significance of the passage of three years.[1] Here the process of poetic investment is even more apparent; the physical or natural object is endowed with the whole civil significance of an agrarian culture. This is not to deny that the 'natural' resemblance is there; it is only to emphasize that, conformably to Vico's own notion of the poetic character, it is there as the result of the movement of the human spirit itself. The spontaneous consciousness, Vico remarks, under the urgency of its great need to communicate, is ingenious in the establishment of such relations between its mental vocabulary and natural objects, of which, in this respect, its own body functions as one. But every such expression or hieroglyphic sign, he cautions, is a metaphor, and every such metaphor is a fable in brief; is, in other words, identical in its significative structure with the mental word which it is evoked to signify.[2]

Signs such as these must have been the first scripture of the nations. Vico is concerned above all to emphasize the 'naturalness' of these signs in the sense which has been indicated above. The point of view against which he directs this opinion is the interpretation of the hieroglyph as a conventional symbol of an 'esoteric' wisdom or consciousness. The conventionalistic fallacy concerning the origin and character of scripture has its immediate source in the failure of scholars to perceive that this problem could not be treated independently from the problem of the origin of language.[3] Ultimately it derives from the wider failure to grasp the character of the poetic activity and its place in the life of the human spirit. Once it is perceived that the whole form of the primitive consciousness is dictated by the poetic act, it follows inevitably that every manifestation of that consciousness must exhibit the same quality which he calls 'naturalness' or 'necessity'. This naturalness or necessity is nothing else than the poetic reality itself. The poetic character, the fable, the hieroglyph are all 'natural' in the sense that all are creations of the spontaneous poetic activity. The character or quality which they exhibit cannot be sought in any other source. The inevitability which attends the products of the poetic activity is the sign of its genuinely creative and non-derivative power.

[1] SNS, 431.   [2] SNS, 404.   [3] SNS, 429.

These conceptions of the nature of poetry and myth, of the origin of language and of scripture provide the basis for the canons of the interpretation of the 'obscure times' of human history and thus for the initiation of the positive programme of the 'New Science'. These canons are both negative and positive. The former clear the ground, as it were, by uprooting the conceits, the prejudices, the distortions which had, in Vico's view, impeded even the proper notion of the 'New Science', to say nothing of its actual inception; the latter provide its actual methodological principles.

The negative canons for the interpretation of poetic wisdom embrace, in the first instance, the two 'borie', or 'conceits', the one of the learned, the other of the nations, which Vico formulates among the earliest of the axioms of the 'Elements' of the *Scienza Nuova Seconda*.[1] The conceit of the nations is stated in terms drawn from the testimony of Diodorus Siculus; every nation, he asserts, whether Greek or barbarian, imagines that it, before all other nations, had invented the commodities of human life and that it has retained the memory of its history back to the beginning of the world. This conceit militates directly against Vico's insight into the pluralistic origin of human culture and, consequently, against his principle of eternal, ideal and providential history which is enacted in the history of each nation in time. More directly still, it generates the diffusion theory of the origin and spread of human culture, the notion, that is, that human culture and civilization, arising in one centre, was then carried by divers means to the other nations of the world. It is, as a matter of fact, the impossibilities, the inconsistencies and the absurdities of the process of diffusion which initially arouse Vico's scepticism. Such a process of diffusion involves a complete dis-ordering of the movements of culture and an equally complete des-truction of any sound chronology, which last, he admonishes, must be the firm basis of universal history. For example, it projects backward into the first moments of human history systems of com-munication which could only have been developed at far more recent and advanced stages. The legend of the introduction of the Law of the Twelve Tables from Athens into Rome illustrates the pernicious effect of this conceit. In addition to the implausibility involved in the process of this transfer, it renders impossible the recognition of the actual character of this code and, consequently, the interpretation of the actual structure of the early Roman polity. How are we to believe, Vico asks, that such a transfer was effected

[1] SNS, 125–8.

when all evidence points to the fact that the Roman people lived straitly confined to a miniscule territory and that to the Roman people even the inhabitants of Taranto were strangers and enemies from another world? [1] Only by recognizing the indigenous origin of those laws does it become possible to see them for what they were, the first codification of the heroic law of the peoples of Latium.

The conceit of the learned compounds the confusion induced by that of the nations. This conceit would have it that whatever is known to the learned of a reflective age must be as old as the world itself. The direct product of this conceit is the illusory notion of the 'matchless wisdom' of the ancients, the illusion that they must have possessed a science and a wisdom at least equal to that of later times and thus have dwelt in a veritable 'golden age' of humanity. This conceit leads to the radical distortion of the documents of those first ages and their wisdom. The effort is made to read or interpret them as though they were the products of reflective consciousness and all the enlightenment which humanity has so laboriously collected in its historical process is gratuitously imputed to those early men and times. As a result, the very idea of historical process is made unintelligible and inconceivable and there arises instead a kind of romantic primitivism of the human spirit. Vico illustrates[2] this conceit by the example of the high priest of the Egyptians who translated all Egyptian history into a sublime natural theology, effectively distorting its true character which Eusebius recognized as simply a history, interspersed with fables. And the Greek philosophers, he adds, had done the same to the fables of Greek mythology.

The conceits alike of the nations and the learned are, in reality, but concretions of two general properties of the human mind. Because of its indefinite character, which we have seen to be its distention between finite and infinite, the human mind, wherever it is lost in ignorance, makes itself the measure of all things. Again, by another property of human nature, men, whenever they can form no idea of distant and unknown things, judge them by what is familiar and at hand. Finally, these conceits are supported by a persuasion that the ancients, by some elusive law of affinity or proximity must have been better informed concerning their own antiquities and origins. But the very opposite is, in fact, the case. The Greeks, by far the most enlightened and refined of the ancients were, at the same time, most ignorant of their own antiquities, and Livius confesses as much for the Romans.[3] This persuasion had created in the

[1] SNP, p. 25; SNS, 116. [2] SNS, 46. [3] SNS, 117.

scholars of later times a fatal diffidence toward the instruments and ideas at their disposal for the accomplishment of a task in which the ancients had failed conspicuously. These negative canons, it is clear, rest on one and one basis only, the discovery of the true nature of poetry, and above all the discovery of its necessity as the form of the initial temporal stage of human consciousness. Until this truth concerning poetry was established there could be no means of dislodging those conceits or, for that matter, of perceiving their deceitful character. The positive canons, consequently, must be conceived in their fundamental character as corollaries of this same discovery of poetry.

The first and most basic of these positive canons is that of the true nature and central importance of etymology. This canon follows directly on the discovery of the poetic origin of language and of scripture. In the light of this discovery it should be possible, beginning with the most contemporary forms of words and languages, to retrace the process of their formation even to the poetic moment in which they originally appeared. This process would immediately imply a reconstruction or retracing of the process of events, and of ideas which those words signify. For the process of the historical transformation of the form and the signification of terms must reflect directly the alterations in events and in ideas which they signify. The whole process is one and unitary and it is possible to move from any point within the process along any of its dimensions. The process is amply illustrated by Vico both positively and negatively from the Latin language. Positively, he employs the example of terms which in the golden latinity had attained highly reflective and philosophical significance but which in their origins must have had direct sensible, civil signification: 'cantare', to wit, which from its reflective association with the refined and cultured art of verse and song according to the best classic norms, must be traced back to its first rude significance as incantation, and through this process to the whole rude structure of primitive religion, which consisted in divination and its perversion, witchcraft.[1]

But the word, by the process indicated above, leads inevitably to the myth, the fable, the poetic character; by the same process, the canon of etymology leads to that of mythology. The basic canon for the interpretation of the myth is the insight into the fact that it is a history and above all a civil history. Thus it becomes possible, according to this canon, to set aside all of the naturalistic interpreta-

[1] SNS, 646 et seq.

tions of myths and to see them as relating directly and even exclusively to the process of the incivilment of human life. The interpretation of myths consists, in the last analysis, in the recognition that they signify the heroic characters in their historical dimension and that the heroic characters are themselves, in their most radical principle, simply historical man himself under the aspect of the diverse labours which the process of incivilment entailed.

To these must be added the canon of the acceptance of the 'great fragments of antiquity'.[1] By this term Vico intends those insights and the traditions of the antique mind which have persisted through the accounts of historians and poets. Such are, for example, the 'fragments' of which he avails himself and which are incorporated intimately into the structure of the 'New Science', the Egyptian tradition of the three ages, of the gods, of the heroes and of men, and the Homeric tradition of a 'language of the gods'. These fragments heretofore had seemed unavailable for scientific purposes. Vico's conceptions of the operations of the poetic consciousness make clear that these fragments, like the whole of the content of poetic wisdom, must support and in turn be supported by elements of public truth. On this ground, this canon establishes these fragments as points of departure for scientific investigation of the poetic consciousness which function almost as hypotheses. These hypotheses, converted into fact by the illumination of scientific investigation, are then seen to provide fundamental elements in the architectonic of the 'New Science'. The three ages of the Egyptians find their corroboration in the theories of the modifications of the human mind as time-forms of the human spirit and of the character of the poetic metaphysics which marks the 'primus passus' of human thought; similarly, the Homeric tradition of a language of the gods receives vindication in the theory of the fable as the first language of men and in the civil histories deducible from the fables which form the tissue of the Homeric poems. These great fragments are the stones which the builders of the history and science of civility had cast aside but which Vico makes the head of the corner; and they achieve integral status in the form of his own science.

Finally, there is the canon of comparison. It is this canon which imparts to the 'New Science' that aspect of a comparative anatomy of cultures which many have taken as its true import. This canon rests clearly on Vico's rejection of the monistic theory of the origin of human culture and the diffusion theory of its extension, both con-

[1] SNS, 357; cf. Croce, *op. cit.*, pp. 183–4; Amerio, *op. cit.*, p. 486.

densed in the 'conceit of the nations', and upon his substitution of pluralism and the concept of ideal contemporaneity. Within the frame of reference of these latter principles the canon of comparison suggests itself as the most efficacious means of establishing that uniformity in which ideal contemporaneity and the ideal and eternal history consist, and of elucidating the concepts of providence and common sense. A principal aspect of providence, in Vico's theory, is that it guides humanity by common sense to that uniformity and ideal contemporaneity. This aspect may be established only by the demonstration that the individual nations pursuing the same temporal course exhibit identical eternal properties, while this demonstration in turn must rest directly upon the possibility of comparison between the courses of the nations. This comparison is rendered feasible ultimately by the doctrine of the poetic characters and by that of the fables; more precisely, it rests upon Vico's assertion that the fables are allegories of the poetic characters which have univocal and not merely analogical significance.[1] The force of this assertion is, from the point of view of method, to make comparison possible; for Hercules, if the sense of his fables be univocal and if he be discovered to be a poetic character of all nations (both conditions being asserted as actual by Vico), must indicate an identical moment in the time-courses of the nations and hence establish an eternal property of humanity and civility.

The combined force of these canons is to set in motion the actual, positive programme of the 'New Science'. The programme has as its term nothing less than universal history as seen in the ideal and eternal history which the science would establish. It has its beginnings, as Vico insists every science must have, with the beginnings of its material; that is to say, with the first moment of genuine human thought or consciousness and its expressive creation of the human spirit and transformation of nature. It is this pristine moment of the spirit which the canons, based ultimately on the new theory of poetry, and on its corollaries makes available. By these canons Vico is enabled to achieve that descent into the poetic consciousness of the first men which he proclaims as the most arduous enterprise which human science may attempt and which, in his own case, has cost the effort 'of twenty-five years of continuous and relentless labour'.[2]

[1] SNS, 210.   [2] SNS, 34, 338.

X

HOMER

Vico's concern with the poetry of Homer emerges with the emergence of the idea of the 'New Science' itself; they are, as he said of philosophy and philology, 'geminae ortae', twin fruit of a single birth. Each successive stage in the development of that idea from its hesitant formulation in the 'Nova Scientia Tentatur' of the *Diritto Universale*, through its genial and organic exposition in the *Scienza Nuova Prima*, to its final, 'geometric' demonstration in the *Scienza Nuova* of 1744, is accompanied by a parallel address to the classical critical problem of western humanism. No shadow of doubt is left but that, to Vico's mind, under a certain aspect at least, the 'discovery of the true Homer' and the project of the 'New Science' constitute members of a single argument.

Nor is that aspect difficult to perceive. On the contrary, it is fundamental to the science. Vico expresses it formally in an axiom of the 'Elements': 'Doctrines must take their beginning from that of the matters of which they treat.'[1] Applied to the entire programme of the 'New Science', this axiom, according to all that he has established concerning ideal-temporal process and its scientific reconstruction, directs him to its initial moment. Its matter is humanity, that very presence to himself in idea which is the most intimate and constitutive being of man. But the beginning of that matter, the theory of the modifications of the human mind has established, is to be found in that moment when men began first to think humanly. The doctrine of that matter, humanity, to insure its scientific character and progress, must descend to that first moment of human awareness thence to renew, on the plane of reflection, the laborious Odyssey of the human spirit toward its idea. How arduous that descent must be, Vico never tires of repeating.[2] The 'ingens sylva' of the imagination of primitive man, of the human spirit in its first time-form of consciousness, stretches dark and pathless before the venturing mind; but the descent must be made.

[1] SNS, 314.   [2] SNS, 330–1.

The undertaking of the 'New Science' addresses itself, in principle, to the universal mind of man and has as its end the delineation of the eternal and ideal history of the human spirit in its universality. Concretely, however, Vico assumes the laborious task only with respect to the culture to which his own is indigenous. It is to the first time-form moment of the mind of classical man that he would descend. This is the necessity imposed upon him, as he remarks, by the fact that he was born and educated 'here, and not in Morocco';[1] it is the necessity of his own historical being, his own existence. This necessity does not impugn the character or the promise of the enterprise; on the contrary, it is in strict conformity with the character of the universalism which permeates the 'New Science'. For it follows clearly, from the principle of common sense and of providence, that this inquiry might be initiated within the concrete structure of any culture of sufficient philosophical refinement, and must whatever that context reach the same term, the ideal and eternal history which rules the course of all the nations in all times. The historical and existential restriction to the context of classical culture, to Graeco-Roman culture and its European derivatives is not so much a limit as a mode of concretion which aids rather than impedes the inquiry by indicating its explicit and concrete matter.

At the threshold of the primitive mind of the man of classical culture looms the Homeric structure. It is the portal as towering and, in its way, as fearful as the gates of Dis through which all must pass who would enter that dread domain. The Homeric structure stands on the boundary between the spontaneous and the reflective life of classical man. Between these areas there is no sure passage save by this gate. The Homeric poems constitute, in other words, the primary document of the mind of classical man. This character has been recognized continuously since the dawn of the reflective, historical consciousness; it was a dogma of the Greek 'paideia' from which not even Plato dared depart. Vico's insight is sure, therefore, when he recognizes that the Homeric problem is integral to the problem and the project of the 'New Science'. So far as the 'New Science' might, according to its existential and historical conditions, undertake its own programme it must assume the form of an exegesis of the Homeric structure. The quest of the 'true Homer', consequently, is no fortuitous adjunct of the 'New Science', but its address to its first documentary problem.

Vico's immediate concern with the Homeric structure, the *Iliad*

[1] *Auto.*, p. 48.

and the *Odyssey*, is to establish their character as true historical documents. 'If', he writes, 'the poems of Homer are civil histories of ancient Greek customs, they will be two great treasure houses of the natural law of the nations of Greece';[1] this is the proposition whose truth must be demonstrated. This demonstration, to be successful, must pass through a veritable Scylla and Charybdis of criticism. In a certain sense, as we remarked above, this character of historical document had never been denied the Homeric epics; on the contrary, it had been attributed to them in a hyperbolic degree. 'Plato', Vico writes, 'left firmly fixed the opinion that Homer was endowed with sublime esoteric wisdom, and all the other philosophers have followed in his train.'[2] This esoteric wisdom was of a piece with that 'wisdom of the ancients' with which the conceits of the nations and of the learned conspired to endow the origins of human things. In virtue of this presumptive wisdom the Homeric epics were classically read as reflective histories and given credence for their testimony as to the character of the first human institutions commensurate with a reflective character. Against this conception of the poems, Vico had to leave intact the historical significance of their accounts of the first institutions of classical culture while demonstrating that their testimony could not be of the reflective, philosophical, 'esoteric' character which Plato had imputed to them. Homer must, so to say, be demoted from the lofty stature of the sage to that of vulgar or popular wisdom before the character of his historical testimony could be established truly.

If this be Scylla, Charybdis lay in keeping intact the unapproachable poetic stature of Homer. This stature had become associated, in the tradition of classical criticism, precisely with the esoteric and philosophical character of the Homeric wisdom. This tradition of criticism rested upon the idea that supreme poetry must express, or be the product of, the loftiest reflective consciousness; that poetry was an art based on reflection. To impugn this reflective character is to impugn the poetic supremacy of the Homeric poems. The attitude of classical criticism is reflected in the matter of the Homeric 'lapses'; these are treated as unavoidable flaws in an otherwise perfect fabric, and as due to momentary breaks in an otherwise perfectly controlled, reflective process, intrusive moments of sleep in waking life. But Vico sees them rather as evidences of the genuinely spontaneous character of Homer's poetry; if Homer had not nodded, he could not have been so great a poet. (Nisi ita saepe dormitaret,

---

[1] SNS, 156–7.   [2] SNS, 780.

numquam bonus fuisset Homerus.[1]) Vico's task is to demonstrate that the Homeric poems are primary documents of the first time-form of classical consciousness and at the same time spontaneous structures of the imagination; finally, they must be shown to be the former precisely because they are the latter.

The magnitude of the task does not dismay Vico; on the contrary, in the *Scienza Nuova Seconda* at least, he approaches it with supreme confidence. The source of this confidence is the theory of poetry which he has developed and of the 'metaphysical' criticism which is based on this theory. The force of the one and the other, he is confident, must be to reveal in the Homeric structure precisely the conjuncture of historicity and poetic quality which the structure of the 'New Science' demands. For this reason, the Homeric poems exercise a second important function in the pattern of Vico's thought; they provide the supreme testing grounds for this theory of poetry and, consequently, for the entire movement of the 'New Science'.

The 'metaphysical' criticism of the Homeric structure follows a simple course, adhering strictly to the principles established in the theory of poetry and myth. Its objective is to reveal the Homeric poems as consisting essentially of fables of heroic or poetic characters. Once this has been accomplished, their character as historical documents follows directly, for Vico has demonstrated that all such fables must be civil histories of obscure times. The stages toward this objective are directed by the peculiar circumstances surrounding the traditional interpretation and conception of the poems, but are governed throughout by the explicit principles of the Vichian poetics.

The point of departure of the critical process is the tradition of the natural existence of Homer. Tradition ordains that the two Homeric epics are the work of a single poet; it sets in motion, consequently, the quest for the 'historical' Homer, the attempt to establish his natural identity as distinct from his identity in the poems themselves. Vico's attack upon this tradition is direct. He proposes to establish that Homer was 'an idea or a poetic character of Grecian men in so far as they told their history in song'.[2]

The initial flaw in the traditional conception appears in the image of Homer as a supreme reflective poet and sage composing his epics for the instruction of the populace and creating to this end the figures of his heroes or protagonists and the material of their fables. This is the image of Homer the teacher which dominated the Greek

[1] DU, III, 698. [2] SNS, 873.

191

'paideia' and which, in turn, dictated the 'philosophical' interpretations of the poems which drew from them the maxims of reflective
humanity and civility. But these interpretations, these philosophical
sentences, Vico insists, were all read into Homer by the philosophers
themselves; 'the philosophers did not discover their philosophies in
the Homeric fables but rather inserted them therein'. This image of
Homer as the sage and teacher of an esoteric or reflective and
philosophical wisdom cannot be sustained when confronted by the
content and the spirit of the Homeric narratives. For what is that
content? Whether concerning gods or heroes, it is of a piece, 'crude,
fierce, wild, savage, unreasonable'. Neither gods nor men are such
as a philosopher or sage, bent upon purposes of enlightenment and
instruction of the populace or the vulgar, would hold up for their
admiration and imitation. The gods of Homer are compounded of
the vices, the deceptions, the illusions and the weaknesses of pro-
fligate men. Jove bases his supreme power on force, demonstrating
in the fable of the great chain that he alone is king of gods and men.
His subject gods disport themselves like rioting peasants at a harvest
festival or a feast of wine: Minerva, an image of philosophy and of
the wisdom of Jove in vulgar belief, strikes Mars with a rock and
despoils Venus of her vesture; they stoop to enter the conspiracies
and intrigues of men, and are themselves vulnerable to the injuries
of men: the same rock-wielding Minerva conspires with Diomede,
the prince of liars, to wound both Mars and Venus. Nor do the
heroes sustain reflective scrutiny with better fortune. Ulysses seeks
the poisoned herbs of Ephyra for the tips of his arrows, and the
bodies of the slain are left to the vultures and the dogs against the
primary law of humanity which commands the burial of the dead.
The princes of the *Iliad*, Achilles and Agamemnon, the one the
greatest of the Greek heroes and the image of all virtues, blameless
in Homer's constant nomenclature, the other the leader of the
Greek league, hurl vile epithets at each other 'as servants in popular
comedies would scarcely do nowadays'. And their wisdom in counsel
is on a plane with their public conduct. The same Agamemnon seeks
to regain his honour after the rape of Chryseis by stealing Briseis
from Achilles, while Achilles, to avenge this personal wrong, thinks
himself amply justified in forsaking the common cause and deliver-
ing the Greeks to the fatal hands of Hector. Such content might be
conceived to be the matter of instruction, if it were held up before
the eyes of the populace as reprehensible and occasion of disgust;
but this is not the case in the Homeric poems. For this Homer does

not hesitate to bend this matter to the entertainment of the populace, arousing their admiration and confirming them in their pleasure. 'Nor could the truculent and savage style in which he describes so many, such varied and such bloody battles, so many and such extravagantly cruel kinds of butchery as make up all the sublimity of the *Iliad* in particular have originated in a mind humanized and softened by any philosophy.' The 'historical' Homer, if ever he existed, could not have been the philosopher, sage and teacher of the great Homeric tradition.[1]

He was neither philosopher nor sage because, in fact, he had not existed as a natural person at all. 'The same thing has happened in the case of Homer as in that of the Trojan war, of which the most judicious critics hold that though it marks a famous epoch in history it never in the world took place.'[2] The evidence for this conclusion appears to Vico to be internal to the poems ascribed to Homer. The great discrepancies existing between the *Iliad* and the *Odyssey* on nearly every point had not escaped critical notice. Neither, however, had they aroused the necessary scepticism toward the natural figure of Homer. Instead, critical curiosity had been assuaged by such fancies as that the *Iliad* was the work of Homer's youth, and consequently preoccupied with wars and rivalries, while the *Odyssey*, composed in his old age, reflected the concerns of maturity. And this despite the fact that there is record in Seneca of a celebrated dispute concerning the common authorship of the two epics.[3]

The analysis of the Homeric epics and the comparison of their internal characterisitics leads Vico to two conclusions, destructive of the possibility of the natural figure of Homer. The first is that the poems must have been composed and compiled by various hands through successive ages.[4] The evidence of this is the commixture, throughout the fabric of both epics, of the characteristics of widely disparate cultures. There is, throughout, a constant contrast between refined customs and the wild and savage patterns of behaviour. The refinement of the court of Alcinous stands out in contrast to the rude accoutrements of the heroes of the *Iliad*; the manners of his courtiers, in contrast to the wild, volative, savage demeanour of Achilles and Agamemnon. This contrast is not, however, primarily between the two poems; rather it pervades both, although the description of the wild and savage customs characterizes the *Iliad* more. But such

[1] SNS, 781-9, 873, 901. [2] SNS, 873.
[3] SNS, 789. [4] SNS, 804.

diversity of custom, according to the metaphysical principles which Vico had expounded, necessarily involves distance in time as well. He feels compelled to conclude, consequently—'ne placidis coeunt immitia'—that the poems represent a growth through time in which the earlier elements were taken up and preserved along with the later. Such a process of gradual formation, however, clearly precludes the possibility of a single authorship, not only of both poems, but of either; it argues directly to a popular and spontaneous process, free and innocent of any reflective ordering principle and preserving all elements, unmindful of their discrepancy, by the tenacity and receptivity of the popular memory and imagination.

Although the contrast of refined and more barbarous manners and customs pervades both poems, the latter, as it has been suggested above, characterize the *Iliad*, the former the *Odyssey*. This circumstance justifies Vico in fixing even the popular processes by which they were formed at different stages of Greek history. Developing a theme which, in its narrow and naturalistic sense (that is, as referring to the natural figure of Homer), he had already rejected, Vico remarks, 'Thus Homer composed the *Iliad* in his youth, that is, when Greece was young and consequently seething with sublime passions . . .; but he wrote the *Odyssey* in his old age, that is, when the spirits of Greece had been somewhat cooled by reflection. . . . In this fashion we show that the Homer who was the author of the *Iliad* preceded by many centuries the Homer who was the author of the *Odyssey*.'[1] That is to say, that the different Homers to whom the poems must be referred must be the same Grecian people at diverse stages of their culture. Homer, as the poetic character of Grecian men recalling and narrating their history in song may consequently be said to be the author of both, and by the same token, to have lived at widely distant epochs of the cultural formation of Greece.

The dissolution of the 'historical', or natural, figure of Homer leaves Vico with two poetic structures formed by a natural or spontaneous process of growth and therefore necessarily of popular origin, comprising elements from two distinct epochs of Greek cultural life and, on the basis of the dominance of the characteristics of these epochs in the one and the other of the poems, assigned to different ages. The separation in time, however, and the quality of the customs and manners portrayed are less important for his purposes than the identity of the process by which both have been formed. The *Iliad* and the *Odyssey*, whatever may distinguish and op-

[1] SNS, 879–80.

pose them one to the other, have in common their popular and spontaneous origin; whatever distance in time may separate them, both still belong to the spontaneous age of Greek culture. This is the veritable key to their genuine character, structure and significance for Vico has, in his theory of poetry, established the principles upon which the spontaneous, popular imagination operates. The basic principle is that it operates by 'necessity', which means, concretely, that it does not create idle fictions, but is intent upon narrating to itself its own history. This it does by means of its fables. But the fables of the popular imagination are but its mode of signifying the poetic characters in which its historical experience is imaged forth or crystallized and which are, consequently, the protagonists of its fables. These are the principles, consequently, which must be applied to the structure of the Homeric epics.

Certain obstacles to the direct application of these present themselves. It would be historically ingenuous and, indeed, counter to Vico's own conception of the time-structure of the human spirit, to suppose that the popular imagination might preserve and transmit the fables and the poetic characters unchanged from the first moment of their formation. On the contrary, the process of the transmission and preservation of these elements must be ruled by laws identical or analogous to those which govern the time-ideal movement of spirit itself. Unless it were to be maintained that the Homeric structure is a transcendent document of the first time-form of human consciousness in Greek history (a document, therefore, somewhat analogous to Vico's conception of the Hebrew law),[1] it is necessary to determine what these laws of the transformation of myth are and at what stage in that process the Homeric fables must be fixed. Vico establishes the law of this transformation by the doctrine of the three ages of poets. 'The first was the age of the theological poets who were themselves heroes and sang true and austere fables; the second, that of the heroic poets who altered and corrupted the fables; and the third, that of Homer, who received them in their altered and corrupted form.'[2] The crucial stage of these three is clearly that of the 'heroic poets', for it is here that the actual deformation of the fables from their initial truth and austerity takes place. It is necessary above all to fix the law of this deformation. The widest principle which governs this transformation is stated among the 'Elements'; it is the axiom which asserts that 'because of the indefinite nature of the human mind, wherever it is lost in ignorance

[1] SNP, p. 232; SNS, 310, 396. [2] SNS, 905.

man makes himself the measure of all things'; and even more explicitly in the axiom which follows, 'It is another property of the human mind that whenever men can form no idea of distant and unknown things, they judge them by what is familiar and at hand.'[1] The initial poetic characters and fables, distant in time from the remembering mind, are subject to these wide and general laws of the movement of the human spirit. They are, however, in turn made more specific and concrete by other observations. In another axiom Vico observes, 'Whatever appertains to men but is doubtful and obscure, they naturally interpret according to their own natures and the passions and habits that spring from them.' And this observation is immediately applied to the specific instance of the fable. 'This axiom is a great canon of our mythology. According to it, fables originating among the first savage and crude men were very severe; then, with the long passage of years and change of customs, they were impropriated, altered and obscured in the dissolute and corrupt times even before Homer.'[2] The rule of this dissolution and corruption of customs has been established by earlier axioms. 'Men first feel necessity, then look for utility, next attend to comfort, still later amuse themselves with pleasure, thence grow dissolute in luxury. . . .'[3] 'The nature of peoples is first crude, then severe, then benign, then delicate, finally dissolute.' And as examples of the actual process of deformation of the fables: 'Because religion was important to the men of Greece and they feared to have the gods opposed to their desires as they were to their customs they attributed their customs to the gods and gave improper, ugly, and obscene meanings to the fables.' This process operates even with respect to the physical images of the heroic or poetic characters. 'Jove becomes so small and light that he is flown about by an eagle. Neptune rides the waves in a fragile chariot, and Cybele rides seated on a lion.' Homer, it has been made clear, appears for Vico in the final stage of this process of the deformation of the fables: 'Homer . . . received them in their altered and corrupted state.'[4]

This conception of the corrupt form of the fables in Homer, which Vico has before employed to destroy the notion of Homer's 'esoteric' or philosophical wisdom, now enables him to place Homer in the time-ideal order of Greek culture. The period at which the poems appear, although distinct and widely separated and still within the span of the spontaneous life of spirit, is late in that life. Upon

[1] SNS, 120, 122. [2] SNS, 220-1.
[3] SNS, 241-2. [4] SNS, 221, 402, 808, 905.

the Vichian theory, this fact disqualifies Homer as a witness to the life of the first and obscure times, save in so far as it is possible, beneath the corrupt form of the fable, by an understanding of the laws of its deformation, to discover its original, true and austere form.

All that is said about fable in its corrupted form is applicable to the Homeric epics only in their character as transmitters of the original fables of the race. It does not apply to another and most fundamental dimension of the poems, their own spontaneous character. The Homeric poems not only transmit the initial fables but generate poetic characters and their fables in their own right. This follows simply upon their genuinely poetic character or quality, for it is such creation that the poetic activity consists. Even the corruption of the older fables is, in a sense, evidence of this spontaneous and poetic activity, for in that deformation, the human spirit is still exercising the basic poetic act of investing its natural dimension with its own form. With respect to the poetic characters and their proper fables which are the products of this poetic activity, the Homeric poems possess the same veredicious character as the creations of the first theological poets. They are true histories of that age of which they are the spontaneous expression. In most general terms, the fables which, in the Homeric epics, are subject to the laws of deformation or corruption are precisely these myths of the theological poets, the poetic characters and the fables of the gods. By contrast, the poetic characters of the heroes which are their proper creation emerge from the Homeric poems with pristine poetic force and as true expressions of the 'ethos', not of the age of the gods, but of the age of men, of that age in which gods and men mingled freely together, but in which, at the same time, the stature of the gods had to a great extent been levelled to that of men, or the heroes among men. If this be the case, the Homeric poems, for all their deformation of the theological myths, emerge in the character which Vico had initially set out to vindicate for them, namely, as 'civil histories of ancient Greek customs' of the age, not of the gods, but of heroes. For in Homer, he opines in another place, it is always right to read 'heroes' for 'gods'.[1] It remains, therefore, to identify the basic poetic characters of the Homeric poems and to study their fables in order to interpret the poems as true civil histories of the heroic age of Greek culture, when that culture was still barbarous.

The genuine poetic power of the Homeric epics appears, then, in the creation of poetic characters proper to it; and in this creation

[1] SNS, 156, 157, 437.

Vico, adducing the testimony alike of Aristotle and Horace, declares Homer to be incomparable. The central poetic character of the *Iliad* is, of course, Achilles, of the *Odyssey*, Ulysses. As the composition of the former poem had been ascribed to an earlier period of the heroic age, the age when Greece was filled with sublime passions of heroic valour, he interprets Achilles to be the poetic character of this heroic valour. 'To Achilles, . . . they attached all the properties of heroic valour and all the sentiments and customs arising from these natural properties, such as quick temper, punctiliousness, wrathfulness, implacability, violence, the arrogation of all right to might, as they are summed up by Horace in his description of this character.' To Ulysses, by contrast, and in conformity with his opinion that the *Odyssey* had been composed in the 'old age' of Homer and of Greece, 'When the spirits of Greece had been somewhat cooled by reflection', were attached 'the sentiments and the customs of heroic wisdom, that is, those of wariness, patience, dissimulation, duplicity, deceit, propriety of speech and indifference of action.'[1] These poetic characters, generated by the popular imagination, exercised the same function as the poetic characters of the gods; that is, they expressed civil histories of the people by whose powerful imagination they had been evoked and who spoke that history in those characters. To these two central characters the popular imagination attached the actions of particular men conspicuous enough to rouse attention as influencing the whole course of their history or expressing its peculiar character. As creations of the popular imagination, these figures exhibit that uniformity, or inner coherence, which is not the evidence of their 'natural' existence, but rather of their origin in the common sense of a whole people; they exhibit also that sublimity which is the indubitable mark of popularity or popular origin.

Upon the basis of the interpretation of these heroic characters it is possible, in Vico's view, to evoke the image of the structure of poetic wisdom of the heroic age of Greece in its earlier and its later phases. The entire structure of that wisdom, in all its multiple branches, and even more in its essential *ethos* or quality of humanity, is carried, as it were, in their persons. A most significant instance is the evidence afforded as to the political structure of the heroic ages, which is uniform through both its phases. From the persons of Achilles, of Ulysses and of the lesser chiefs with whom they are surrounded in the course of the narrative, Vico draws evidence of

[1] SNS, 809, 879.

his thesis which, against the background of the dominant political theories of his day, seemed to him nothing less than revolutionary, that the first government after the stage of the family composed only of parents and offspring, was that of a theocratic aristocracy; that is, rule by an intrenched minority who sustained their power and jurisdiction by claim to special access to the gods by augury and divination, poetically expressed by the figure of divine descent. This political structure had its roots in the absolute power of the father over his consort and offspring; it found its immediate occasion, however, in the circumstances of *asylum*, according to which institution others than the proper offspring were admitted to the family in the status of *famuli*. The relationship which prevailed between the *famuli* and the heads of families is the basic pattern of all heroic law and of heroic jurisprudence; the power of the family head was absolute and he was justly called king in this character as he was called priest by virtue of his power over the auspices.

The aristocratic structure arose from the confederation of family heads under pressure of revolt on the part of the *famuli*, who were the *plebs* of the earliest cities. To the union of the heads of families there was extended the same quality of authority, the same jurisprudence as prevailed in the family. Thus Homer 'calls each hero of whom he sings a king'; but this is intelligible, Vico believes, only as the term is understood in the heroic jurisprudence, that is, as members of 'reigning senates' made up of 'so many family kings'.[1] This is the polity he sees reflected in the Homeric narratives, where Achilles is the natural equal of Agamemnon and where the decisions of the heroes in war and peace are determined in general councils, presided over by the wisdom of Nestor, who is the poetic figure of the accumulated spoken wisdom of history and tradition. Thus Homer becomes for Vico a basic document in his attack on the thesis of Bodin that the first polities were monarchies and upon the contractual theory of the origin of polity as generally sustained in the eighteenth century.

To return, however, to the subject of the Homeric poems themselves, Vico believes that by his conception of their popular character he has at a stroke achieved two ends. In the first place, he has resolved the perplexities and contradictions which surrounded the 'Homeric question' since classical times and which had been made vocal by Plato and by Horace. In the second he had secured the primary document of the 'New Science'.

[1] SNS, 557, 584.

The essential ambiguity of the 'Homeric problem' lay in the fact that all critics had recognized the inimitable and sublime quality of the Homeric poems, but had been unable to identify its true source or principle. Similarly they had been unanimous in recognizing the verediciousness of the narratives, and of poetry in general, but had been unable to determine the principle of that quality. To sustain the one insight and the other, they had had recourse to the fiction of the 'esoteric' or philosophical wisdom of Homer. But such esoteric or philosophical wisdom is in direct contrast to all of the qualities which all recognizes as constituting the very sublimity and incomparability which they admire. The whole force of Vico's argument, taken as referring directly to this ambiguity of the 'Homeric problem', is to furnish this principle which all had sought and thus to preserve to Homer the sublime poetic character which was his. This he had done by establishing that poetry is in its essential character the form of vulgar or spontaneous, and not of reflective or philosophical wisdom; and that, consequently, on the hypothesis of the popular origin of the Homeric poems, it is possible and necessary to recognize as proper and essential to their sublimity all those qualities which had been in such manifest contradiction to their reflective origin. Thus 'Homer, lost in the crowd of the Greek peoples is justified against all the accusations levelled at him by the critics . . . on account of his base sentences, vulgar customs, crude comparisons, local idioms, licences in metre, variations in dialect, . . . his having made men of gods and gods of men.' 'In addition to these, all those . . . pre-eminences fall to him which have been ascribed to him by all the masters of the art of poetry, declaring him incomparable in his wild and savage comparisons, in his cruel and fearful descriptions of battles and deaths, in his sentences filled with sublime passions, in the clarity and splendour of his style. All these were properties of the heroic age of the Greeks . . . , the age of vigorous memory, robust imagination and sublime invention. . . .' And finally, 'his title is assured to the three immortal eulogies that are given him: first of having been the organizer of Greek polity or civilization; second, of having been the father of all other poets; and third, of having been the source of Greek philosophies'. For 'it was poetic wisdom itself whose fables provided the occasions for the philosophers to meditate their lofty truths. . . .' 'None of these eulogies could have been given to the Homer hitherto believed in.'[1]

Above all Vico had secured to the purposes of the 'New Science'

[1] SNS, 882, 901.

a primary document in whose availability the theoretical conceptions of the 'New Science' found their vindication, and its positive programme its inception. 'In virtue of our discovery we may ascribe to him an additional and most dazzling glory, that of having been the first historian of the entire gentile world who has come down to us. Wherefore his poems should henceforth be highly prized as being two great treasure houses of the customs of early Greece.'[1] The conditional proposition of the twentieth axiom of the 'Elements' is, for Vico, thus converted into fact and the world of vulgar wisdom, of which his doctrine of poetry, vindicated in the Homeric epics, is the key, lies open to him.

[1] SNS, 156–7, 902 et seq.

XI

THE THEORY OF THE STATE

GOETHE, reviewing the vast work of his artistic life, the poems, the plays and the novels which have made his name immortal, dismissed them as fragments. He was judging them, of course, in relation to the total vision which commanded his mind and imagination, upon which his spiritual gaze was always fixed, but of which his compositions evoke but fleeting intimations. In this respect, there is a genuine affinity between Goethe and Vico. The exalted quality of vision marks Vico's thought as well and that vision, as his English translators have remarked,[1] is forever with him in all its dazzling totality. The glimpses of that whole which he affords the reader are, however, fleeting and infrequent. His intention is to depict the total movement of providence as it guides history to the existential realization of the total idea of man in the structures of society and culture. In order to make a beginning in this matter, however, he must descend into the 'ingens sylva' of the mind of primitive man, thence to trace the first time-forms of the human spirit. Poetic wisdom, which is only a moment, and hence a fragment, of the life of the human spirit in history, thus comes to pre-empt the chief attention of his actual composition and research. Nevertheless, the vision of the whole does, from time to time, shine through and nowhere, perhaps, so clearly as in his treatment of the theory of the state.

The problem of the state is central to the concern of the 'New Science', of course, because of the continuity of Vico's thought with classical political humanism. For political humanism, it has been suggested above, man is essentially social. Humanity is the power to generate and to sustain the structures of community. The state is a fundamental social structure, so fundamental, indeed, that some philosophers have not hesitated to make it co-terminous with society. Concern with the social nature of man, consequently, includes necessarily the problem of the state and of government. This

[1] Bergin and Fisch, *The New Science of Giambattista Vico*, p. ix.

general concern is strengthened in Vico's case by his concern with jurisprudence. The state is the immediate social context of law; from the point of view of jurisprudence it is difficult to resist the temptation to identify law and sociality. The enterprise of the 'New Science', growing directly out of the speculative problems of jurisprudence, immediately contemplates the problem of the state. Finally, in the treatment of the problem of the state the principles and method of the 'New Science' are deployed to the widest limits of their power; above all the concept of history as the synthesis of time and idea is thrown into brilliant relief. This synthesis, as has been seen, imposes the ideal of a science which will be at once history and philosophy. In the matter of politics, it imposes the complex task of defining the normative idea of the state, of establishing the actual course of the transformation of the positive structure of political power through time and, finally, of demonstrating the essential unity of the one and the other.

In conformity with this conception of science and the concrete task which it imposes in the matter of politics, the Vichian theory of the state takes its point of departure in the critique of an historical proposition which, Vico feels, has been expressed with special force and influence by Jean Bodin.[1] It is the proposition that the first form of human government must have been monarchical and that monarchy was succeeded by stages of tyranny, of free and popular government and finally by aristocracy. This proposition, to Vico's mind, conceals beneath an historical error fallacies both of method and of theory. The fallacy of method is that which he has already identified as the 'conceit of the learned'; the concept of monarchy is introduced into the primitive context according to its civil, reflective form. The fallacy of theory is the conclusion that polity must and could have arisen only by force or fraud—a conclusion fraught with dogmatic anarchism. To this dual error he opposes his own basic principle and maxim: polity, like all human institutions, must have arisen 'ipsis rebus dictantibus'.

The circumstances, or the facts in the case, he believes, dictate that the first form of society must have been the family. The men of the feral wandering had been compelled by the thunders of Jove, as he had suggested in his account of the formation of the poetic figure of the god,[2] and by the sense of the divine presence thus awakened, to fix their habitations, to take fixed mates, to generate certain offspring and thus to establish the domestic economy. Since this is the

[1] SNS, 1009–19; 552.   [2] SNS, 379, and cf. Chapter IX.

case, the seeds of polity, its first form and its inchoate idea, must be sought within the structure of the family. It is impossible, however, to grasp the process by which polity emerged if it be supposed, with Bodin for example, that the family included only parents and their certain offspring. Among other things, this would involve the supposition, which Vico finds unacceptable, that in the process of the formation of the state, the sons must have risen against the fathers, as well as the wider thesis, already rejected by Vico, that the much-debated origin of the state must have been by force and fraud. In order, consequently, to render comprehensible the manner in which the state arose from and within the structure of the family, he advances the thesis that the family must have been constituted, not of parents and offspring alone, but of the 'famuli' as well, and must, as a matter of fact, have received its designation from this circumstance.[1]

The 'famuli', in Vico's account, were those men who had sought the protection of the founders of the families as asylum against the rigours and the perils of the feral state. Outside the initial unit of parents and offspring, those who still wandered in the feral state fell into two classes, the strong, and the weak who were their natural prey. Against these strong the weak appealed for protection to those who had established fixed and fortified abodes. The protection and the asylum which the fathers afforded could be sustained only by the conquest and destruction of those 'impious strong' against whose tyranny the weak had appealed for succour. Thus was born the natural office of the fathers, which remained the guiding ideal of Roman government even to imperial times and with it the family in the full sense of the term, parents, offspring and those who had been received into asylum.

This initial structure of group life did not constitute polity, but it contained the elements out of which polity and the state arose. It did not constitute polity because there existed within this structure no glimmering of a common good and, consequently, no action for a common good. The sole utility and good of this initial society were the good and the utility of the father, the 'res patria'.[2] It would be an error, Vico believes, to introduce into this context the quality of the relationship between father and son which characterizes the family in civil, and even in heroic, times. To the father of this family, his offspring as well as his consort were literal extensions of his own being. They could not constitute with him the 'locus' of a common

[1] SNS, 552 et seq.; 257.　　　　　　　　[2] SNS, 256, 584.

good, because in order to do so, the offspring would have to be recognized as possessing a principle of independent being and identity. Nor could the 'famuli' establish a common good with the father; in return for his protection and asylum they could offer, in their feral state, only themselves. They became, in consequence, his chattel, subject wholly and absolutely to his will and constituting a portion of his private good. Nevertheless, it is the presence of the 'famuli' within the domestic economy which occasions the emergence of the common good upon which polity was founded.

The relationship between the father and the 'famuli' was one of absolute subservience to absolute lordship. It was based on the fact of power resident wholly and only in the father and on the fact of absolute need which drove the weak to his asylum. Such a relationship, obviously, could be sustained only so long as its initial, generating conditions persisted. Once these began to deteriorate, once, that is, the need for that protection disappeared, the situation must prove explosive. The very stability, moreover, of the domestic economy made it inevitable that those conditions should disappear. Cradled in this stability, the 'famuli' must awaken first to the harshness of the rule of the fathers and secondly to a sense of their own power, though it were only the power of numbers. The spectre of revolt arose at this juncture to trouble the regal power of the father and it was this spectre alone, Vico believes,[1] which was able to evoke in the rude minds of the fathers some image of a common utility and good and with it a first inchoate idea of polity.

The common good and the polity thus engendered must have been exceedingly limited in range. It is the characteristic of the strong, Vico writes,[2] to relinquish nothing of what they have won by their courage, but rather to yield, under necessity or utility, but little and that little reluctantly. So it must have been with the fathers and the 'monarchical' power which they enjoyed and which rested upon their own strength and valour. In the first place, it is inconceivable to Vico that this common good should appear between the fathers and their 'famuli'. The force of his maxim of the strong forbids him to believe that the fathers, in the presence of the threat or of the fact of the revolt of their 'famuli', would turn to their appeasement, in the first instance at least. On the contrary, it compels him to believe that they would turn rather to compact with their peers, the other fathers, and to the formation of a common league against a common danger. This was in substance the first image of a common

[1] SNS, 584.   [2] SNS, 261.

good, mutual protection against the spectre of revolt and this the first form of polity, the order of the fathers in compact to this end.[1] This common good was but the actuality of the power of the fathers viewed as establishing a basis of unity among them. To the order, that is, the body of the fathers as the agency of this common good, the heads of families must yield only so much of their autonomy as the imminence of danger and the conditions of successful common action demanded. That this must be a minimal and erratic concession would seem to follow obviously from the force of that same maxim of the strong and the situation created is illustrated, Vico believes, by the conduct of the heroes of the Greeks before Troy. For the character of these heroes and the relations between them, he believes, must have been such as he is describing. Passionate attachment to personal honour, as a symbol of autonomy, punctiliousness in relations with their peers, easy rebellion under fancied wrong are the marks of their community. The eminence of the order could be commensurate only to the present danger out of which the sense of the common good arose. Nevertheless, it is sufficient and constant enough to establish the notion of a common good and of a right to some degree distinct from the autonomy of the fathers and thus to secure the idea and the fact of polity.

This account of the formation of the first polity 'ipsis rebus dictantibus' permits Vico to advance two further propositions in the historico-philosophical science of the state, the one philological, of the order of the 'certum', the other philosophical, of the order of the 'verum'. The first polity could not have been monarchical, as Bodin, for example, held, but must have been aristocratic; thus the first proposition.[2] The aristocracy he intends is simply the order of the fathers convened and leagued together for the prosecution of their common good. Its essential character lay in the fact that it was a congress of peers. Within this congress the fathers retained their original autonomy, surrendering only so much as the common good could exact. They remained, therefore, 'monarchs' in their domestic economies, that is, over the areas of their private utility and good. Over the common good, however, power inhered in the order and specifically to the council of peers, such as Vico recognizes in the heroic 'boulé' of the Homeric poems.[3] Political authority, consequently, was distributive as the common good it guarded was distributive. The second proposition concerns the 'verum' or the idea of political authority and the state; the state or polity is the order by

[1] SNS, 950, 1005.   [2] SNS, 1005.   [3] SNS, 67; cf. also 624.

which a common good is prosecuted conceived substantively, that is, in its transcendency to the order of private good over which the common good assumes eminence and the agencies of that private utility over which the state assumes jurisdiction and control. In its idea, consequently, the state embraces two factors, a common good and the order and agency generated for its pursuit or preservation. These stand as functions of each other and the form of the state will be regulated by the conception of the common good which is entertained. Society generates agencies of polity commensurate with its conception of the common good, neither greater nor less.

The conception of the common good which generated and sustained the primitive aristocratic polity was, as Vico has suggested, exceedingly limited. It was, in brief, the preservation of the autonomy of the fathers against the threat of the revolt of their 'famuli', who were, Vico remarks, the 'plebs' of the heroic commonwealths. It was, essentially, a conservative idea. It envisaged no positive common goal except the conservation and protection of an already existing power and autonomy. Its basic principle, consequently, must be described as negative rather than positive. It found expression in the circumstance reported by Aristotle in a passage which Vico, in his frequent citations of it, invariably calls 'golden': the patricians of the heroic cities swore eternal enmity against the 'plebs', that is, against their own 'famuli'.[1] Concretely, this enmity could only be the rigid exclusion of the awakening 'plebs' from participation in the power of the fathers. Its action was to cause the bases of the autonomy, which had now become the common good of their order, to harden into the rigid and exclusive privileges of a caste and to limit political action to the vindication of these privileges.

Since the common good of the aristocratic order was simply the autonomous power of the fathers viewed under a certain aspect, i.e. its possible violation at the hands of the 'famuli' or 'plebs', the privileges into which this common good crystallized could be only the original substance of the 'res patria' viewed now, in its turn, through the order of the fathers. These, as Vico has pointed out in a number of contexts,[2] were four, the three 'principles' of the 'New Science', religion, matrimony and burial, and their adjunct, deriving from the structure of the domestic economy, property. Religion, as he has pointed out, provides the ultimate basis of society and hence of humanity itself, for it was the divine presence alone which first drove the men of the feral wandering to the establishment of the

[1] SNS, 271 (Axiom LXXXVI).   [2] SNS, 11–12, 330, 337.

family and this presence alone has power to hold them in that restraint upon which life in the group depends. This first religion was essentially divination, or the religion of the auspices, for the first men, according to the principles of poetry and of the formation of the poetic characters, understood the heavenly phenomena as signs and commands. Their most primitive art or science, consequently, was the interpretation of these signs for the guidance of their own good and utility. Thus arose the first, the priestly office of the fathers which was the fount of their power and authority, for these sprang from their power to read the auspices of Jove.[1] Translated into the area of the common good, this priestly office became an attribute and function of the aristocratic order. The auspices of the common good defined the source of the power of the order, of the specifically political power and authority therefore, just as it had those of the fathers. From this office, consequently, it was the aim of aristocratic polity to exclude the 'famuli' or the 'plebs'. The auspices became the basis of the specifically political power of the aristocratic order and its fundamental rubric became 'Auspicia Jovis esse sua'.[2] The poetic character of the auspices was the image of divine origin. The patricians were the 'sons of the gods'. And thus it was that the rubric of plebian revolt became in turn the formula 'a caelo non esse (patres) dimissos'.[3]

Similarly, the other elements of the power of the father were transformed into the pillars and the substance of aristocratic privilege and power. The selection of fixed mates, into which the first men were driven by the shame or modesty engendered by the sense of the divine presence, constituted the first act of marriage; the natural expression of the motive which compelled this action, the sense of the divine presence, was the celebration of the union with the special invocation of that presence. Thus were born the 'solemn nuptials' whence flowed the certainty of offspring and social identity, both primitive characters of the domestic economy. With the establishment of the first polity, solemn nuptials became in turn a radical character of the aristocratic order and the social identity of which they were the source the special mark of the patrician; he was able to name his father.[4] By contrast the 'plebs' or the 'famuli' remained in the practice of promiscuous and unblessed unions, 'more ferarum'

[1] SNS, 523.
[2] SNS, 525, 604; cf. also 985, 'Auspicia incommunicata plebi sunto'.
[3] SNS, 415: '(Patres) non esse caelo dimissos'.
[4] SNS, 530: 'Qui potest nomine ciere patrem', cf. 433, 587.

and in the confusion of identity which characterized the feral state.[1] To this continued social anonymity the policy of the aristocratic order deliberately condemned them as the mark of their less than human stature. The power to do this was in the hands of the patricians because the auspices, without which solemn nuptials could not be celebrated, were theirs. In like manner burials with religious rites were denied the 'plebs' while real property, which was the material substance of the fathers' power, was placed beyond their presumption. The 'famuli' worked the lands of the fathers, which had been won from the 'ingens sylva', for the good of the fathers. These elements defined concretely the common good of the aristocratic order which it was sworn to vindicate against the awakening self-consciousness of the 'famuli'.

This structure of the aristocratic state was naturally surrounded, or embodied in, a system of symbols, spontaneously generated to signify its peculiar quality and character. One of these symbols has already been mentioned, the divine descent of the heroes. Even more effective must have been the linguistic symbol, because it signified even more powerfully the ultimate basis of aristocratic power. This basis, it has been noted, was religious and consisted in possession of the auspices. Power over the auspices was essentially linguistic or semantic; it consisted essentially in the power to read and to interpret in policy and action the signs of the divine will and intention. The purest expression, consequently, of the exclusion of the 'plebs' from the power of the aristocratic order was their exclusion from the language of the auspices, the language of the gods spoken by the heroes, as Homer remarks. Homer distinguishes more than once this language of the gods from the language of men. This distinction must be read, Vico believes, as the identification of a language of the aristocratic order based on auspicial symbols and set in contrast to the 'vulgar' tongue, the language of men, or of the 'plebs'. This language of the gods or of the auspices was guarded by the aristocratic order as the innermost fortress of the power it enjoyed. When this fortress fell, when, that is, the patricians were compelled to express the law in the 'language of men', the vulgar tongue, the reign of the heroes, in Vico's account, was at an end.

The first polity as thus depicted by Vico presents the aspect above all of a compact of privilege. In fact, however, he understands it to be much more. It harbours the first form of equity, civil equity, which finds political expression in the 'reason of state'. Civil equity

[1] SNS, 567: of the plebians 'agitabant connubia more ferarum'.

is the recognition of a common good restricted to one stratum or segment of society or social organization, which, in virtue of this good, constitutes the commonwealth in its proper sense. The 'reason of state' is the administration of the social order for this restricted common good and it persists, even when a universal common good is recognized, as a claim to an especial competence in one segment of society for the government of the whole. This is the form of equity which characterized the Roman government both in strictly aristocratic times and in the times of popular liberty when the senate was still deferred to. In the former times the senate administered the commonwealth for the good of the patricians; in the latter, while admitting a common good of all the people, it still retained political power by reason of a claim to special wisdom in council. Civil equity and the reason of state are the true marks of aristocratic and heroic polity.

This concept of a civil equity contains within itself its contradictory, the concept of an equity not subject to these restrictions. It implies dialectically an equity which rests upon the vision of a common good truly common to all and of a common wisdom in the pursuit of this good resident in all, or in the council of all. Such, Vico says,[1] would be natural equity reflecting a common good based on the common nature of men, inherent singly and distributively in all. The political expression of this natural equity would be popular government, that is, decision and action in union by all the people for the common good of all.

Civil equity and natural equity, with their corresponding political expressions, define for Vico the ideal terms of the historical movement of polity. Polity moves in history from the more limited to the less limited, from the restricted to the inclusive notion of the common good and from a limited to an all inclusive agency for the common good. In this movement it obeys the same ideal and eternal law by which the whole of history moves from the partial to the total presence of man. Natural equity represents the total presence of man to himself under the aspect of a common good proper to all, while civil equity represents a presence of man to himself, under the same character, the common good, which is at the same time partial absence. And here, in the area of polity, as in the whole of history, the movement between partial presence and total presence generates the phenomenology of the state, that is, the order of the temporal appearance of the concrete forms of the state in their relationship to

[1] SNS, 1086.

its idea. The abstract principle of this phenomenology is that every concrete form of polity, or of the state, represents a particular appreciation of the idea of the state, while its concrete motive force is the ever-present tension between social groups intent upon the preservation of a limited common good and those which, though dimly and still only partially, envisage a common good common to all.

The historico-philosophical proposition which expresses these insights is Vico's statement that, as the initial form of polity must have been aristocratic, because aristocracy expresses the mode under which the common good must have appeared to men in their first civility, so this form must have been succeeded, and must always be succeeded, by popular government.[1] In its first form, as it might effectively dislodge aristocracy, this popular government must itself have been exceedingly limited and restricted. Natural equity could have appeared to the first plebians only under the immediate and concrete form of the penetration of the privileges of the regnant aristocratic order. Returning, therefore, to the concrete terms of his analysis, the 'eternal enmity' between the patricians and the plebs, the common good which the plebs of the heroic commonwealths claimed for themselves could have been, concretely, only those positive elements which aristocratic polity reserved to its own order.

The immediate point of conflict between the opposing elements of the heroic commonwealth must then have been property. Natural equity has its historical birth in agrarian revolt.[2] All real property, he has suggested, in the family was held as the private good and domain of the father, the material, economic basis of the 'res patria', dictated by the settled mode of habitation and the limits it imposed on the mobility of the family. In the feral state food was sought or hunted, an enemy was evaded by flight; in the domestic economy the one and the other were alike impossible. Cultivation of the land succeeded forage and the hunt and the enemy had to be met and overcome at the limits of the cultivated fields. Just as the whole of the domestic economy, from the auspices of the family gods to the persons of the consort and the offspring, was the extension of the being of the father and the domain of his private right, so too were these cultivated fields. The acceptance of the 'famuli' into asylum could not change this; they worked the land for the good of the father. The league of the fathers in the aristocratic commonwealth conceived this real property as an element of the common good it sought

[1] SNS, 927. [2] SNS, 599–618, especially 612–13.

to conserve. Access to the products of the fields must have been the first object of the assault of the 'plebs' on the aristocratic privilege. It was a minimal conception of natural equity. According to Vico's maxim of the strong it had to be met, when it could no longer be repressed, by a minimal concession, the concession of bonitary rights in the fields. At the threshold between civil and natural equity there appears agrarian revolt and agrarian reform. When this threshold is crossed, as it was by the concession of bonitary rights, the process of the transformation of aristocratic polity in the direction of popular had begun.

The real barrier between the aristocratic order and the 'plebs' was not, however, in Vico's eyes, property. It was, rather, solemn marriage or 'connubium', for this it was which effectively and radically distinguished the orders. 'Connubium' or solemn marriage effected in the divine presence and under the auspices endowed the patricians with social identity; by contrast the promiscuous generation of the plebians in unsanctified unions condemned them to social anonymity. It was the demand of the 'plebs' for participation in 'connubium', consequently, and not mere agrarian revolt, which marked the genuine awakening of the 'plebs' to a community of human nature with the patricians and hence to natural equity.[1] Demanding the 'connubium' was the equivalent of demanding social identity; even more, since 'connubium' was effected through the auspices, this demand was an approach to the auspices themselves. For this reason, plebian aspiration to solemn marriage must have met with fiercer resistance than agrarian revolt, for it struck much closer to the roots of aristocratic power, just as it marked in the plebian consciousness a profounder sense of natural equity than that expressed in the desire for direct participation in real property and its fruits.

Real property and solemn marriage marked the outer frontiers of aristocratic polity, however, and not its innermost stronghold and source. These lay rather in religion and consisted essentially in command of the auspices. So long as this remained inviolate the polity could not change radically. Until this command of the auspices itself, in one manner or another, became the demand of the awakening plebian consciousness, the emergence of natural equity must remain partial and incomplete. The demand for 'connubium' approached dangerously close to the auspices, but still did not attain to

[1] SNS, 598: 'The plebians in making this demand were in effect asking for Roman citizenship whose natural principle was solemn nuptials . . .'; cf. also 513, 566-9, 586.

them directly. The aristocratic order, because it appreciated the auspices as the ultimate source of its power, had surrounded them with a barrier of restrictive symbolism more exclusive and repellent than any other social form. The auspices, as it has been remarked, designated an essentially linguistic and semantic process, the interpretation of natural signs, poetically conceived as divine, and the translation of these into principles of policy. The most direct expression of the linguistic and semantic character of the auspices was the restriction of the language of the auspices to the order of the fathers. The laws which expressed the policy based on the auspices were, consequently, expressed in a sacred language forbidden and inaccessible to the plebians. This, in Vico's view, is the civil origin and significance of that distinction between the language of the gods and the language of men to which Homer, for example, refers. Language, the sacred language of the laws based on the auspices, was the ultimate symbolic bastion of aristocratic polity. That polity succumbed and natural equity emerged fully at the crucial point in history when the aristocratic order was forced to express the law in the common language of men and not in the sacred language of the auspices. The philological importance of this event cannot, from Vico's point of view, be overstated. It marks effectively and existentially the end of civil equity and the emergence of natural equity. The expression of the laws in the common tongue reflects at once the sense or awareness of a common good which is truly common and the demand for a polity which should be commensurate to that good, namely, a popular government. It marks the culmination of the process by which the notion of a restricted common good and the form of polity which expresses it, is superseded by a notion of the common good as universal and inhering in the common nature of men. It marks the end of the 'reason of state', for it expresses the insight that the determination of policy in pursuit of the common good is not the office of a few but of all.

Natural equity and the form of polity, popular government, which it implies, would thus appear to be the ideal and existential terms, respectively, of the historical process of polity. Popular government, that is to say, would seem to be the concrete form of polity in which the idea of natural equity finds perfect existential actualization. Natural equity constitutes the total presence of man to himself in his social, and therefore specifically human, character, under the form of a common good proper to all in virtue of a common human nature. Popular government would seem to translate this presence into a pattern of action, into an historical institution, expressing the principle that the common good of all is the proper action of the action and decision of all. This is not, however, wholly the case in Vico's theory. Certain contradictions develop which make it necessary, in his view, to dissociate the one from the other and to abandon the existential form, popular government, in order to retain and to conserve the ideal value, natural equity, a universal common good. The resolution of these contradictions leads him to the 'royal law' by which the normative concept of polity is finally determined.[1]

The contradictions are two and appear both in the ideal and in the existential order. The first is the tendency of natural equity to resolve itself into private utility, or to appear synonymous with it; the second, the tendency of popular government, because of the confusion of natural equity and private utility, to breed tyranny. Together, these contradictions render nugatory and actually reverse the entire ideal-temporal process which Vico has sought to depict.[2]

Natural equity tends to a confusion of the common good with private utility by very reason of its insistence that the common good be genuinely the good of all, that it has its roots in a common human nature, realized substantially in every man and therefore distributively present in human society. This pulverization of the common good, so to say, into the infinite plurality of mankind, or at least into the indefinite plurality of an historical society, lays it open to the operation of that force of human nature which Vico has made the subject of one of the axioms of the 'New Science' and by which man seeks always and in the first place his own utility.[3] He becomes capable of social action only when it appears to him that the common good and his own utility coincide. When the common good is presented to him, as natural equity does present it, as pervading distributively the pluralism of human subjects or persons, he tends, inevitably, not to identify his utility with that larger good, but to contract the common good to the limits of his private concern. Classical utilitarianism, which flourished after Vico, perceived this fact as well as he, and sought a remedy in the consoling notion that, both in economics and in ethical and political action, the pursuit of private utility must prove ultimately to be the road to the common good. Natural equity must thus appear fraught with the possibility

[1] SNS, 1007-8.
[2] The degeneration of popular commonwealths into tyrannies; cf. SNS, 292 (Axiom XCV), and also 288-9.
[3] SNS, 241 (Axiom LXVI).

of anarchism, for everyone, contracting the common good to his private utility, becomes in fact the enemy of the common good and of polity.

Anarchism is, however, itself antipathetic to human nature. Out of the situation of anarchy toward which the confusion of the common good with private utility tends, there arises rather tyranny. Tyranny, in Vico's sense, is essentially the displacement of the common good by a private utility strong enough to become dominant. This must be the result of the reduction of the common good to private utility. By this reduction popular government opens the way to the conception of polity as the contest of wills in pursuit of private goods or interests. In such a contest those must inevitably dominate who most clearly recognize and most ruthlessly exploit the fundamental confusion. The most ambitious and the most dissolute, Vico says,[1] must assume actual control of the polity and will exercise this usurped power for private ends which they will identify unambiguously with the common good. This ambition of the ruthless is abetted by the sloth of the less forceful, whose whole energy is consumed in the pursuit of more immediate interests and who will, consequently, either tolerate or even applaud such usurpation. Only the most extraordinary conditions and circumstances can prevent popular government from taking this path to tyranny, but such conditions do not, in Vico's conception, rule the course of history.

Nevertheless, natural equity is not impugned by these contradictions to which it gives rise. It expresses still, for Vico, the ideality of human polity and the term toward which the process of polity in history must move. What is now clear is that natural equity does not find adequate concretion in popular government. It needs as its agency a form of polity in which the common good and private utility are effectively distinguished and reconciled. The failure of popular government lies in its inability to make this distinction and to effect this reconciliation. Society, to execute the insight of natural equity, must generate a form of polity in which the common good is effected without prejudice to private utility. It demands, in other words, a government of the people for the people, but not by the people. It is at this juncture of their historical life, consequently, that nations following a 'royal law' which brings them 'to rest under monarchies'.

Monarchy represents for Vico the normative and ideal form of polity or the state because it is able to achieve the mediation between

[1] SNS, 288–9, 1007.

common good and private utility which natural equity demands. Monarchy has its 'rationale' wholly in a common good; the monarch, appearing at the moment of the greatest confusion of common good and private utility, takes all of the general concern into his own hands and thus releases private persons for pursuit of private interest.[1] The monarch, so to say, assumes the common good into his person, and becomes thus its incarnation and substantial symbol. In order to exercise this function, the monarchy must be demonstrably without private interest. If the tyrant imposes a private utility in place of the common good, the monarch, by contrast, divests himself of private personality to become the personification of the common good. Monarchy demonstrates this disinterestedness, instinctively, as it were, seeking its popular basis. In the first place, it releases private energies for the pursuit of private concern within a firm framework of polity. Further, if the monarch is to vindicate his own identity with the common good, he can tolerate no inequalities before himself; for this reason, Vico writes, 'monarchs seek to make their subjects all equal'. Before monarchy, all agencies within the state appear in a common character, whether individuals or corporations, that of agencies of private interest before the instrument of the common good. Finally, the monarch can sustain his position only so long as he may demonstrate that the common good which he embodies is indeed but the extension and guarantee of the private interests and liberties of his subjects. The monarch thus appears, to Vico's mind, as the shield of popular liberty and of private utility against any pretension to privilege; at the same time he appears as the personification of a common good which is defined in and through private interest and in which, consequently, all opposition between them is mediated. But this is natural equity itself, that the good of all be sought in and through the good or utility of each. For this reason, Vico believes, monarchy closes the time-ideal process of polity, realizing in itself the idea and the existential form of human government.

Vico has thus constructed a pure phenomenology of human polity; that is, the order of the temporal succession of its concrete forms based on the inner articulations of its idea. In his own words, he has constructed an ideal, eternal history of human polity, upon which the temporal order of the forms of polity in the life of nations is predicated. In this specific material, consequently, the enterprise of

[1] SNS, 1008: 'Takes all public concerns . . . into his own hands, leaving his subjects free to look after their private affairs.'

the 'New Science' is realized with an amplitude lacking in any other area; for the object of the 'Science' is precisely the construction of such ideal, eternal history in every area of human social process and finally with respect to the idea of man. In this material Vico has carried the process of the temporal formation of the presence of man to ultimate point, civil polity. The theory, or historico-philosophical concept, of the state consequently provides the most illuminating instance of the actual operation of the theory of history which is the speculative and methodological principle of the 'New Science'.

INDEX

Absence: and pseudo-myth 63; in human spirit 77

'aequum bonum': 44, 46, 47, 49, 55, 63

aestheticism: two forms of 85; opposed by Vichian theory of poetry 85

agent, legislating: 46, 47, 48

alienation: 2, 40

Alvarez: 13

Amerio, Franco: 5n., 87n., 166n., 186n.

anarchism: juridical 38; political 215

anticurialism: 17

Antigone: 51

'arbitrium': 161 ff.

aristocracy: 20, 202 ff.

Aristotle: 17, 41, 106, 198

Arnauld: 16

atheism: denied in primitive peoples 95; as hypothesis 97

Augustine, St.: 17, 79

Augustinianism: and paradox 79; and relation of finite and infinite 79

Aulisio, Domenico: 21

auspices: as source of aristocratic polity 207; as object of plebian revolt in early commonwealths 213; sacred linguistic character of 213

authority: in positive law 36 ff.; part of 'verum' of law 42; philology as science of 58; element of civil wisdom 82; and philology 161–2; Scienza Nuova as philosophy of 162

'authors', Vico's: 18–19

Autobiography, of Vico: occasion and composition 11 ff.

Bacon, Francis: 15, 67

barbarism: of sense 124, 135, 138; of reflection 124, 135, 138; returned, in Middle Ages 131; and the Enlightenment 139

Bergin, Thomas Goddard: 1n., 202n.

Bodin, Jean: 203, 204, 206

Bourguet, Louis: 11

Calogero, Guido: 152n.

Campanella, T.: 15

Canisius: 13, 36

Capasso, Nicola: 26

Cardinal, M. F. d'Althann: 26

Caravita: 18, 26

causality, and history: 102, 104; tautology of 104

'certum' of law 36; in science of humanity 55; and philology 146–7; recovery of, from nature 147; convertibility with 'factum' 147, 148, 151; and 'fact' 149; and 'arbitrium' 161

chance: 49

character, poetic (or heroic): and truth 172; and class-concept 172; and memory 175; and abstraction 175; time structure of 175; ontological structure of 176; and presence 178; and alienation 178; of Jove 173; of Solon 176; of Homer 194; of Hercules 179, 187

chronology: as problem of universal history 129

circularity: of spirit, as interpretation of 'ricorso' 131; in structure of Scienza Nuova 145; of philosophy and philology 146

Cirillo, Nicola: 11

civility, as 'division of times' 126–7

classes, logical; and poetic character 172

Clement XI, Pope: 22

Colonna, Camillo: 14

complex, sense-phantasy: 87

conceit: of nations 183; of learned 184

INDEX